eKNOW 2023

The Fifteenth International Conference on Information, Process, and Knowledge Management

April 24th – 28th, 2023

Venice, Italy

eKNOW 2023 Editors

Eric J.H.J. Mantelaers, Zuyd University of Applied Sciences, Sittard, the Netherlands

Susan Gauch, University of Arkansas, USA

Printed from e-media with permission by:

Curran Associates, Inc.
57 Morehouse Lane
Red Hook, NY 12571

Some format issues inherent in the e-media version may also appear in this print version.

Printed with permission by Curran Associates, Inc. (2024)

International Academy, Research, and Industry Association (IARIA)
412 Derby Way
Wilmington, DE 19810

Phone: (408) 893-6407
Fax: (408) 527-6351

petre@iaria.org

Additional copies of this publication are available from:

Curran Associates, Inc.
57 Morehouse Lane
Red Hook, NY 12571 USA
Phone: 845-758-0400
Fax: 845-758-2633
Email: curran@proceedings.com
Web: www.proceedings.com

Table of Contents

eKNOW 2023

Forward

The Fifteenth International Conference on Information, Process, and Knowledge Management (eKNOW 2023) was held in Venice, Italy, April 24 - 28, 2023. The event was driven by the complexity of the current systems, the diversity of the data, and the challenges for mental representation and understanding of environmental structure and behavior.

Capturing, representing, and manipulating knowledge was and still is a fascinating and extremely useful challenge from both theoretical and practical perspective. Using validated knowledge for information and process management and for decision support mechanisms raised a series of questions the eKNOW 2023 conference was aimed at.

eKNOW 2023 provided a forum where researchers were able to present recent research results and new research problems and directions related to them. The topics covered aspects from knowledge fundamentals to more specialized topics such as process analysis and modeling, management systems, semantics processing and ontology.

We take this opportunity to thank all the members of the eKNOW 2023 Technical Program Committee as well as the numerous reviewers. The creation of such a broad and high-quality conference program would not have been possible without their involvement. We also kindly thank all the authors who dedicated much of their time and efforts to contribute to the eKNOW 2023. We truly believe that, thanks to all these efforts, the final conference program consists of top quality contributions.

This event could also not have been a reality without the support of many individuals, organizations, and sponsors. We are grateful to the members of the eKNOW 2023 organizing committee for their help in handling the logistics and for their work to make this professional meeting a success.

We hope that eKNOW 2023 was a successful international forum for the exchange of ideas and results between academia and industry and for the promotion of progress in knowledge management research. We also hope that Venice provided a pleasant environment during the conference and everyone saved some time for exploring this beautiful city

eKNOW 2023 Chairs

eKNOW Steering Committee
Susan Gauch, University of Arkansas, USA
Martijn Zoet, Zuyd University of Applied Science, The Nederland
Samia Aitouche, Laboratory of Automation and Manufacturing (LAP), University Batna 2, Algeria
Eric J.H.J. Mantelaers, Zuyd University of Applied Sciences, Sittard, the Netherlands

eKNOW 2023 Publicity Chair
Laura Garcia, Universitat Politècnica de València (UPV), Spain
Javier Rocher Morant, Universitat Politecnica de Valencia, Spain

eKNOW 2023

COMMITTEE

eKNOW Steering Committee

Susan Gauch, University of Arkansas, USA
Martijn Zoet, Zuyd University of Applied Science, The Nederland
Samia Aitouche, Laboratory of Automation and Manufacturing (LAP), University Batna 2, Algeria
Eric J.H.J. Mantelaers, Zuyd University of Applied Sciences, Sittard, the Netherlands

eKNOW 2023 Publicity Chairs

Javier Rocher Morant, Universitat Politecnica de Valencia, Spain
Laura Garcia, Universitat Politecnica de Valencia, Spain

eKNOW 2023 Technical Program Committee

Rocío Abascal Mena, Universidad Autónoma Metropolitana - Cuajimalpa, Mexico City, Mexico
Raoua Abdelkhalek, LARODEC | Institut Supérieur de Gestion de Tunis | Université de Tunis, Tunisia
Malak A. Abdullah, Jordan University of Science and Technology, Jordan
Marie-Hélène Abel, Sorbonne universités - Université de technologie de Compiègne, France
Awais Adnan, Institute of Management Sciences Peshawar, Pakistan
Nitin Agarwal, University of Arkansas at Little Rock, USA
Joyce Aguiar, Center for Psychology at University of Porto (CPUP), Portugal
Abdullah Fathi Ahmed, University Paderborn, Germany
Samia Aitouche, University Batna 2, Algeria
Arnulfo Alanis, Instituto Tecnológico de Tijuana | Tecnológico Nacional de México, Mexico
Abdulwahab Alazeb, University of Arkansas, USA
Mohammed Alqahtani, University of Arkansas, USA
Mohammad T. Alshammari, University of Hail, Saudi Arabia
Bráulio Alturas, Instituto Universitário de Lisboa (ISCTE-IUL) | ISTAR-Iscte (University Institute of Lisbon), Portugal
Gil Ad Ariely, Lauder School of Government, Diplomacy and Strategy - Interdisciplinary Center Herzliya (IDC), Israel
Mohamed Anis Bach Tobji, ESEN – University of Manouba | LARODEC Laboratory – ISG of Tunis, Tunisia
Mário Antunes, Polytechnic of Leiria, Portugal
Jorge Manuel Azevedo Santos, Universidade de Évora, Portugal
Michal Baczynski, University of Silesia in Katowice, Poland
Zbigniew Banaszak, Koszalin University of Technology, Poland
Basel Bani-Ismail, Oman College of Management and Technology, Oman
Dusan Barac, University of Belgrade, Serbia
Peter Bellström, Karlstad University, Sweden
Hajer Ben Othman, National school of computer science - University of Manouba, Tunisia
Asmaa Benghabrit, Moulay Ismaïl University, Meknès, Morocco
José Alberto Benítez Andrades, University of León, Spain
Julita Bermejo-Alonso, Universidad Isabel I, Spain
Shankar Biradar, Indian Institute of Information Technology Dharwad, India

Carlos Bobed, University of Zaragoza, Spain
Karsten Boehm, University of Applied Sciences, Kufstein, Austria
Zorica Bogdanovic, University of Belgrade, Serbia
Gregory Bourguin, LISIC | Université Littoral Côte d'Opale(ULCO), France
Loris Bozzato, FBK-Irst | Fondazione Bruno Kessler, Trento, Italy
Bénédicte Bucher, University Gustave Eiffel | ENS | IGN | LaSTIG, France
Ozgu Can, Ege University, Turkey
Qiushi Cao, Swansea University, UK
Lorenzo Capra, State University of Milano, Italy
Massimiliano Caramia, University of Rome "Tor Vergata", Italy
Vítor Carvalho, 2Ai-EST-IPCA / Algoritmi Research Center - Minho University, Portugal
Dickson K.W. Chiu, The University of Hong Kong, Hong Kong
Ritesh Chugh, Central Queensland University, Australia
Anacleto Correia, Naval Academy, Portugal
Miguel Couceiro, University of Lorraine | CNRS | Inria Nancy G.E. | Loria, France
Juan Pablo D'Amato, Universidad Nacional del Centro de la PRov (UNCPBA) / CONICET, Argentina
Anca Daniela Ionita, University Politehnica of Bucharest, Romania
Gustavo de Assis Costa, Federal Institute of Education, Science and Technology of Goiás, Brazil / LIAAD - INESC TEC, Portugal
Joaquim De Moura, University of A Coruña, Spain
Cláudio de Souza Baptista, University of Campina Grande, Brazil
Sylvie Despres, Université Sorbonne Paris Nord, France
Giuseppe A. Di Lucca, University of Sannio | RCOST (Research Center on Software Technology), Italy
Vasiliki Diamantopoulou, University of the Aegean, Greece
Mihaela Dinsoreanu, Technical University of Cluj-Napoca, Romania
Gokila Dorai, Augusta University, USA
Tomasz Dudek, Maritime University of Szczecin, Poland
Sourav Dutta, Ramapo College of New Jersey, USA
Tygran Dzhuguryan, Maritime University of Szczecin, Poland
Tome Eftimov, Jožef Stefan Institute, Ljubljana, Slovenia / Stanford University, Palo Alto, USA
Kemele M. Endris, L3S Research Center, Hannover, Germany
Fairouz Fakhfakh, Universiy of Sfax, Tunisia
Lamine Faty, Université Assane Seck de Ziguinchor, Senegal
Amélia Ferreira da Silva, Centre for Organizational and Social Studies of Porto Polytechnic, Portugal
Joan Francesc Fondevila, Universitat de Girona / Universitat Pompeu Fabra, Spain
Igor Garcia Ballhausen Sampaio, Instituto de Computação (UFF), Brazil
Susan Gauch, University of Arkansas, USA
Dipesh Gautam, Institute for Intelligent Systems (IIS) | The University of Memphis, USA
Alfonso González Briones, University of Salamanca, Spain
Malika Grim-Yefsah, University Gustave Eiffel | ENSG (Ecole Nationale des sciences géographique - Géomatique), France
Markus Grube, VOQUZ IT Solutions GmbH, Germany
Teresa Guarda, Universidad Estatal Peninsula Santa Elena - UPSE / Universidad de las Fuerzas Armadas – ESPE / ALGORITMI Research Centre | ESPE | UPSE, Ecuador
Michael Guckert, Technische Hochschule Mittelhessen, Germany
Carolina Guerini, Cattaneo University Castellanza (Varese) / Sda Bocconi, Milan, Italy
Gunadi Gunadi, Gajayana University, Malang, Indonesia
Juncal Gutiérrez-Artacho, Universidad de Granada, Spain

Mounira Harzallah, LS2N | University of Nantes, France
Manuel Herranz, Pangeanic, Spain
Stijn Hoppenbrouwers, HAN University of Applied Sciences, Arnhem / Radboud University, Nijmegen, Netherlands
Marjan Hosseinia, University of Houston, USA
Farah Jemili, Higher Institute of Computer Science and Telecom (ISITCOM) | University of Sousse, Tunisia
Richard Jiang, Lancaster University, UK
Maria José Sousa, ISCTE-Instituto Universitário de Lisboa, Portugal
Maria José Angélico Gonçalves, P.Porto/ ISCAP / CEOS.PP, Portugal
Katerina Kabassi, Ionian University, Greece
Yasushi Kambayashi, Nippon Institute of Technology, Japan
Jean Robert Kala Kamdjoug, Catholic University of Central Africa, Cameroon
Dimitris Kanellopoulos, University of Patras, Greece
Michael Kaufmann, Hochschule Luzern, Switzerland
Ron Kenett, Samuel Neaman Institute for National Policy Research - Technion, Israel
Noureddine Kerzazi, ENSIAS Mohamed V University in Rabat, Morocco
Sandi Kirkham, Staffordshire University, UK
Wilfried Kirschenmann, Aldwin by ANEO, France
Agnieszka Konys, West Pomeranian University of Technology in Szczecin, Poland
Christian Kop, Alpen-Adria-Universität Klagenfurt | Institute for Applied Informatics, Austria
Jarosław Korpysa, University of Szczecin, Poland
Olivera Kotevska, Oak Ridge National Laboratory (ORNL), Tennessee, USA
Milton Labanda-Jaramillo, Universidad Nacional de Loja, Ecuador
Birger Lantow, The University of Rostock, Germany
Chaya Liebeskind, Jerusalem College of Technology - Lev Academic Center, Israel
Erick López Ornelas, Universidad Autónoma Metropolitana, Mexico
Isabel Lopes, UNIAG & Polytechnic Institute of Bragança - ALGORITMI Research Centre, Portugal
Khoa Luu, University of Arkansas, USA
Pierre Maillot, INRIA, France
Paulo Maio, ISEP - School of Engineering of Polytechnic of Porto, Portugal
Carlos Alberto Malcher Bastos, Universidade Federal Fluminense, Brazil
Sheheeda Manakkadu, Gannon University, USA
Federica Mandreoli, Universita' di Modena e ReggioEmilia, Italy
Eric Mantelaers, RSM Netherlands / Maastricht University / Zuyd University of Applied Sciences / Open University, Netherlands
Elaine C. Marcial, Universidade de Brasília, Brazil
Claudia Martínez Araneda, Universidad Católica de la Santísima Concepción (UCSC), Chile
Yobani Martínez Ramírez, Universidad Autónoma de Sinaloa, Mexico
Michele Melchiori, Università degli Studi di Brescia, Italy
Fernando Moreira, Universidade Portucalense, Portugal
Vincenzo Moscato, University of Naples "Federico II", Italy
Tathagata Mukherjee, The University of Alabama in Huntsville, USA
Rajesh Kumar Mundotiya, University of Petroleum and Energy Studies, Dehradun, India
Mirna Muñoz, CIMAT, Mexico
Phivos Mylonas, Ionian University, Greece
Susana Nascimento, NOVA University of Lisboa, Portugal
Samer Nofal, German Jordanian University, Jordan
Issam Nouaouri, LGI2A | Université d'Artois, France

Takao Terano, Chiba University of Commerce / Tokyo Institute of Technology / University of Tsukuba, Japan
Giorgio Terracina, University of Calabria, Italy
Michele Tomaiuolo, Università di Parma, Italy
George Tambouratzis, ILSP/Athena Research Centre, Greece
Christos Troussas, Department of Informatics - University of Piraeus, Greece
Esteban Vázquez Cano, Universidad Nacional de Educación a Distancia (UNED), Spain
Marco Viviani, University of Milano-Bicocca, Italy
Hans Weigand, Tilburg University, Netherlands
Rihito Yaegashi, Kagawa University, Japan
Shuichiro Yamamoto, International Professional University in Nagoya, Japan
Erdem Yörük, Koç University, Turkey / University of Oxford, UK
Zurinahni Zainol, Universiti Sains Malaysia, Malaysia
Brahmi Zaki, Taibah University, KSA
Cecilia Zanni-Merk, INSA Rouen Normandie, France
Elmoukhtar Zemmouri, Moulay Ismail University, Meknes, Morocco
Yu-Dong Zhang (Eugene), University of Leicester, UK
Qiang Zhu, University of Michigan - Dearborn, USA
Beata Zielosko, University of Silesia in Katowice, Poland
Magdalena Zioło, University of Szczecin, Poland
Martijn Zoet, Zuyd University of Applied Science, The Nederland
Mounir Zrigui, Faculté des Sciences de Monastir, Tunisia

Copyright Information

Computational Grounded Theory

An Experiment: Human versus Machine

Clint Wolfs
Lectoraat Future-Proof Financial
Zuyd Hogeschool
Sittard, Netherlands
Clint.Wolfs@zuyd.nl

Eric Mantelaers
Lectoraat Future-Proof Financial
Zuyd Hogeschool
Sittard, Netherlands
Eric.Mantelaers@zuyd.nl

Martijn Zoet
Lectoraat Future-Proof Financial
Zuyd Hogeschool
Sittard, Netherlands
Martijn.Zoet@zuyd.nl

Rick Reijnders
Lectoraat Future-Proof Financial
Zuyd Hogeschool
Sittard, Netherlands
Rick.Reijnders@zuyd.nl

***Abstract*— Grounded theory has been a fundamental concept within qualitative research for decades. While human creativity forms an important element during the creation of new theories, there have been suggestions in which computers might support this creative process. As a result, the computational grounded theory framework was introduced. Currently, there is a lack of studies that evaluate practical performance implications of computational grounded theory approaches. This paper aims to contribute by evaluating the differences between a manual and an automated keyword extraction process; a process that is considered to be important during the first stage of the open coding process. Results indicate that the outcomes of the automated process are - to some extent - in line with the outcomes of the manual process. Nonetheless, phi coefficients do not exceed 0.21, meaning that the results do not perfectly agree with each other. As a result, some keywords might be left out while other unimportant words may be labeled as being a keyword. Therefore, although automatic keyword extractors can be helpful during the open coding process, results should still be cautiously interpreted. Moreover, the results indicate that elements of the computational grounded theory framework can be implemented in practice, without significant different results.**

Keywords*— Computational grounded theory; automatic keyword extractors; qualitative research; theory development; coding process; validity; reliability; RAKE; PRE; SRE; TRE; MRE; Yake!; KBERT

I. Introduction

Content analysis is an established method in scientific research. One of the main challenges with content analysis in general, and hand-coding techniques in particular, is the resources (in terms of cost and time) associated with the data collection and data analysis. Therefore, one can question the scope and depth of textual data analysis. As a result, researchers have been investigating ways to minimize resources while maintaining reliability, validity and reproducibility. In addition, a more efficient process enables the researchers to collect and analyze more (diverse) data sources to begin with.

Two fields that have changed content analysis (and continue to do so) are (1) information science and (2) computational linguistics [1]-[6]. Both apply supervised machine learning, as well as unsupervised machine learning to text analysis. This has led to a debate on how to incorporate such methods in existing research processes and methods without compromising scientific integrity. More specifically, it has led to the question how computational linguistics can result in higher reliability, validity and reproducibility of the results.

Nelson [7] proposes a methodological framework called computational grounded theory which consists of three steps: 1) pattern detection using unsupervised methods, 2) pattern refinement using guided deep reading and 3) pattern confirmation using natural language processing. These steps consist of techniques that support the traditional coding process within grounded theory: 1) open coding, 2) axial coding and 3) selective coding. Often, these techniques are tested by comparing and evaluating the information retrieval of specific algorithms. However, for practical application, a comparison to the results of human coding is preferred [9]. Nonetheless, Nelson [7] states that human comparison has not been performed very often.

This paper aims to extend the understanding of the application of unsupervised methods for open coding. While we in line with previous research consider multiple unsupervised techniques, we compare these techniques to the results of human coding and treat this coding as our benchmark. With these premises, the specific research question addressed is: "How do the results of unsupervised methods compare to human coded results?"

The remainder of this paper is organized as follows. First, section 2 discusses the literature review which is followed by the explanation of the research method in section 3. Section 4 describes the data collection and the results are presented in section 5. Section 6 the conclusions and corresponding discussion. Lastly, limitations and propositions for future research are presented in section 7.

II. LITERATURE REVIEW

As previously mentioned in the introduction, [7] propose a methodological framework in which computers might assist during the traditional process of grounded theory. The automated process of keyword extraction can be a practical interpretation of computer assisted grounded theory.

A. *(Computational) Grounded Theory*

Grounded theory is considered to be a fundamental concept within qualitative research. In contrast to the research often conducted within the quantitative field, grounded theory does not seek to prove or disprove theories that remain to be untested [9]. Rather, the aim of grounded theory is to construct theories [9] that can be tested using traditional quantitative research methods. Grounded theory consists of three main phases, being open coding, axial coding and selective coding [10]. During the open coding process, key words or key phrases that are believed to be related to some phenomenon are extracted from the qualitative data [11]. Through systematic analysis and constant comparison of the coded data, the relationships between phenomena can then be investigated during the axial coding process [11]. Thereby, overarching categories are created. Lastly, one single core category that overarches multiple of the underlying categories is created during the selective coding process [10].

Despite of the proposed methodological framework of [7], the coding process often remains a manual process. In addition to the relatively high labor intensity of this manual process and the subjectivity across coders, there are also plausible limitations in terms of reproducibility [7]. Inconsistencies within coded elements from individual coders could lead to suboptimal and inaccurate results. As a result, independent coders (try to) follow guidelines and be as consistent as possible during the coding process [12]. Additionally, a retrospective assessment of the quality of the coding process is considered to be very important [13]. In its most simplistic form, the reliability of multiple coders can be assessed by computing the percentage of agreement. However, it is argued that this (relatively simple) measure can be misleading since it does not take coincidence into account [14]. As a result, Krippendorff proposed a more conservative method to determine the reliability by taking random chance into account [14]. Nonetheless, while these measures can be helpful, they are examples of repressive measures and checks. If these measures lead to the conclusion that the coding process is inconsistent, the labor-intensive coding process has to be redone in order to prevent unsubstantiated theory development. It would be more useful if inconsistencies can be minimized to begin with. A certain type of automation might form a plausible preventive measure.

B. *Automatic Keyword Extraction*

As previously mentioned, key words are selected at the beginning of the open coding process. Since these selected keywords form the foundation of the grounded theory process, it is important that these keywords are the result of a consistent process. By using a machine instead of a human, inconsistencies might be minimized. The selection of keywords is a process that could be done automatically in a variety of different manners. Automatic keyword extraction is the process in which an algorithm identifies the keywords within a collection of texts (corpus). These keywords should represent the most useful information within the corpus [15]. With the manual open coding process in mind, automatic keyword extraction algorithms could not only simplify this labor-intensive process but could also establish more consistent results. As of now, there are numerous algorithms available that each has its own approach in determining whether or not a word is a keyword [15].

C. *Types of Automtic Keyword Extractors*

Similar to manual coding, it is possible to use multiple estimators and aggregate their decision. Within this study, there are seven independent algorithms that will be used to estimate whether or not a word is a keyword: Rapid Keyword Extraction (RAKE), Position Rank Extractor (PRE), Single Rank Extractor (SRE), Topic Rank Extractor (TRE), Multipartite Rank Extractor (MRE), Yet Another Keyword Extractor (Yake!) and Key Bidirectional Encoder Representations from Transformers (KBERT).

RAKE assumes that key phrases usually occur in the beginning of a text corpus [16]. Because of this assumption, one important parameter is the phrase delimiter (',' and '.' for example) which is used to create so called 'candidate experessions'. These candidate expressions are part of a sentence/text corpus. Moreover, a second important parameter is a list with stopwords. This list is used to 1) remove irrelevant words from the tokenized corpus and 2) split the corpus to create the candidate expressions. The final score is calculated using both the words (exluding stopwords) and the candidate expressions. In addition, RAKE differentiates itself from comparable algorithms due to its simplicity [17], computational efficiency, speed and the ability to work on individual documents [16] Nonetheless, the plausible lack of stopwords (which is a parameter) might influence the output, resulting in less relevant results [16].

PRE is a graph based approach in which a vertex represents a token and an edge represent a relationship between vertices [15]. For each individual word, PRE establishes a graph [18]. Moreover, PRE considers (in addition to word position) also the word frequency [16]. Based on this information, words that occur relatively often and early within the corpora, receive a greater probability of being a keyword [16]. This means that the assumption of RAKE could also be applicable to PRE [16]. In terms of performance, PRE seems to perform better compared to the TextRank alternative.

SRE generates a graph for each document based on the words in that document. Moreover, it computes the corresponding word scores that drive the decision on whether or not a word is considered to be a keyword [19].

Similar to SRE and PRE, TRE is also a graph-based approach. However, it tries to achieve better performance by assuming that each document relates to a specific topic. Indeed, the addition of this assumption generally leads to a better performance in terms of the precision and recall evaluation measures, compared to TRE [20].

MRE is built upon the foundation of TRE and therefore has similar assumptions. However, whereas TRE simply tries to find relationships between words based on different topics, MRE also tries to differentiate the importance of the relationships between words within those topics [21]. Results indicate that this approach leads to better performance, compared to SRE, PRE and TRE [18].

Whereas PRE seemed to perform better compared to TextRank, Yake! seems to perform better than RAKE, TextRank and SRE. Comparable to most algorithms, Yake! starts with tokenizing the text corpus based on specified delimiters. Based on this list of words, five features are extracted: casing (does the word start with a capital letter, excluding the words at the start of a sentence), word position, word frequency, relatedness to context and the proportion of sentences that include the word. Due to the word position feature, the assumption that more relevant words occur in the beginning of a text corpus is (again) applicable. The five features are then aggregated into one number which will then be used to determine a final score [22].

KBERT originates from the Bidirectional Encoder Representations from Transformers (BERT) algorithm which can be used for the creation of word embeddings [23]. The input for the BERT algorithm includes three main elements: token, segment and position [24]. Therefore, BERT differentiates itself from most other word embedding architectures that merely use word vectors as input [24]. Initial performance results of a (fine-tuned) BERT classification model seem to be high with an accuracy of 97.6% according to a recent study [24].

As previously mentioned, most literature focusses on performance comparison between algorithms [7] while a comparison to the results of human coding is preferred [8]. Therefore, this paper aims to evaluate plausible differences between manual and automated keyword extraction. In the end, while automated results might be more reliable, it does not mean that the results are valid. A comparison with a manual process is in this context the only way to also take validity into consideration. Therefore, the following hypothesis will be tested:

H1.) There is no significant association between the results of the automated and manual text coding process.

III. RESEARCH METHOD

The goal of this study is to evaluate plausible differences between manual and automated text coding. More specifically, this paper aims to identify the differences between the automated and manual keyword extraction. While the consistency of the automated process will be higher, it does not mean that the algorithms identify the correct key words to begin with. Therefore, it is important to compare the automated results to the results of human coding. Texts will be assessed by the seven independent algorithms and two individual researchers.

A. *Keyword Extraction*

Regarding the automated keyword extraction, seven algorithms will be used to identify the most unique and relevant words within the text corpus (keywords). For each text corpus, the results of these independent algorithms will be compared to each other.

With regard to the manual keyword extraction process, two researchers will be selecting the most unique and relevant words from the same text corpus. For reliability concerns, the results of both researchers will be tested for consistency using the inter rater reliability coding method. In the situation of a disagreement, both researchers will directly discuss and adjust coding accordingly.

B. *Comparison*

In order to meet the primary objective of this study, the results of the manual and automated coding process need to be compared. This comparison will be made on two levels. First, the results of the manual coding procedure are compared to the results of each individual algorithm. In addition, the results of the manual coding process will be compared to an aggregated result. More specifically, if at least five out of seven algorithms identify a word as being a keyword, we conclude that the general automated approach identifies the word as a keyword.

In addition to descriptive statistics, differences between the categories will be tested on significance and effect size. While significance will be tested by a chi-square test, effect size will be determined by both a phi coefficient and an odds-ratio respectively.

IV. DATA COLLECTION

The data that will be used for this study, is formed by a collection of titles of news articles and online blogs. These data have been collected by the research group Future-Proof Financial of Zuyd Hogeschool. Over a period of thirteen months (January 10th 2021 - February 4th 2022), the data have been collected. Because the news articles and online blogs are collected from websites of accounting firms, most news articles are related to accounting. On a daily basis, the URLs of articles and blogs have been automatically collected via the use of web scrapers. Using the URLs of all the blogs and articles, the titles can be extracted. The selection of accounting firms is based on a verified registration of accounting firms that is maintained by the Dutch government.

The final data table consisted of 29.672 rows that each represents an URL to an article or blog that was posted by one of the 181 sources (websites). Due to duplicate titles, 177 sources remain of which 19.209 URLs have been collected and will be taken into consideration during the analyses.

V. RESULTS

During the analysis, the 177 sources resulted in 19.209 titles and thus unique URLs. Moreover, all the titles combined consisted of 213.127 words which, on average, counted 6.28 characters. Figure 1 shows the relative distribution frequency for the number of characters in the words. While inspecting Figure 1, it is important to note that the Dutch language does not include spaces in word compositions. For example, 'small-scale investment deduction' is written as one single word: 'kleinschaligheidsinvesteringsaftrek'. Furthermore, the 213.127 words and 19.209 titles resulted in an average of 11.1 words for each title (i.e., text corpus). Figure 2 provides the relative distribution frequency for the number of words in the corpus. Since some publishers chose to use a brief introduction as title section, the distribution is severely right-skewed. Lastly, out of these 213.127 words, only 15.779 words were found to be unique throughout the whole data set.

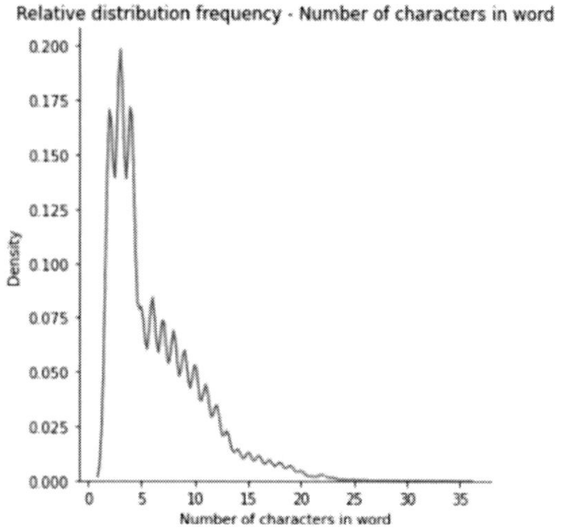

Figure 1. Relate distribution frequency of number of characters in words

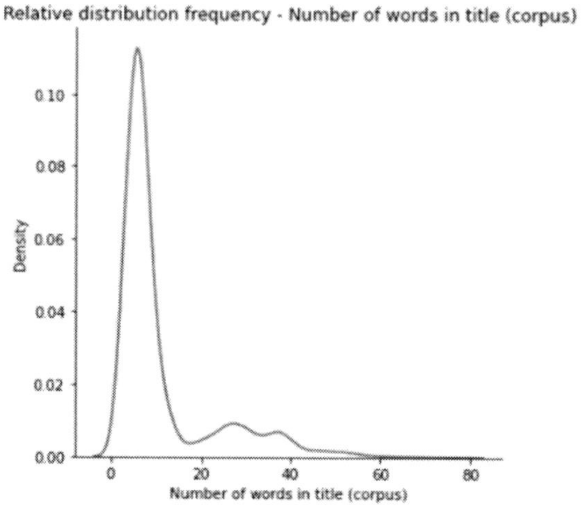

Figure 2. Relative distribution frequency of number of words in corpus

With regards to the statistical tests, all results turned out to be highly significant with chi-square values that range between +/- 3.000 up to +/- 10.000. This would imply that the expected frequencies differ significantly from the observed frequencies, meaning that the algorithms either significantly agree or disagree with the manual results. With phi coefficients ranging between 0.12 and 0.21, we can conclude there is not an extraordinary high or low association. Nonetheless, the positive coefficients indicate that the algorithms significantly agree with the manual results. A minimum of 2.49 and a maximum of 4.34 for the odds ratios confirm that it is more likely that the algorithms do not indicate the word as a keyword, given that the manual

TABLE I. STATISTICAL RESULTS - AUTOMATED V.S. MANUAL RESULTS

Comparison	Chi-square	p-value	degrees of freedom	n	phi coefficient	odds ratio
Aggregated assessment vs. Manual assessment	7.798.193	0.0	1	213127	0.191	4.019
RAKE vs. Manual assessment	2.984.758	0.0	1	213127	0.118	2.486
YAKE vs. Manual assessment	8.836.122	0.0	1	213127	0.205	4.335
PRE vs. Manual assessment	9.847.433	0.0	1	213127	0.215	4.206
SRE vs. Manual assessment	6.961.978	0.0	1	213127	0.181	3.633
MRE vs. Manual assessment	6.672.700	0.0	1	213127	0.177	3.475
TRE vs. Manual assessment	6.293.304	0.0	1	213127	0.172	3.379
KBERT vs. Manual assessment	6.564.973	0.0	1	213127	0.176	3.433

process did not indicate it as a keyword either. For example, the odds ratio of 4.34 indicates that it is 4.34 times more likely that Yake! does not indicate a word as being a keyword, given that the manual process did not indicate the word as a keyword either. Interesting to mention is that Yake! (X2 (1, 213,127) = 8,836.12, $p < 0.01$, $\varphi = 0.204$) and PRE (X2 (1, 213,127) = 9,847.43, $p < 0.01$, $\varphi = 0.215$)

TABLE II. CONTINGENCY TABLE – AUTOMATED AGGREGATED RESULTS | MANUAL RESULTS

	Aggregated assessment | Yes	Aggregated assessment | No
Manual assessment | Yes	6,548 / 3.1%	13,830 / 6.5%
Manual assessment | No	20,316 / 9.5%	172,433 / 80,9%

turned out to have the highest phi coefficient, while both are less computationally intensive compared to KBERT. Moreover, Yake! and PRE are also the only algorithms that – in terms of effect sizes - outperform the aggregated assessment (X2 (1, 213,127) = 7,798.19, $p < 0.01$, $\varphi = 0.191$) where at least 5 out of 7 algorithms have to agree before indicating it as a keyword. Table I shows the contingency table for the comparison between the manual results and the automated, aggregated assessment. Table II provides the results for each individual algorithm and the aggregated assessment. Table II shows that, regardless of the algorithm used, the results of the automated process are significantly associated with the results of the manual process. More specifically, the table shows only positive phi coefficients, meaning that manual and automated results are significantly in line with each other. This implies that we can reject the hypothesis stated above.

VI. DISCUSSION AND LIMITATIONS

Even though initial results seem promising, there are also several limitations to take into account while interpreting these results and corresponding conclusions. First of all, the data are related to one single area of expertise. While this eases the process of selecting coders for the manual text coding process, it also limits the degree to which the conclusions should be taken into consideration. It might be that results are optimal within the financial/accounting expertise but not so in the medical field. Moreover, only Dutch articles have been covered by the text coding process. This might limit the representativeness of the results. Most important reason is that most keyword extraction algorithms rely (to some extent) on the position of words. As a result, the algorithms might become inaccurate if a certain language relies on a different structure. Lastly, while the titles were often completely written in the Dutch language, there were instances in which a title also used English terms. This might have limited the accuracy of our results since most algorithms require defining the language of the text corpus.

VII. CONCLUSION AND FUTURE WORK

While the theoretical framework of computational grounded theory has been published several years ago, it seems that practical applications are mostly purely within the algorithmic field. As a result, a comparison between the performance of algorithms and the performance of the manual process is often left out. Moreover, while algorithms form an application of automation and therefore deliver more reliable results, it does not mean that algorithms also deliver valid results. By comparing manual and automated results, this study attempted to apply one single element of computation grounded theory in practice, outside of the purely algorithmic field. The effect sizes imply that, while the results of the manual and automated process are significantly associated, the phi coefficients are not necessarily extraordinary high or low. Nonetheless, no algorithm was found to be negatively associated with the results of the manual process, indicating that the manual and automated results are more often in line with each other than that they are not. This indicates that validity – to some extent – is warranted. As a result, automatic keyword extractors can be a helpful technique during the open coding process.

By automating the identification of important words that are labeled in the next stage of the coding process, the consistency across manual coders might be improved. Moreover, it seems to be plausible that the use of automatic keyword extractors leads to a less resource intensive process. Nonetheless, automatic keyword extractors should be used cautiously since it is likely that there still are false positives (found keywords that are not necessarily important) and false negatives (important words that are not found by the algorithm). This might have severe consequences for the next stages of the coding process and therefore, severe consequences for the theory development as a whole.

With regards to future work, limitations that are stated in the previous section could be taken into consideration. In addition to these limitations, this study solely focuses on one single part of the proposed computational grounded theory framework. It would be useful to investigate and compare machine and human performance with regards to other individual elements of the computational grounded theory framework. Lastly, it would be interesting to evaluate machine and human performance with regards to the computational grounded theory framework as a whole.

REFERENCES

[1] C. A. Bail, "Inside the Rituals of Social Science," Theory and Society, vol. 43, no. 3–4, pp. 465–482, Jul. 2014, doi: https://doi.org/10.1007/s11186-014-9216-5.

[2] R. Biernacki, "The cultural environment: measuring culture with big data," Reinventing Evidence in Social Inquiry, pp. 1–26, 2012, doi: https://doi.org/10.1057/9781137007285_1.

[3] P. DiMaggio, M. Nag, and D. Blei, "Exploiting affinities between topic modeling and the sociological perspective on culture: Application to newspaper coverage of U.S. government arts funding," Poetics, vol. 41, no. 6, pp. 570–

606, Dec. 2013, doi: https://doi.org/10.1016/j.poetic.2013.08.004.

[4] J. W. Mohr and P. Bogdanov, "Introduction—Topic models: What they are and why they matter," Poetics, vol. 41, no. 6, pp. 545–569, Dec. 2013, doi: https://doi.org/10.1016/j.poetic.2013.10.001.

[5] P. A. Reed and J. E. LaPorte, "A content analysis of AIAA/ITEA/ITEEA conference special interest sessions: 1978-2014," Journal of Technology Education, vol. 26, no. 3, Jul. 2015, doi: https://doi.org/10.21061/jte.v26i3.a.2.

[6] K. M. Meyer and T. Tang, "#SocialJournalism: Local news media on twitter," International Journal on Media Management, vol. 17, no. 4, pp. 241–257, Oct. 2015, doi: https://doi.org/10.1080/14241277.2015.1107569.

[7] L. K. Nelson, "Computational grounded theory: A methodological framework," Sociological Methods & Research, vol. 49, no. 1, pp. 3–42, Dec. 2020, doi: https://doi.org/10.1177/0049124117729703.

[8] K. Benoit, M. Laver, and S. Mikhaylov, "Treating words as data with error: Uncertainty in text statements of policy positions," American Journal of Political Science, vol. 53, no. 2, pp. 495–513, Dec. 2009, doi: https://doi.org/10.1111/j.1540-5907.2009.00383.x.

[9] J. Mills, A. Bonner, and K. Francis, "The development of constructivist grounded theory," International Journal of Qualitative Methods, vol. 5, no. 1, pp. 25–35, Mar. 2006, doi: https://doi.org/10.1177/160940690600500103.

[10] A. Moghaddam. "Coding issues in grounded theory," Issues In Educational Research, vol. 16, no. 1, pp. 52–66, Apr. 2006.

[11] C. Goulding, "Grounded Theory: some reflections on paradigm, procedures and misconceptions," working paper, University of Wolverhampton., Telford, UK, 1999 [Online]. Available: https://wlv.openrepository.com/bitstream/handle/2436/11403/Goulding.pdf?sequence=1&isAllowed=y

[12] J. Nassar, Viveca Pavon-Harr, M. Bosch, and I. McCulloh, "Assessing data quality of annotations with krippendorff alpha for applications in computer vision," Dec. 2019.

[13] K. Krippendorff, " Computing Krippendorff's Alpha-Reliability," working paper, University of Pennsylvania., Philadelphia, PA, USA, 2011 [Online]. Available: https://repository.upenn.edu/cgi/viewcontent.cgi?article=1043&context=asc_papers

[14] M. Zoet, J. Versendaal, P. Ravesteyn, and R. Welke, 'Alignment of business process management and business rules', 2011.

[15] S. Beliga, A. Meštrović, and S. Martinčić-Ipšić, "An overview of graph-based keyword extraction methods and approaches," Journal of Information and Organizational Sciences, vol. 39, no. 1, pp. 1–20, 2015.

[16] M. G. Thushara, Tadi Mownika, and Ritika Mangamuru, "A comparative study on different keyword extraction algorithms," in 2019 3rd International Conference on Computing Methodologies and Communication (ICCMC), Dec. 2019, pp. 969–973. doi: https://doi.org/10.1109/ICCMC.2019.8819630.

[17] S. Anjali, N. M. Meera, and M. G. Thushara, "A graph based approach for keyword extraction from documents," in 2019 Second International Conference on Advanced Computational and Communication Paradigms (ICACCP), Dec. 2019, pp. 1–4. doi: https://doi.org/10.1109/ICACCP.2019.8882946.

[18] M. Ravikiran, "Finding black cat in a coal cellar – keyphrase extraction & keyphrase-rubric relationship classification from complex assignments," Dec. 2020.

[19] X. Wan and J. Xiao, "Single document keyphrase extraction using neighborhood knowledge.," in AAAI, 2008, vol. 8, pp. 855–860.

[20] A. Bougouin, F. Boudin, and Béatrice Daille, "TopicRank: Graph-based topic ranking for keyphrase extraction," in International Joint Conference on Natural Language Processing (IJCNLP), Dec. 2013, pp. 543–551. Available: https://hal.archives-ouvertes.fr/hal-00917969

[21] F. Boudin, "Unsupervised keyphrase extraction with multipartite graphs," in Proceedings of the 2018 Conference of the North American Chapter of the Association for Computational Linguistics: Human Language Technologies, Volume 2 (Short Papers), 2018, pp. 667–672. doi: https://doi.org/10.18653/v1/N18-2105.

[22] R. Campos, Vítor Mangaravite, A. Pasquali, Alípio Mário Jorge, C. Nunes, and A. Jatowt, "YAKE! Collection-independent automatic keyword extractor," pp. 806–810, 2018, doi: https://doi.org/10.1007/978-3-319-76941-7_80.

[23] Y. Wang, L. Cui, and Y. Zhang, "How can BERT help lexical semantics tasks?," Dec. 2019.

[24] M. Tang, P. Gandhi, Md Ahsanul Kabir, C. Zou, J. Blakey, and X. Luo, "Progress notes classification and keyword extraction using attention-based deep learning models with BERT," Dec. 2019.

Technological Support for Correcting Exams: The Continuum Paradigm

Next step forward to build a holistic continuous audit model

Ed Curfs and Eric Mantelaers
Future-Proof Auditor
Zuyd University of Applied Sciences
Sittard, the Netherlands
ed.curfs@zuyd.nl
eric.mantelaers@zuyd.nl

Martijn Zoet and Clint Wolfs
Future-Proof Financial
Zuyd University of Applied Sciences
Sittard, the Netherlands
martijn.zoet@zuyd.nl
clint.wolfs@zuyd.nl

Abstract—**Continuous Monitoring, Continuous Auditing, Continuous Assurance, Continuous Reporting and the Continuum Paradigm (CP) are the elements in which research has been performed over 30 years. A major part of the research was focused on individual elements of the CP. However, no research has been performed with the purpose to identify if it is possible to build a holistic audit model based on the CP. Researchers noticed that there are no global standards available yet, approved by the stakeholders in relation to Continuous Assurance or Continuous Reporting. In this paper, we developed and built a simplified and holistic CP, the case study, for the four building blocks of the CP: Continuous Monitoring, Continuous Auditing, Continuous Assurance and Continuous Reporting. The case study is based on an exam for the post-doc education program for Financial Auditing at Dutch Universities. An exam has been selected as this makes it possible to verify the performance of the model by verification of the machine (case study) versus the manual results. The overall conclusion is that there is a correlation between the results of the machine and the manual results of the examinators. However, the score of the machine is structurally lower than the manual scores of the examinators. The case study proves that it is possible to build an audit model, with reference to the technological support for correcting exams, based on the CP.**

Keywords–case study; continuous monitoring; continuous auditing; continuous assurane; continuous reporting; continuum paradigm; reporting; forensic; financial auditing; financial data and non-financial data; machine review; manual review; sustainability reporting; testscripts.

I. INTRODUCTION

Due to cost-reduction programs, the increase of the labor costs, the shortage of skilled and educated professional financial auditors, increase the need for implementation (AI), ChatGTP, data analytics, process mining and also the further development of the CP. These advances are resulting in the creation of added value for the management of organizations and their stakeholders.

However, the process of the implementation of the CP is on-going for more than three decades [1] [8] [9]. Nonetheless, a holistic continuous audit model based on the CP has not yet been designed, built, and implemented. In the past, research has mainly been focused on non-financial data [1]-[3] although the first goal of the CP is to provide assurance of financial data, the annual statement of a company or even 'continuous' published financial figures of the company. Based on the current development in law and regulation, the importance to get insight in a holistic continuous audit model increases. For the individual elements of the CP, a lot of research has been performed [1]-[3][5][6][8]. The goal of this case study is to develop the CP as a holistic system in a pragmatical way. Based on the outcome of the case study, professionals and researchers will gain a better understanding of the actual status and the missing building blocks to achieve a successful implementation of the CP at a larger scale.

The remainder of this paper is structured as follows. Section 2 summarizes the results of the literature review. The research method is described in Section 3. In Section 4 the data collection is described. The results are described in Section 5. Section 6 describes the conclusion. Finally, the paper concludes in Section 7 with the limitations and future research.

II. LITERATUE REVIEW

The four building blocks of the CP are (1) Continuous Monitoring (CM), (2) Continuous Auditing (CA), (3) Continuous Assurance (CAss), and (4) Continuous Reporting (CRe). A lot of research has been performed to each element from several different views and perspectives, however, so far, no research has been performed on all the elements of the CP as a whole.

The need for ongoing, timely assurance of data and information utilizing CM, CA, CAss, and CRe is becoming more apparent. To improve the readability of the article the abbreviations are presented in Table I.

In the last decades, Vasarheyli, Kuenkaikaew, Alles and Willems performed research in the area of CM, CA, CAss, and CRe [1]. This research was mainly related to financial data and limited to one single element of the CP, e.g., CM or CA. Due to new applicable law and regulation non-financial data becomes more and more relevant. These new developments, in combination with the IT developments and the shortage on the labor market, place pressure on further development of a holistic system of the CP as an audit model.

To build a holistic CP [1][8][9], making use of real data, has not been achieved yet since the following standards are missing. Global accepted standards with regards to CM, audit and assurance standards related to classification of CA, and reporting standards for CRe are not yet defined and approved by the related international bodies.

Alles et al. performed research in the area of Continuous Monitoring of Business Process Controls (CMBPC) [2]. Architecture has been developed to build a complete independent CMBPC system running on top of the Siemens' own enterprise information system. This pilot showed that it is feasible for a large internal audit department to implement a vast array of CA-type procedures to mitigate business risks in certain high impact areas, and to achieve labor savings through automation of internal audit tasks. Based on a detailed investigation of this pilot the outcome is that certain SAP reports related to logical access, including all parameters and changes of these parameters, have been developed, including red flags. These red flags require further investigation of the internal auditor of Siemens. This task results in a judgment of the auditor, is related to CA and is associated to audit the reliability and sustainability of the internal control system. This is one of the four so-called General IT controls. The elements CM, CAss and CRe were not part of this pilot.

Kogan, Sudit and Vasarhelyi investigated the status of Continuous Online Auditing (COA) in 1999 [3]. The outcome of the program of research was that further research needed to be performed in the areas of general architecture. In addition, future research should explore and design standard formats for enterprise data to facilitate data capture for COA. Furthermore, future research should focus on investigating the trade-offs, exploring the extent to which the auditor can rely on COA and investigating whether the use of COA is more likely to be initiated by internal than external auditors.

Recent research has been performed by Canning et. al [4] in the area of processes of auditability sustainability assurance. The purpose of the case study was to provide a better understanding of how financial audit concepts are translated in the sustainability assurance arena. A total of fourteen semi-structure and in-depth interviews were conducted with sustainability assurors who had financial audit training and experience or were specialists in other areas. These interviews were conducted between the period March and July 2013. Based on the information received, the audit of non-financial data is mainly performed manually, making limited use of IT solutions. Furthermore, it became clearer that financial auditors also choose to switch from financial audit in order to specialize in non-financial audit domains as for example corporate sustainability reporting. Explicitly examining their intrinsic motivations for switching, their experiences, and the influence they seek to bring to bear on assurance practices in new spaces, including materiality assessments, would be a fruitful avenue for future research.

The interest for the CP increases and research has been performed also regarding Forensic Continuous Auditing (FCA) by Kearns and Barker [5]. The conclusion of the research was that there are cogent reasons for adopting a system of forensic continuous auditing. Experience has shown that the traditional financial audit is not an effective mechanism for uncovering fraud [5]. The forensic continuous audit system resulted in creation of control reports.

Eulerich and Kalinichenko [6] investigated the current state and future directions of CA research and one of the conclusions was that very specific applications for CA were investigated and the pragmatical added value for a general internal audit function may be limited. This situation cannot be acceptable and requires further research and investigation. The focus should be on pragmatical and practical applications for CA. Based on our review of the available research, we noted that limited results have been booked regarding the development and design of a holistic audit model based on the CP. We would like to investigate if there are pragmatical simplified cases available to perform a holistic test that takes all elements of the CP into account.

TABLE I. OVERVIEW RELEVANT ABBREVIATIONS OF THE ARTICLE

Abbreviation	*Description*
CA	Continuous Auditing
CAss	Continuous Assurance
CM	Continuous Monitoring
CMBPC	Continuous Monitoring of Business Process Controls
CP	Continuum Paradigm
COA	Continuous Online Auditing
CRe	Continuous Reporting

Based on the literature review it can be concluded that all elements of the CP have been heavily investigated as stand-alone components. No attempt has been made to investigate several elements simultaneously or build a simple model to prove the CP design and concept as a holistic audit model. The main reasons that no integrated holistic research has been performed are: (1) there are no global standard for monitoring internal controls, (2) there are auditing standards, for internal and external auditors, however these are always tailored per engagement / customer, (3) there are assurance standards, for internal and external auditors, however the professional judgment of the auditor is a complex process, based on data of several sources, and (4) there are reporting standards, auditors opinion, however these are the results of the auditing standards and the professional judgement of the auditor.

The goal of this research is to build, an audit model based on a case study. The model of the case study and the relation with the basic principles of the CP will be explained in detail in Section 3.

III. RESEARCH METHOD

The goal of this research is to build a holistic audit model based on the CP. The first step was to find an example or process that could be used to investigate all or nearly all buildings blocks of the CP. To make this possible, the team of three researchers investigated the options for simple processes that currently are performed manually. The team of researchers existing of 1) a junior researcher, with broad experience in internal and external auditing, 2) a senior researcher (PhD) with broad experience as external auditor and 3) a senior researcher with broad experience on business rules management has been established. In addition, the processes should contain both financial as well as non-financial data. Moreover, it should be technically possible to automate the manual process. Lastly, the manual tasks should be linked to the building blocks of the CP.

The case study should provide insight in how a manual process could be transferred to a holistic audit model, based on the building blocks of the CP. This manual process should be based on the following tasks, (1) monitoring of a subject, (2) auditing of a subject, (3) defining achieved level of assurance based on the pre-defined standard and (4) reporting of the outcome. A manual process that could be used, is for example the review and judgment of written exams. By automating this process, it would be possible to compare the results of the manual process and the results automated process. The most important reasons for selecting the process of a written exam are (1) this is a simple process and (2) the tasks to be performed manually can be linked one to one to the building blocks of the CP.

In the manual process, an examiner is reading ten or more written exams, exam by exam and answer by answer. In practice, this task is performed over a period of several days as a stand-alone task. If the task can be performed for more than two exams simultaneously, it could be defined as a continuous task. The next task, the assessment of the content on one answer versus the content of the standard solution guidance has been linked to the building block CA. Audit is the verification of an outcome, result versus a pre-defined accepted standard. For the case study, the standard used is the standard examination guidance. The following manual task, calculation of the result of a written exam has been linked to the building block CAss. The outcome of an exam can be compared to the outcome of a financial audit. The auditor provides a certain level of assurance. In basic terms, there are two options (1) a qualified opinion or (2) a not-qualified opinion. The next manual task of recording the final result of a written exam per candidate corresponds to the building block CRe. More specifically, the knowledge level per topic per candidate is reported.

The CP includes the judgement process in the combination of the building blocks CM, CA and CAss. In Table II a high-level overview is presented with regard to the relationship between the building blocks of the CP and the manual tasks performed by reviewing written exams. There is a one-to-one relationship between the assessment process and the four building blocks of the CP.

The goals of the public auditor exams (as applicable in the Netherlands) are development to verify the level of actual competences about e.g., risk management, internal control, customer acceptance, materiality, audit approach, law and regulation, audit methodology, audit techniques, and professional judgement. The development of professional judgement is to improve the process as well as the quality of decision making, as investigated by Vaassen and Bröcheler [7]. Their research has been performed in 1996 and is based on the internal control exams. The research approach has partly been used as a reference for the development of the script. The script is a computer script that automates the manual assessment process. The script makes use of predefined topics. A topic is related to a task a financial auditor performs. Table V provides an overview of the 18 defined topics. The script also contains the counting mechanism per question and the counting mechanism in total, based on the allocated points per word, figure and abbreviation per question. This results in a standard score per question, is shown inTable III. In addition, this results in a score per topic, which illustrates the knowledge level per topic.

TABLE II. ELEMENTS IN SCOPE TEST SCRIPT

The Continuum Paradigm			
CM	*CA*	*CAss*	*CRe*
The Exam Gambit morning and afternoon session of the population in total 33.	*The test cript based on the standard examination guidance made by the developer of Exam Gambit. The test script has been developed and reviewed by the 3 researchers.*	*Based on the points per question and the valuation as defined in the test script per candidate a results is presented.*	*The results per candidate is presented in an overview of achieved knowledge level per topic.*

Since this research is based on the internal control exams, we searched for exams with more or less the same design, structure and review process. The researchers decided to select the evaluation process of Financial Auditing exams made by students of the Dutch post-doc program Auditing. The reasons that this evaluation process has been selected are that the following data are available: (1) a case and written exams as input and subjects to be audited, (2) the rating methodology and method, (3) a standard examination guidance prepared by an independent audit professional, (4) general accepted guidance and rules for evaluation of the cases and defining the final judgement.

The next step was to select a representative exam to build the case study. Based on the selected exam, universities can be contacted to request the results made by the student for that specific exam. The Dutch National Exam Auditing of summer 2022, Exam Gambit, has been selected to build a model for the four building blocks (CM, CA, CAss and CRe) of the CP.

The main reason for selecting the Exam Gambit is that this is the most recent exam and represents the instances required by the auditing profession as well as the program of requirements defined by the Dutch Auditing Profession. This exam has also been selected as this relates to financial data as well as non-financial data. Exams in the context of, for example, psychology studies, teacher training, law studies, engineering studies, construction studies, chemical studies, languages, are less suitable because they often do not relate financial and non-financial data. The researchers are of the opinion that the CP should be created via a case study for both types of data. In the near future, due to developments related to the development of global law and regulation, both will require continuous attention. Furthermore, the data elements of the Exam Gambit (two parts, morning, and afternoon session) are available. These are the exam, the standard examination guidance of the Exam Gambit, the valuation of the questions of the morning and afternoon Exam Gambit, the rating / assurance level of the National Exam (the regulation), the exams made by the students and the guidance how the results are presented to the accountable Professor of the university and the students.

The researchers are aware of the fact that building a case study for one exam of a post-doc program still is not a fully continuous process of monitoring the results and performance of a student during the whole post-soc program. However, this will be a simpler task to be automated. A calendar, a timetable of the post-doc program and results of a student are the data elements to be combined into one dashboard.

A. *Manual Judgement Process*

The case for the Auditing exam is prepared by one of the seven universities in the Netherlands accountable for the post-doc program Auditing. Cases are made on a rotation base. Each exam exists of a morning session and an afternoon session. For each session, the candidates can spend 3 to maximum 3,5 hours, depending on the standard defined by the exam developer. The morning and afternoon session of the Exam Gambit counted each four questions and for each session, 50 points were allocated. In case the candidate collects for one session more than 27.5 points in total and for the other more than 22.5 points in total, resulting in 50 points out of 100, the candidate passes the exam Auditing successfully.

The evaluation and judgement process for the exams Auditing have been the same process for several decades. The team of examinators are receiving the exams of maximum 10 students. Each case is reviewed by two independent examinators. One of the examinators is in the lead and receives the results of the second examinator.

B. *Automated Judgement Process*

The script designed is based on the standard examination guidance. The standard examination guidance (the answer) is based on two components per question. One component is referring to the regulation and standards and the second component is referring to the activities to be performed. The professional international auditing standards as well as the Dutch, 'Controle en Overige Standaarden' (COS), and the Dutch laws and regulations such as 'Richtlijnen Jaarverslaggeving' (RJ) are applicable. For each question, the applicable regulations have been defined and per regulation a decision rule has been created.

In the standard scheme guidance is provided regarding the standards, financial figures and per question a description of the correct answer in general. Per answer the standards, the main key-words and the financial figures have been used to define the decision rules. One standard or one man key-word or one financial figure results each in a decision rule. For question 1 in total 102 decisions rules have been developed.

For each question, the total points to be granted, based on the standard examination guidance, have been divided by the defined number of decision rules per answer. In Table III, the final maximum score per question is presented.

The draft script has been prepared by one researcher and two researchers reviewed independently the (draft) scripts, during each stage of the development process. The first version of the script, existing of 1,004 decision rules for the Exam Gambit, has been tested making use of the 6 cases of University I. Out of the 33 cases ad-random the cases of three candidates have been selected that passed the exam and three candidates that did not pass the exam. Based on the analysis performed, the researchers notified that 249 predefined decision rules were not mentioned in one of the 6 cases prepared by these candidates. These 249 decision rules influence negatively the score per candidate with 17.5 points out of 100. The first test script has been validated and cleansed, resulting in 755 decision rules

TABLE III. STANDARD SCORE AND SCORE TEST SCRIPT

Question	Session	Score based on standard scheme	Number of decision rules	Score per decision rule
1	Morning	10	102	0.0980390
2		10	76	0.1315790
3		10	97	0.1030930
4		20	177	0.1129940
Total Score Morning		50	452	
5	Afternoon	15	45	0.3333300
6		10	82	0.1219510
7		15	75	0.2000000
8		10	101	0.0991000
Total Score Evening		50	303	
Total		100	755	

The outcome of the second test was reliable and could be used for the total population of 33 candidates, 66 cases. The designed CP has been accomplished for the 66 cases. The results and outcome have been presented in this article.

C. *Relationship manual versus automated Judgement Process*

The manual process consists of providing the cases to the reviewers, the manual review, the manual calculation of the rating, the manual judgement and manual reporting of the outcome. This process normally takes several weeks. The relation between the automated versus the manual process is that based on the case study, it can be concluded that the monitoring task (collection of the written exams), the review task (audit), the judgement task (assurance) and the final outcome (reporting) of exams (monitoring) can be performed simultaneously and continuous for an unlimited number of exams. The automated process takes less than one minute for 66 exams. The automated process can be repeated at any time, any moment and at any location.

D. *Link to future performance of the auditor*

During the evaluation of the first version of the test script the researchers thought that it might be also possible to define a relationship between the tasks a financial auditor performs on a day-to-day basis and the Exam Gambit. The defined topics are related to audit elements, audit work, audit approach, audit techniques. These are all tasks that a financial auditor will perform during an engagement. For each decision rule (in total 755) a topic has been defined During the first attempt accomplished by one of the researchers' 25 topics were defined and allocated. The review of the other two researchers resulted in final 18 topics. See Table V the 18 topics that have been defined. About these 18 topics the same rating methodology has been used as for the 755 decision rules.

IV. DATA COLLECTION

There are seven universities in the Netherlands providing educational skills and training for the post-doc program Auditing. We contacted the University I with the request to provide to us the cases Gambit prepared by the candidates.

University I provided us with the following data: (1) the total population of the candidates are 35. Two of the candidates did not participate in the Auditing exam summer 2022, (2) the exams of 33 candidates who completed the morning and afternoon session of the Case Gambit, summer 2022, (3) the results per candidate for the Exam Gambit. The results according to the first, as well as the second examiner have been provided. All the provided data have been anonymized in line with applicable global law and regulation.

The overall exam results of all seven universities in the Netherlands normally varies between 60% and 75% of the total population that passes the Auditing exam. The candidates are a mix of candidates that make the Auditing exam for the first time and repeaters. The number of repeaters per auditing exam is a small part of the population. For the auditing Exam Gambit at University I, 19 candidates passed the Exam successfully (58 %) and 14 candidates did not (42 %).

V. RESULTS

By designing and building a script for an exam, it is possible to combine the following building blocks of the CP: CM, CA, CAss and CRe into one model. The case study proves that it is possible to achieve a holistic audit model based on the CP. The manual process of reviewing written exams can be automated based on the CP. The case study can be repeated for all written exams during the complete study program of several years at any university. However, this was not part of the case study as this is only one the many exams a student needs to pass.

TABLE IV. CORRELATION RESULTS

	Total decision rules	Result machine	Result manual
Total decision rules	1.0000000	0.8329330	0.5669460
Result machine	0.8329330	1.0000000	0.6237030
Result manual	0.5669460	0.6327030	1.0000000

FIGURE 1. RELATIONSHIP RESULTS AUTOMATED VERSUS MANUAL

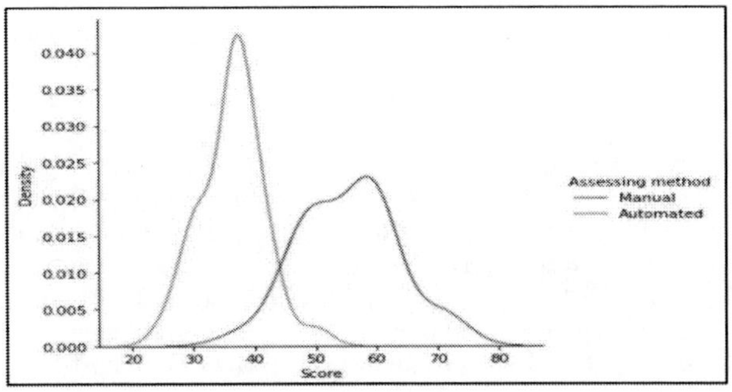

The results of the case study based on the population of 33 cases University I are (1) there is a correlation between the results of the machine (case study) and the results of the corrector (value of 0.6237030, see Table IV), (2) the scores of the machine are structurally lower than manual scores of the examinators (see Figure 1.) and (3) it has been proven that it is possible to build a pragmatic integrated CP.

Out of the original defined 1,004 decision rules, 249 decision rules have been removed after the review of the other two researchers.

TABLE V. KNOWLEDGE LEVEL PER TOPIC FOR ALL EXAMS

Nr	Topic	%
0	Initial audit engagement	65.00%
1	Audit statement	38.96%
2	Dat oriented audit apporach	25.25%
3	Internal control	45.03%
4	Materiality	29.76%
5	Reporting	42.42%
6	Acceptance of the engagement	28.01%
7	Quality assurance	30.23%
8	System oriented audit	45.45%
9	Tendency	67.42%
10	Law and regulation	44.68%
11	Audit work related to opening balance	23.43%
12	Audit work related to findings	47.33%
13	Audit work related to financing Gambit	38.18%
14	Audit work related to financial regualtion (shift) risk	45.26%
15	Audit work related to provisions	25.33%
16	Audit work related to projects	38.66%
17	Audit work related to shifting turnover and costs	9.09%

Based on the 18 topics and the evaluation of the scores of these topics, it is possible to provide insight in the average knowledge of the total population of these (individual) students. For example, the topic (0) Initial audit engagement results in a score of 65 %. The result 65 % implies that the average knowledge level per student is good. In case the result for a topic is below 50 % it could mean that the current knowledge of the student regarding this topic is not up to standard or that the education of this topic is not sufficient.

VI. CONCLUSION

Based on the results of the investigation, it became clear that building a holistic audit model, useful for financial auditing is a very complex process and that global standards regarding monitoring, auditing, assurance and reporting for building a model are missing. Due to these factors, the researchers decided to find options and scenarios to be used to design a holistic audit model based on the CP. On the other hand, because global accepted standards for CM, CAss and CRe are missing, and that each organizations have its own tailor-made processes and systems in place, one standard CP for example the automotive industry will not fit in. The boundary condition will be that all companies of a specific industry need to align their business standards with the specific elements of their processes and systems of the industry.

The outcome of the case study is that this is the first time that the building blocks of the CP have been developed as a holistic audit model. This is a simplified model and provides insight in the missing elements per building blocks for further successful developments in the area of the implementation of the CP for auditing.

The results of the case study are (1) there is a correlation between the results of the machine (case study) and the results of the corrector (value of 0.6327030, see Table IV), (2) the scores of the machine are structurally lower than manual scores of the examinators (see Figure 1). There is also a correlation between total decision rules and result machine (value 0.8329330) and the result manual (value 0.5669460). The correlation of the machine result is higher than the manual result. The next result (3) it has been proven that it is possible to build almost a holistic audit model based on the CP model.

By an automated evaluation of an exam, the researchers made it possible to also provide insight in the development level of students about specific tasks a financial auditor performs during the operational process of auditing the financial statements of a client. Automated evaluation of written exams makes it possible to provide insights over more demission's than the standard evaluation. This data could be used to improve the overall quality of the education program as part of the post-doc program and to coach the student in a more focused and tailor-made approach. The long-term result could be that the maturity level of the next generation of Certified Public Auditors increases.

VII. LIMITATIONS AND FUTURE RESREACH

The case study is the first attempt to design and build a holistic audit model based on the CP, for financial as well as non-financial data. However, there still are several limitations that should be taken into consideration while interpreting the results.

The first limitation is related to the representation – the significancy of the correlation. The difference between the machine and examinators has not been verified based on statistical testing. This testing is needed to achieve the representatives of our results. A second limitation relates to the validation of the decision rules. Out of the 755 decision rules, 128 decision rules have still not been used in the tested 66 cases. This could imply that the knowledge level of the students is low or that the decision rules are not valid. Moreover, it could also be that the standard examination guide provided by an independent professional in auditing is incomplete or overcomplete. Another explanation could be that the expectation level of the professional is not in line with the achieved knowledge level.

Based on this research and the case study, further research is needed to identify if the CP is the best way for continuous monitoring the performance of processes of organizations and more specifically, the financial audit process. Another option could be that the money part of the good and money model of Starreveld [10] will be a better and more practical hybrid option. This conceptual model has the advantages that the continuous monitoring is based on the following data: (1) incoming payments, (2) outgoing payments and (3) development of one or several general ledgers accounts: for example, bank and external obligations (loans). These financial data are available on a minute-to-minute base and a major part of the data are structured, which is founded on global standards. These financial data are transferred from the company and the external finance companies daily. Therefore, all the related process risks, internal controls and data transfer do not need to be continuous monitored, audited, and assured to achieve reasonable assurance of these financial data. Correspondingly, data of previous years is available, and these data can be used as an assurance framework to identify major deviations or out of the benchmark postings.

REFERENCES

[1] M. A. Vasarhelyi, M. Alles, S. Kuenkaikaew, and J. Littley, "The acceptance and adoption of continuous auditing by internal auditors: A micro analysis," International Journal of Accounting Information Systems, vol. 13, no. 3, pp. 267–281, Sep. 2012, doi: 10.1016/j.accinf.2012.06.011.

[2] M. Alles, G. Brennan, A. Kogan, and M. A. Vasarhelyi, "Continuous monitoring of business process controls: A pilot implementation of a continuous auditing system at Siemens", International Journal of Accounting Information Systems, vol. 7, Issue 2, pp. 137-161, June 2006. [Online]. Available: https://www.sciencedirect.com/science/article/abs/pii/S1467089506000273 (accessed Mar. 21, 2023)

[3] A. Kogan, E.F. Sudit, and M. A. Vasarhelyi, "Continuous Online Auditing: A Program of Research", Journal of Information Systems, vol. 13, pp. 87-104, 1999, doi: 10.1108V9781787434134.

[4] M. Canning, B. O'dwyer, and G. Georgakopoulus, "Processes of auditability in sustainability assuranace – the case of materiality construction", Accounting and Business Research, vol. 49, no. 1, pp. 1-27, 2019. doi: 10.1080/00014788.2018.1442208.

[5] G. S. Kearns, and K. J. Barker, "Developing a Forensic Continouos Audit Model" , ADFSL Conference on Digital Forensics, Security and Law, 2011, doi: 10.15394/jdfsl.2011.1094.

[6] M. Eulerich and A. Kalinchenko, "The Current Stae and Future Directions of Continuous Auditing Research: An Analysis of the Existing Literature", Journal of Information Systems, vol. 32, no. 3, pp. 31051, 2018, doi: 10.238/isys-51813.

[7] E.H.J. Vaassen and V.K. Bröcheler, "The influence of a decision support tool and experience on the assessment of AO/IC descriptions", De Accountant, nr. 1, September 1996. [Online]. Available from: https://pure.uvt.nl/ws/portalfiles/portal/1399788/Invloed.pdf (accessed Mar. 23, 2023).

[8] E. Curfs, E. Mantelears, and M. Zoet, "How to Plot Current Pilots on the Audit Maturity Model? The CP," in Proc. eKNOW 2022, pp. 12-17.

[9] E. Mantelaers and M. Zoet, "Association for Information Systems AIS Electronic Library (AISeL) Continuous Auditing: A Practical Maturity Model," 2018. [Online]. Available: https://aisel.aisnet.org/mcis2018/40 (accessed Feb. 01, 2023).

[10] R.W. Starreveld, O.C. van Leeuwen and H. van Nimwegen, "Administrative information management", Deel 1: Algemene grondslagen, 5th edition, 2002, ISBN 90 207 3052 5.

Usage of Audit Data Analytics within the Accountancy Sector

Lotte Verhoeven and Eric Mantelaers
Research Centre – Future-proof Auditor
Zuyd University of Applied Sciences & RSM Netherlands Accountants N.V.
Sittard/Heerlen, the Netherlands
lotte.verhoeven@zuyd.nl
eric.mantelaers@zuyd.nl

Martijn Zoet
Research Centre – Future-proof Financial
Zuyd University of Applied Sciences
Sittard, the Netherlands
martijn.zoet@zuyd.nl

Abstract— **Evidence from the various reports and articles as well as the importance of the audit process shows that adjustment and/or improvement of the current approach within the accountancy sector is necessary. Research demonstrates that technology can contribute to an improvement of audit quality. Additionally, previous research increasingly recognizes that audit data analytics is likely to transform the conduct of the audit significantly. The goal of this research is to study how Audit Data Analytics is currently used within the audit. In order to answer this question, a survey was distributed via the Dutch National Accountants Association, focusing on how Audit Data Analytics is used in the accountancy sector. However, the results and the non-chronological order of the data analysis types indicate a misinterpretation or lack of understanding of the data analysis types (implemented in the survey) and their chronological order.**

Keywords-audit data analytics; audit quality; process mining; process mining algorithms.

I. Introduction

Audit quality consistently received substantial attention from regulators and academics over the past years due to numerous audit scandals. Caused by a lack of independent oversight and enforcement, various accounting and audit scandals took place in the beginning of the 21st century. Recent reports from the Dutch Authority for the Financial Markets (AFM), and recent published reports from, among others, the Future Accountancy Sector Committee (CTA) and the Accountancy Monitoring Committee (MCA), show that the quality of annual audits is inadequate [1]–[4]. Internationally the lack of audit quality is also visible. In the Brydon report, Brydon states that the audit quality is insufficient and improvements including new reporting duty with respect to fraud and more auditor transparency are recommended [5]. Evidence from the various reports and articles as well as the importance of the audit process shows that adjustment and/or improvement of the current approach within the accountancy sector is necessary [6]. Research demonstrates that technology can contribute to an improvement of audit quality [7].

This research, therefore, focuses on the current usage of Audit Data Analytics (ADA) within the audit. The goal of this research is to achieve a view of the application of ADA within the financial audit. To achieve this, this paper answers the following main question: *How and to what extent is Audit Data Analytics currently used by auditors/accountants?*

The remainder of the paper is organized as follows: Section II describes the relevant literature regarding audit quality and ADA. In Section III, the research method is described, followed by the data collection and analysis in Section IV. Finally, the results, conclusion and future work are presented in Sections V and VI respectively.

II. Literature Review

Audit quality is a very broad concept and can be defined in various ways. DeAngelo describes audit quality as "the market assessed joint probability that a given auditor will both discover a breach in the client's accounting system and reports the breach" [8]. Whereas the Government Accountability Office uses a more extensive approach and states that high audit quality is achieved when performed according to the corresponding standards and no material misstatements due to error or fraud are present [9]. The legal definition of audit quality is on the other hand very concise, as it states audit quality as either "audit failure" or "no audit failure" [10]. In conclusion, audit quality is a broad concept and difficult to summarize in a single definition. Next to that, these different definitions show that audit quality is not yet recognized universally across the world. As mentioned before, evidence from the various reports and articles as well as the importance of the audit process shows that adjustment and / or improvement of the current approach within the accountancy sector is necessary [1]–[4][6].

Previous research shows that technology/ADA can contribute to an improvement of audit quality [7]. By automating certain audit analyses, more time and resources can be allocated to the interpretation of these analyses. This maximizes the dual aspects of audit quality: independence and expertise [7][8]. Additionally, previous research increasingly recognizes that ADA is likely to transform the conduct of the audit significantly [11]–[13]. As Barr-Pulliam et al. state: "The use of advanced testing methods such as ADAs can occur at any stage of the audit and can significantly transform the process of auditing financial statements, resulting in enhanced audit effectiveness and audit efficiency – both elements and signals of audit quality" [11]. To support the individual and personal judgement of the auditor, ADA could provide a solution. ADA is a method of using data analysis techniques to evaluate financial information and assess the accuracy and reliability of an organization's financial statements. This involves collecting and examining large amounts of data, and using statistical and computational tools to identify patterns, trends, and anomalies that may indicate potential problems or issues. Data-driven audits are becoming increasingly familiar within the accountancy sector, due to innovation, increase in technology/data and the pursuit of continuous assurance [14]. Data-driven 'control' is also used by the AFM (regulator), as they want to implement data-driven supervision to enhance the efficiency and effectivity of the supervision of audit firms. To achieve this, the AFM will structurally request data from the audit firms to gain insight into the current quality control and risk characteristics [15].

Despite the fact that the use of ADA within the audit practice is relatively new, various previous research has been performed. The Financial Reporting Council (FRC), regulator to auditors, accountants and actuaries and setter of UK's Corporate Governance and Stewardship Codes, conducted a review of the use of technology in the audit of financial statements. Within this review, the FRC found that ADA was currently used mostly for risk assessment and the audit of revenue and that advanced ADA was only used sporadic [16]. This was also highlighted by Eilifsen et al. who explored the use of ADA in current audit practice in Norway. Eilifsen et al. found that despite the positive attitude with regards to the usefulness of ADA, the use of 'advanced' ADA is rare [17]. Eilifsen et al. also found that this is caused by its complexity and lack of implementation guidelines and confidence in the ability of ADA to provide sufficient and appropriate audit evidence. It is suggested that this is likely to persist until ADA will be incorporated in the audit methodologies and ADA is explicitly supported and accepted by supervisory bodies and standard-setters [17]. However, this research focuses not only on the use of ADA, but also on the sequentially of its use.

III. Research Method

The goal of this research is to study how ADA is currently used within the audit. In order to answer this question, a survey was distributed focusing on how ADA is used in the accountancy sector. The survey is distributed via the Dutch National Accountants Association (NBA) across members of the Accounttech working group, a total of 7,008. The members of the NBA are spread over several accountancy firms in the Netherlands and consists out of accounting consultants/auditors (AA in Dutch), chartered auditors (RA in Dutch) and people working in the accountancy sector.

The survey consists of 20 questions which are divided into seven subsections. These subsections relate to 1) composition/descriptive (general), 2) the scope of ADA, 3) assessing the possibility to detect misstatements, 4) sequentially, 5) possibility to assist decisions, 6) materiality and 7) phase of the audit in which ADA is used. The questions are answered on a likert-scale basis [18], in which answers range from '1 – I never use it', to '7 – I always use it'. Likert scales are considered a good fit for analytical purposes, due to their relatively large number of categories [19]. In addition, the respondents were able to answer: 'I don't know' or 'Not relevant'. For the purpose of this research the latter two are classified as '1 – I never use it'.

By formulating the survey questions, the Value Through Analytics (VTA) model from Zoet is used [20]. This model concretizes data analytics into subtypes. The VTA model incorporates the six different types of analyses from Leek and Peng (2015), namely: The 1) descriptive, 2) explanatory, 3) inferential, 4) predictive, 5) causal, and 6) mechanistic [21]. The VTA model also includes the three types of process mining as described by Van der Aalst (2011): discovery, conformance and improvement [22].

The VTA model is a tool to classify data analytics into different categories [23] and is shown in Figure 1. The VTA model distinguishes 54 different types of data analysis which can be derived by walking through the three circles within the model. The inner circle starts with the question: "What do I want to analyze?" In which a 1) process, 2) decision or 3) object can be chosen. The second circle questions "Why do I want to analyze?" Which can be answered by 1) discovery, 2) conformance, and 3) improvement. Finally, the outer circle asks the question "To what extent do I want to analyze it?" The last question indicates the choice to the following types of data analytics: 1) descriptive, 2) explanatory, 3) inferential, 4) predictive, 5) causal, and 6) mechanistic. Additionally, the types of analysis within the VTA model are layered in sequence, which indicates that if an inferential analysis can be carried out, one should also be able to carry out a descriptive and explanatory analysis.

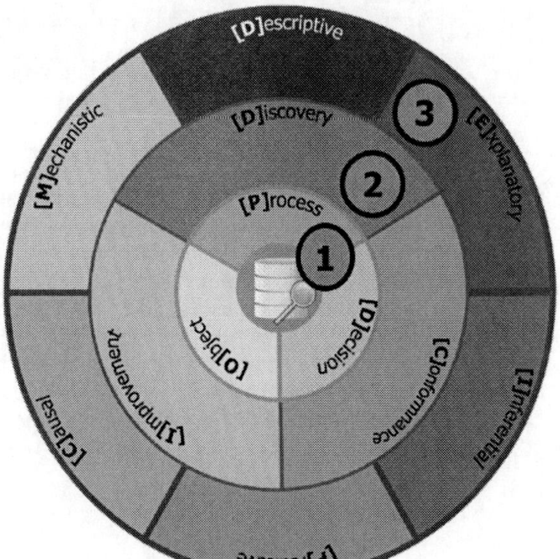

Figure 1. Value Through Analytics model [20]

To assess which competences can be utilized with the help of ADA, a so-called analysis quotient can be computed, which visualizes the type of questions that can be answered [23]. An example of this is shown in Figure 2, in which the questions are set against audit organizations. Grey indicates that an audit organization cannot perform the analysis, green indicates that the type of analysis is standard procedure within each audit. Blue indicates that the analysis is used within every audit, but expertise is needed. Purple indicates that the analysis is executed by only one employee for their own use, but the results are not communicated throughout the team. Finally, yellow indicates that it is not executed for every audit [23].

The survey questions were set up by Dr. Mantelaers (chartered auditor) and Dr. Zoet, founder of the VTA model [20]. In order to validate and refine the survey questions and to ensure the correct questioning a pilot test was conducted by five master students (Accounting and Control – Maastricht University). Moreover, the pilot test was executed by two members of the Accounttech group, of which one is related to the Post-Master IT-Auditing & Advisory (Erasmus University Rotterdam).

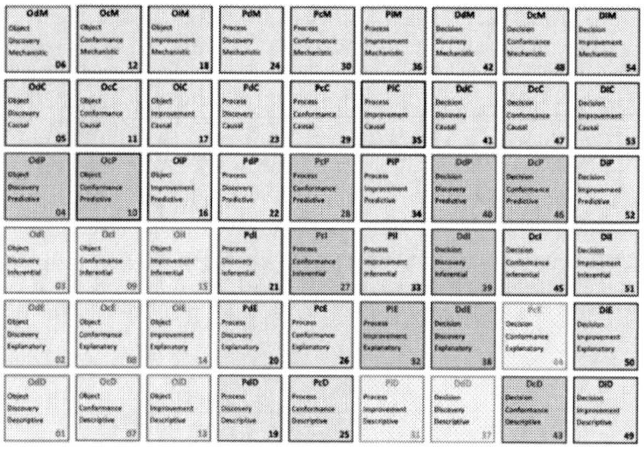

Figure 2. Periodic system types of analyses [23]

Within the survey questions, a particular sequence is followed related to several 'levels' of ADA usage in practice, which can be linked to the data analysis types/levels in the VTA model. In Table I the survey questions are linked to the type of data analyses derived from Figure 2. Each question focuses on the frequency of use of the ADA types as mentioned in Table I. As the questions and data analysis types, are listed in a chronological order, this implies that if an auditor uses ADA type five, the auditor will also be expected to be able to perform ADA type two and four.

TABLE I. SURVEY DESIGN

Survey question	ADA type	ADA description
7.1	2	Object – Discover – Explanatory
7.2	4	Object – Discover – Predictive
7.3	5	Object – Discover – Causal
7.4	7	Object – Discover – Descriptive
7.5	8	Object – Discover – Explanatory
8.1	19	Process – Discover - Descriptive
8.2	20	Process – Discover – Explanatory
8.3	25	Process – Conformance – Descriptive
8.4	26	Process – Conformance – Explanatory
8.5	37	Decision – Discover – Descriptive
8.6	43	Decision – Conformance - Descriptive

The sequentially of the data from the survey will be analyzed with the help of process mining algorithms. For the use of this research, a heuristic analysis will be performed due to the scope of possible responses and outcomes. A heuristic analysis eliminates any redundant details and exceptions and focuses on the main behavior [24].

IV. DATA COLLECTION AND ANALYSIS

The survey was distributed to a population of 7,008 respondents in total, of which 203 responded, a response rate of 2,90%. The response rate is relatively low, possibly caused by the non-committal nature and scope of the survey. Moreover, surveys are frequently distributed within the Accounttech working group and NBA, which also causes the low response rate. From a NBA perspective this can be considered a representative response rate. The survey was distributed in the first half of 2021. The respondents consist out of 167 males and 36 females, of which 72 are a chartered auditor (RA in Dutch) and 39 accounting consultants (AA in Dutch). Around 25% of the respondents works for one of the Big 4 Auditing Firms (EY, PWC, Deloitte and KPMG). The most common jobs within the respondents are external auditor (chartered auditor and accounting consultants), accountant in business or public/internal auditor. However, the work experience varies across the respondents as is shown in Table II.

TABLE II. WORK EXPERIENCE RESPONDENTS

Work experience (in years)	Number of respondents
< 5	3
5 - 10	22
10 – 20	72
20 – 30	58
> 30	48
Total	**203**

To analyze the outcomes of the survey a heuristic process mining algorithm is applied by using three input variables. These input variables consist out of 1) case concept name, represented by the respondents ID, 2) concept name, represented by the question number and 3) the timestamp, represented by the answer based on the likert scale. To ensure the chronological order a timestamp is added to the data by converting the likert scale. In which '7 – I always use it' is matched to the earliest timestamp, as it is always used (used now). '1 – I never use it' is matched to the latest timestamp, since its use will be furthest in the future. The options in between (two to six) are matched accordingly.

V. Results

The analysis distinguishes 132 types of unique variants within a total of 203 respondents (65.0%). A total overview of the data analysis types in order of usage is shown in Figure 3. The numbers 7.1 until 8.6 refer to the questions of the survey, the link to the data analysis types is shown in Table II. As the likert scale was converted to a timestamp in order to perform these analyses, the order of the questions depends on the usage of the specific ADA. For example, question 7.1 relates to the use of data analysis: Object – Discover – Explanatory. 60.6% of the respondents (n=123) indicated that this analysis is always used (likert scale – 7). Due to the rating of '7 – I always use it', this data analysis type is matched to the earliest timestamp and therefore shown at the start of the path in Figure 3.

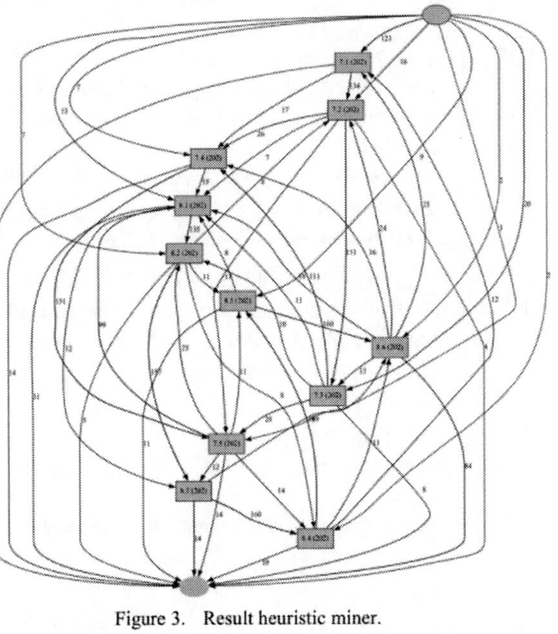

Figure 3. Result heuristic miner.

Due to the high number of unique variants (65,0%), an overview of the top ten variants is shown in Table III. For clarity purposes, the number of occurrences per unique variant is added.

TABLE III. TOP 10 VARIANTS

												Number of occurences
Variant 1	7.1	7.2	7.3	7.4	7.5	8.1	8.2	8.3	8.4	8.5	8.6	58
Variant 2	7.1	7.2	7.3	7.4	7.5	8.2	8.3	8.4	8.5	8.6	8.1	4
Variant 3	7.1	7.2	7.3	8.1	8.2	8.3	8.4	8.5	8.6	7.4	7.5	3
Variant 4	8.1	8.2	8.3	8.4	8.5	8.6	7.1	7.2	7.3	7.4	7.5	2
Variant 5	7.2	7.3	7.4	7.5	8.1	8.2	8.3	8.4	8.5	8.6	7.1	2
Variant 6	7.1	7.3	8.1	8.2	8.3	8.4	8.5	8.6	7.2	7.4	7.5	2
Variant 7	7.1	7.3	7.4	7.5	8.1	8.2	8.3	8.4	8.5	8.6	7.2	2
Variant 8	7.1	7.2	7.5	8.1	8.2	8.3	8.4	8.5	8.6	7.3	7.4	2
Variant 9	7.1	7.2	7.3	7.5	8.1	8.2	8.3	8.4	8.5	8.6	7.4	2
Variant 10	7.1	7.2	7.3	7.4	7.5	8.5	8.6	8.1	8.2	8.3	8.4	2

The most common variant (variant 1) occurs 58 times. This variant is, also chronologically seen, the most logical variant, as the occurrence of the questions are in a chronological order (7.1 to 8.6). This means that the data analysis types, intertwined in the questions, are used in the (expected) chronological order. However, this is only applicable to 28.6% of the respondents (n=58). The number of occurrences for the other variances is widely spread as can be seen for variant two to ten (max. four occurrences per variant). The results from variant two show that question 8.1 (related to data analysis type Process – Discover – Descriptive) is used less compared to question 8.2 to 8.6 (related to the more advanced data analysis types). In variant three to ten a non-chronological order is also apparent, indicating that the more 'basis' analysis types are carried out less frequently than the more 'advanced' types. However, variant four indicates that analyses with regards to a process and/or decision (questions 8.1-8.6) are frequently used, and analysis regarding an object (questions 7.1-7.5) less frequently, despite the fact that most of the analyses regarding 'Objects' are expected to be used standard in every audit, as can be derived from Figure 2.

As the results vary widely, an additional analysis solely on the external auditors (chartered auditor and accounting consultants) as they are expected to have the most experience with regards to audits. Within the total sample, 111 external auditors and 79 unique variants are identified (variance of 71.2%). Compared to the total sample, an even higher variance can be recorded.

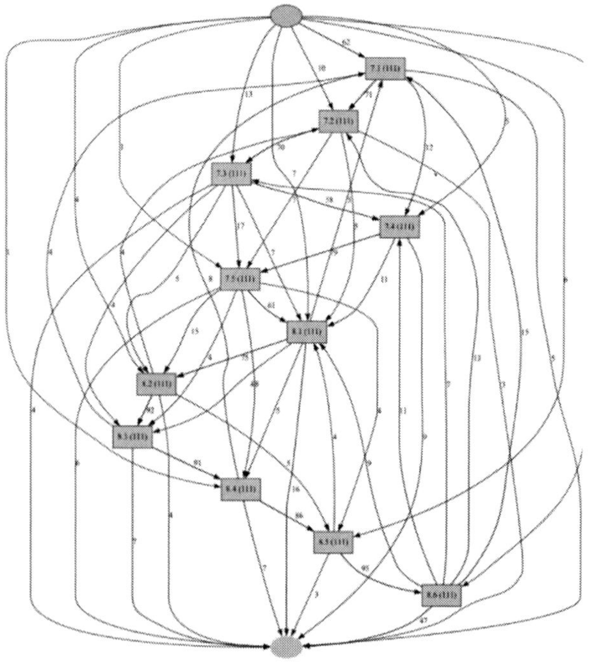

Figure 4. Result heuristic miner external auditors.

Due to the high number of unique variants (65.0%), an overview of the top ten variants is shown in Table IV. For clarity purposes, the number of occurrences per unique variant is added.

TABLE IV. TOP 10 VARIANTS EXTERNAL AUDITORS

												Number of occurences
Variant 1	7.1	7.2	7.3	7.4	7.5	8.1	8.2	8.3	8.4	8.5	8.6	31
Variant 2	7.1	7.3	7.4	7.5	8.1	8.2	8.3	8.4	8.5	8.6	7.2	2
Variant 3	7.1	7.2	7.3	7.4	7.5	8.2	8.3	8.4	8.5	8.6	8.1	2
Variant 4	8.6	8.5	7.2	7.1	7.3	7.4	7.5	8.2	8.3	8.4	8.1	1
Variant 5	8.6	7.2	7.3	7.1	7.4	7.5	8.1	8.2	8.3	8.4	8.5	1
Variant 6	8.5	8.6	8.2	8.3	8.4	7.2	7.5	7.3	7.4	8.1	7.1	1
Variant 7	8.5	8.6	8.1	8.2	8.3	8.4	7.1	7.2	7.5	7.4	7.3	1
Variant 8	8.5	8.6	7.3	7.5	8.1	8.2	8.4	7.1	7.4	7.2	8.3	1
Variant 9	8.5	8.6	7.1	7.2	7.3	7.5	8.2	8.3	8.4	8.1	7.4	1
Variant 10	8.5	8.6	7.1	7.2	7.3	7.4	7.5	8.1	8.2	8.3	8.4	1

The most common variant (variant 1) occurs 31 times. This variant is, also chronologically seen, the most logical variant, as the occurrence of the questions are in a chronological order (7.1 to 8.6). However, this is only applicable to 27.9% of the respondents (n=31). The number of occurrences for the other variances is widely spread as can be seen for variant two to ten (max. two occurrences per variant).

VI. CONCLUSION AND FUTURE WORK

In this article, we aim to answer the main question: *"How and to what extent is Audit Data Analytics currently used by auditors/accountants?"* With the help of a survey distributed across members of the NBA working group Accounttech, an overview was given of the use (and its extent) of ADA. The insights derived from our study provide a better understanding of how and to which extent ADA is currently used by auditors/accountants and specific external auditors. However, the results and the non-chronological order of the data analysis types indicate a misinterpretation or possible lack of understanding of the data analysis types (implemented in the survey) and their chronological order. Remarkable are the similar results within the external auditor group, as they are expected to have the most experience regarding audits. Future research could therefore focus on concretizing (and creating an understanding of) the data analysis types. This could be achieved by creating a more practice-oriented survey. Moreover, in future research we would like to include the answers: *'I don't know' or 'Not relevant'* in the results and follow up on these answers to identify the underlying reasons and expand our results/knowledge.

ACKNOWLEDGEMENTS

We would like to thank Michelle van Wamelen for collecting the data. Moreover, we would like to thank the NBA working group Accounttech for collaborating on this survey.

REFERENCES

[1] MCA, "Accountancy Monitoring Committee," 2020. https://www.monitoringaccountancy.nl/ (accessed Mar. 24, 2023).

[2] Future Accountancy Sector Committee, "Confidence in Control Final Report of the Committee on the Future of the Accountancy Sector | Parliamentary Document | Central Government," 2020. https://www.rijksoverheid.nl/documenten/kamerstukken/2020/01/30/vertrouwen-op-controle-eindrapport-van-de-commissie-toekomst-accountancysector

[3] AFM, "AFM supervisory agenda 2022," 2022.

[4] AFM, "Research reports on supervision of audit firms | Audit firms | AFM Professionals." https://www.afm.nl/nl-nl/sector/accountantsorganisaties/rapporten-publicaties (accessed Mar. 24, 2023).

[5] D. Brydon, "Assess, assure and inform: improving audit quality and effectiveness," UK Government, 2019. [Online]. Available: https://www.gov.uk/government/publications/the-quality-and-effectiveness-of-audit-independent-review

[6] Future Accountancy Sector Committee, "Reliance on Audit," *Minist. van Financ.*, 2020, [Online]. Available: https://www.rijksoverheid.nl/documenten/kamerstukken/2020/01/30/vertrouwen-op-controle-eindrapport-van-de-commissie-toekomst-accountancysector

[7] E. Mantelaers, "An Evaluation of Technologies to Improve Auditing," Open University, 2021.

[8] L. E. DeAngelo, "Auditor Size and Audit Quality," *J. Account. Econ.*, vol. 3, no. 3, pp. 183–199, 1981, doi: https://doi.org/10.1016/0165-4101(81)90002-1.

[9] Government Accountability Office, "Public Accounting Firms: Required Study on the Potential Effects of Mandatory Audit Firm Rotation," Government Printing Office, Washington D.C., 2003.

[10] J. R. Francis, "What do we know about audit quality?," *British Accounting Review*, vol. 36, no. 4. pp. 345–368, 2004. doi: 10.1016/j.bar.2004.09.003.

[11] D. Barr-Pulliam, H. L. Brown-Liburd, and K. A. Sanderson, "The Effects of the internal control opinion and use of audit data analytics on perceptions of audit quality, assurance, and auditor negligence.," *A J. Pract. Theory*, vol. 41, no. 1, pp. 25–48, 2022, [Online]. Available: https://doi.org/10.2308/AJPT-19-064

[12] G. Salijeni, A. Samsonova-Tadderu, and S. Turley, "Big Data and changes in audit technology: contemplating a research agenda," *Account. Bus. Res.*, vol. 49, no. 1, pp. 95–119, 2019.

[13] M. Cao, R. Chychyla, and T. Stewart, "Big Data analytics in financial statement audits," *Account. Horizons*, vol. 2, no. 29, pp. 423–429, 2015.

[14] J. van Buuren and W. Wijma, "On quality assurance of data-driven control methodology," *Maandbl. Voor Account. en Bedrijfsecon.*, vol. 96, no. 1/2, pp. 15–25, 2021.

[15] AFM, "Legislative letter." 2021. [Online]. Available: https://www.rijksoverheid.nl/documenten/kamerstukken/2021/04/21/kamerbrief-wetgevingswensen-dnb-en-afm

[16] FRC, "The use of technology in the audit of financial statements," 2020.

[17] A. Eilifsen, F. Kinserdal, W. F. J. Messier, and T. E. McKee, "An Exploratory Study into the Use of Audit Data Analytics on Audit Engagements," *Am. Account. Assoc.*, pp. 1–23, 2020.

[18] R. Likert, "A Technique for the Measurement of Attitudes," *rchives Psychol.*, no. 140, pp. 1–55, 1932.

[19] L. H. Kidder, C. M. Judd, and E. R. Smith, *Research methods in social relations*, 5th ed. CBS College Publishing, 1986.

[20] M. Zoet, "VTA-model," *2018.* https://martijnzoet.com/2018/10/22/het-value-through-analytics-vta-model/ (accessed Feb. 01, 2023).

[21] J. Leek and R. D. Peng, "What is the question?," *Science Magazine*, pp. 1314–1315, 2015.

[22] W. M. P. Van Der Aalst, "Process Mining," in *Discovery, Conformance and Enhancement of Business Processess*, 2011, pp. 215–217.

[23] E. Mantelaers and M. Zoet, "Data-analysis (III)," 2021. https://www.accountant.nl/vaktechniek/2021/1/data-analyse-nader-geanalyseerd-iii/ (accessed Mar. 27, 2023).

[24] A. J. M. M. Weijters, W. M. P. van der Aalst, and A. K. A. de Medeiros;, "Process Mining with the HeuristicsMiner Algorithm," *Beta Work. Pap.*, no. May, 2006.

Tools Based on Word Embedding to Make Easy the Analysis of Emotions in Spanish Text

Jorge Silva Pedreros, Alejandra Segura-Navarrete, Christian Vidal-Castro
Information Systems Department
Universidad del Biobío, UBB
Concepción, Chile
email: jorge.silva1602@alumnos.ubiobio.cl, asegura@ubiobio.cl, cvidal@ubiobio.cl

Claudia Martínez-Araneda
Computer Science Department
Universidad Católica de la Santísima Concepción, UCSC
Concepción, Chile
email: cmartinez@ucsc.cl

Abstract— **In the context of the analysis of emotions of text obtained from the web and social networks, this article aims to describe the development process of a tool to support this analysis based on the embedding of words. The main motivation has to do with the need to offer a tool for text preprocessing and emotion analysis for the Spanish language integrated into a single web application. The web application for the analysis of emotions, called fastText-embedding-viewer integrates three modules: The first corresponds to an Application Programming Interfaces (API) called corpus-preproc for text preprocessing that includes a collection of functionality, such as whitespace normalization, modifier and mark removal, lowercase folding, punctuation trimming around words and words without alphabetic characters, and content extraction main HTML and Cascading Style Sheets (CSS); the second corresponds to a novel module that allows obtaining similar words and analogies based on word embedding; and the third enables the analysis of emotions via a supervised machine learning model created using fastText for an input sentence. Promising results were obtained in the preliminary evaluation of the web application.**

Keywords-word embedding; analysis of emotions; fastText.

I. INTRODUCTION

Currently, there are numerous works on the area of analysis of emotions, either applying a lexicon, machine learning (ML), or a hybrid approach. It has been shown that when ML approaches are combined with the use of a lexicon, the performance of the classifiers improves [1]. The analysis of emotions in texts has several associated subtasks, such as tokenization, part of speech (POS), lemmatization, stemming, and elimination of stopwords, for continuing with the detection of emotion itself. Nevertheless, there are numerous tools for the analysis of emotions, that is, detection of polarity {positive, negative, neutral}, aimed at knowing the preferences of a customer in relation to a product or service or various related topics. Most of the time, the support tools for the pre-processing and analysis tasks are not integrated, which makes it difficult to manage them, in addition to not being available for the Spanish language, which limits their work in a diversity of Corpus. Therefore, this work shows the development of a web application that integrates various modules, among which are the complete text preprocessing and analysis of emotions for the Spanish language using the word embedding fastText algorithm [2][3].

Sections 2 and 3 discuss the relevant concepts of word embedding and related works where applications that perform an analysis of emotions similar to that documented in this work are included. Section 4 describes the tools that have been developed, e.g., preprocessing, and the architecture of the web application for detection of emotions based on the word embedding fastText algorithm. Then, we describe an evaluation of quality the web application. The acknowledgement and conclusions close the article.

II. BACKGROUND

The analysis of emotion corresponds to the area of subjectivity analysis in AI that has the objective of classifying a text into one of the positive, negative or neutral categories. The analysis of emotions, on the other hand, attempts to classify a text into one or more emotions according to the selected taxonomy. The taxonomies of emotions (Figure 1) have the objective of simplifying the analysis of the large number of human emotions. Emotion is a multifaceted experience, typical of humans and animals [4], that combines consciousness, bodily sensation, and behavior, reflecting the personal significance of different situations [5]. As represented in Figure 1, there are several proposals for taxonomies to classify emotions. As the categories increase, the recognition of an emotion and, consequently, its automatic detection becomes more complex. The analysis of subjectivity in texts is usually based on lexicons or ML models. These two approaches allow the classification of texts into different emotions or feelings. The first uses annotated semantic lists or hierarchies to classify texts. In simple terms, the words of the lexicon present in a comment are used to detect the predominant emotions or feelings.

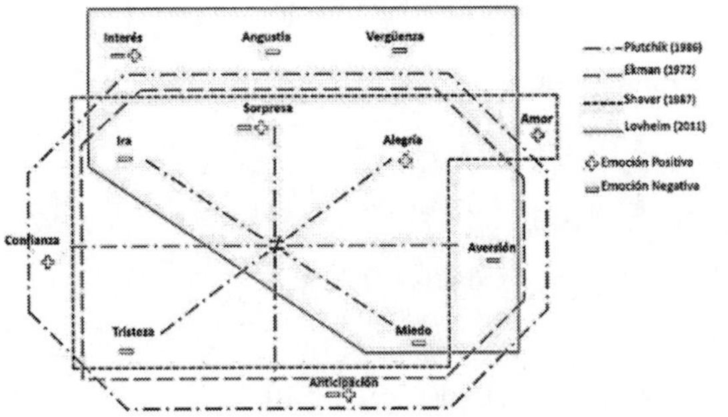

Figure 1. Representation of the four most common emotion taxonomies [6].

The oldest example is the General Enquirer [7], which uses a lexicon of positive and negative words to label the affective valence of texts. EmoLEX [8] is a lexicon of words labelled with the eight primary emotions of Plutchik [9]; RedPal is a semantic hierarchy developed by [10] that also uses Plutchik. ML-based analysis uses ML techniques to label emotions, e.g., the XED dataset [11], where the Support Vector Machine (SVM) technique and Bidirectional Encoder Representations from Transformers (BERT) are used to predict emotions through Plutchik.

There is also the possibility of combining the above approaches to create a hybrid model and improve the performance of automatic analysis. An example is Emo2Vec [12], where lexicons in Mandarin Chinese are used to postprocess word embedding, predicting a subset of emotions with the hourglass model [13]. Study [14] combines Global Vectors for Word Representation (GloVe) and Long Short-Term Memory (LSTM) to predict emotions with the Eckman taxonomy. It is also relevant to mention XED, which uses a corpus of manual development to develop an SVM model and fine-tuning for BERT.

In this study, we used the El Mercurio online (EMOL) unannotated Corpus for the unsupervised fastText model and the XED annotated Corpus for the supervised model.

III. RELATED WORK

The analysis of emotions in texts has several associated subtasks, such as tokenization, POS, lemmatization, stemming, and elimination of stopwords, for continuing with the detection of emotion itself, which is a classification task using an approach based on lexicons, machine learning or hybrids. Nevertheless, there are numerous tools for the analysis of emotions, that is, detection of polarity {positive, negative or neutral}, aimed at knowing the preferences of a customer in relation to a product or service or various related topics. Among these are tools including MonkeyLearn, Lexalitics, Amazon Comprehend, Google cloud NLP, Aylien, MeaningCloud, Rosette, OdinText Text Analytics, Repustate, and BiText [15].

Within the literature review that we have carried out, we identify various tools that in addition to polarity, are capable of detecting the specific emotion that is reflected in an emotion intensity value, normally on a scale of -1 to +1, such as Synesketch, Receptiviti, IBM Watson Natural Language, EMTk and Text2Emotion.

- **Synesketch:** Corresponds to an open-source engine for the recognition of textual emotions. Its entry corresponds to one or more sentences and analyses emotional content in terms of emotional categories based on the Ekman taxonomy, intensity, and polarity (valence). The recognition technique is based on a refined method of keyword detection that uses a word lexicon based on WordNet, a lexicon of emoticons, common abbreviations and colloquial expressions, and a set of heuristic rules. The recognition ends with a visualization of the emotions in an animated graphic. The emotional weight of each word and each emotional type is calculated as the ratio between the number of emotional synsets (of a given emotional type) and the number of all synsets to which the word belongs, decreased by the average penalty of all its emotional synsets [16]. For example, for the entry "I will not be lovesick!", the output is a vector of weights [joy = 1,0, 0, 0, 0, 0], where negation processing and the amplifier were included.

- **Receptiviti:** API based on an emotion engine called SALLEE (Syntax-Aware Lexica L Emotion Engine) detects the emotions and feelings expressed in a text. It is designed to qualify the emotions that a person is expressing, which can include the emotions that they are feeling at present, emotions that they have felt in the past, those that they hope to feel in the future, or those that they see or assume that others are feeling. Each emotion can be defined as negative, neutral or positive. SALLEE is particularly effective in capturing emotions from social media posts, short text samples, casual language use and media such as conversations or text messages. For example, for the input "That was the best movie", the output is a string in JSON format with the following content.

```
{
 "dictionary_measures":
 {
   "admiration": 0.2,
   "goodfeel": 0.2,
   "sentiment": 0.2
 }
}
```

where the calculation formula for one of the emotions (admiration) is described by (1):

$$\frac{count(admiration)}{count(goodfeel; badfeel; ambifeel; nonemotion)} \quad (1)$$

Equation (1) returns a score of 0.2 for the emotion of admiration, which means that approximately 20% of the statements were characterized by showing admiration. The goodfeel score for this sentence is

0.2, and the sentiment score is also 0.2 (on a scale of -1.0 to +1.0). This occurs because the word "best" expresses a positive emotion without amplifiers, softeners or negations. The score is relatively low because better is not a particularly strong emotion word [17].

- **Emotion Mining Toolkit (EMTk)**: Is a set of modules and datasets that offers a comprehensive solution to extracting feelings and emotions from a text. The toolkit is written in Java, Python and R and is published under an open-source licence from MIT. The modules are based on previously developed tools, Senti4SD and EmoTxt [18], whose codes have been refactored and optimized, respectively. The emotion detection module includes classification models trained in our datasets and used for the detection of emotions from text. EmoTxt identifies emotions in a corpus of input in CSV format, with one text per line, preceded by a unique identifier. The result is a CSV file that contains the text ID and the predicted label for each element of the input collection. EmoTxt can also be used to train a new classifier from a set of data, for which it must have a collection of texts labelled with emotions [19].

- **IBM Watson™ Natural Language Understanding:** This web service uses linguistic analysis and machine learning to extract meaning and metadata from unstructured text data. It explores text data using text analysis to extract categories, classifications, entities, keywords, sentiments, emotions, relationships, and syntax [20]. For example, for the input in JSON format:

```
{"html":
"<html><head><title>Fruits</title></head><body
><h1>Apples and Oranges</h1><p>I love apples! I
don't like oranges.</p></body></html>",
"features": { "emotion": { "targets": [ "apples",
"oranges"]
  }
 }
}
```

The output in the same format is:

```
{"language": "en",
 "emotion": {
  "targets": [{
    "text": "apples",
    "emotion": {
     "sadness": 0.028574,
     "joy": 0.859042,
     "fear": 0.02752,
     "disgust": 0.017519,
     "anger": 0.012855
    }
},
{
    "text": "oranges",
    "emotion": {
     "sadness": 0.514253,
     "joy": 0.078317,
     "fear": 0.074223,
     "disgust": 0.058103,
     "anger": 0.126859
    }
}
]  "document": {
    "emotion": {
     "sadness": 0.32665,
     "joy": 0.563273,
     "fear": 0.033387,
     "disgust": 0.022637,
     "anger": 0.041796
    }
   }
  }
}
```

- **Text2emotion**: This is a Python package to detect emotions from textual data. It processes any textual data, recognizes the emotions embedded in it, and provides the output in the form of a dictionary. It is well suited, with five basic emotion categories: happy, angry, sad, surprise, and fear [21].

A summary of all these tools is provided in Table I.

TABLE I. TOOLS FOR ANALYSIS OF EMOTIONS IN WRITTEN TEXTS

Features	**Tools**				
	Synesketch	***Receptiviti***	***EMTk***	***IBM Watson NL Understanding Text Analysis***	***Text2Emotion***
Preprocessing	No	Partially	Yes, it uses Stanford CoreNLP	Yes	Yes
API available	No	Yes	No	Yes	Yes
Licence	GNU	Commercial	MIT open source	Commercial	MIT open source
Output	Emotion intensity and visualization	Emotion intensity and valence	CSV (Text_id, emotion_label)	Emotion intensity	Emotion Intensity
Analysis base on	Word lexicon, emoticon lexicón, heuristic rules	Dictionaries	Emotion Lexicon from WordNet affect and supervised machine learning model	Linguistic and machine learning approach	Machine learning approach
Languages supported	English	English	English	English, French	English
Authors	[16]	[17]	[18][19]	[20]	[21]
URL	https://www.krcadinac.com/work/projects/synesketch/	https://www.receptiviti.com/emotions	https://hub.docker.com/r/collabuniba/emtk	https://www.ibm.com/demos/live/natural-language-understanding/self-service/home	https://text2emotion.herokuapp.com/

Table I shows that the main motivation of this work is justified given the scarcity of preprocessing and emotion analysis tools existing for the Spanish language.

IV. TOOLS DEVELOPMENT

Next, the development of a text preprocessing API and a web application for the analysis of emotions and detection of analogies based on the fastText model is described. The web application operates as a client of the API.

A. Development of preprocessor module (API)

A common problem in Natural Language Processing (NLP), machine learning and any specialty that works with large volumes of plain text is the great variety of forms in which these are represented and expressed. The development of an API to execute the ad hoc preprocessing task allows the integration of several functionalities to solve the problem of cleaning and normalizing the corpus. Among the functionalities are the following:

- Parallel processing of files in a directory.
- Text is automatically converted to UTF-8 if the original encoding is in the Encoding Standard.
- NKFC and whitespace normalization.
- Removal of modifiers and marks.
- Lower-case folding.
- Trimming of punctuation around words.
- Replace words with <unk> placeholder if they meet any of the following criteria:
    - Word has an at sign @.
    - Word lacks alphabetic characters.
    - Word has two punctuation chars in a row, such as http://.
- HTML code is parsed, and CSS selectors can be used to:
    - Remove undesired elements.
    - Insert newlines after paragraphs and line breaks.
    - Extract the main content of an HTML document.

Table II summarizes the functionalities and shows some examples, excluding coding conversion, since it only applies to the internal representation of the text:

TABLE II. PREPROCESSING TASKS

Task	Input	Output
Unicode normalization[a]	ℋ𝒪l𝒜 muNdó	HOlA muNdo
Parsing and cleaning HTML code	<p>uno<p> dos <script>3===2	uno\ndos
Tokenization	Lorem ipsum. Dolor sit	Lorem ipsum\nDolor sit
Removal punctuation marks	y foo dice, ... cómo (es posible)	y foo dice cómo es posible
Replacement of custom tokens[b]	El reporte 3442 de foo@example.com está en http://example.com/report	El reporte de está en
Lower-case folding	Zenda sobrevivió al COVID-19	zenda sobrevivió al covid-19

[a] This stage also includes the normalization of word and sentence separators.
[b] A replacement token is inserted to preserve the distance between words.

To complete this preprocessing phase, an ad-hoc tool was developed for the preprocessing of text and HTML corpus called corpus-preproc available from [22], this tool will be a module of the web application described below.

B. Development of web application

The architecture of the available application is based on the controller view model, as shown in Figure 2. Docker platform on Ubuntu 20.04, whose host has the following hardware.

- Processor: Intel®Xeon® CPU E3-1220 v3 @ 3.10 GHz.
- RAM: 16 Gb.
- Disk memory: 285 Gb.

1) Back-end of application: For back-end of application, the microservices architecture is used. Figure 2 shows that to guarantee a level of security, Cloudflare Access services are used, which allow authenticating users by sending an OTP key by email, in this case, only accepting the domain ubiobio.cl. We also use Cloudflare Tunnel, a service that hosts sites without opening ports, which allows hosting a site with a standard port using the infrastructure provided by the university. In addition, it is observed within the security layer that the supervised word embedding server (ServerfastText) has been launched.

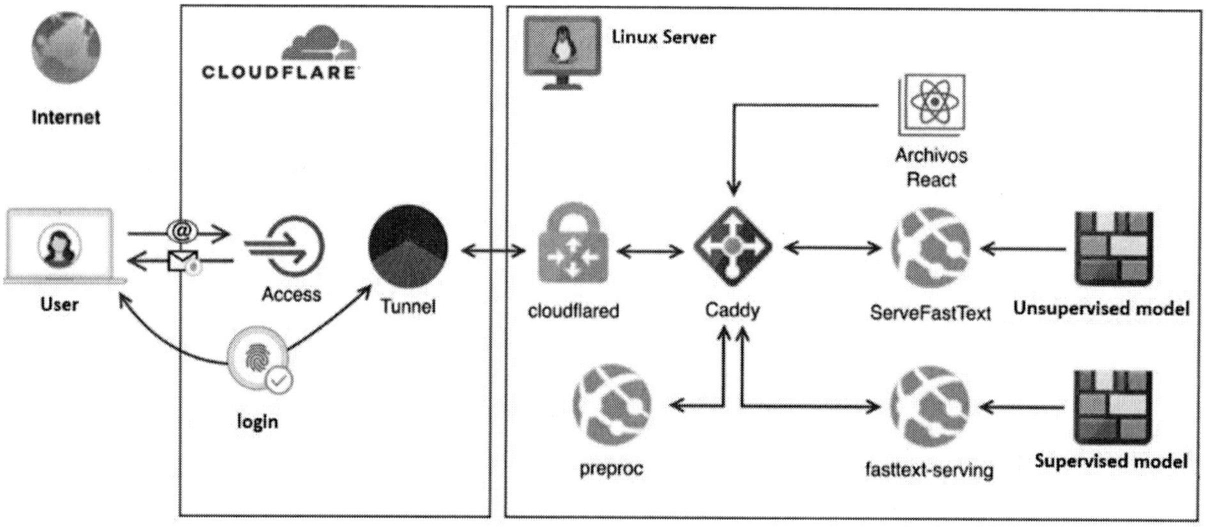

Figure 2. Web application architecture (back-end).

The reverse proxy and server for React assets (Caddy) and the Cloudflare client (Cloudflared) are static binaries. This makes provisioning very easy, requiring only the binaries, the compiled React files, the models and the configuration of Cloudflare and Caddy in a GNU/Linux distribution.

2) *Front-end of application:* As shown in Figure 3, the fastText-embedding-viewer application has three modules. The first is a preprocessor client (described in Section 4.A), the second is the word embedding module, where similar words and analogies are obtained, and the third module, oriented to the analysis of emotions, is where the emotional profile of a sentence, based on Plutchik's taxonomy, is obtained. The view of front-end can be seen in Figure 3 available from [23].

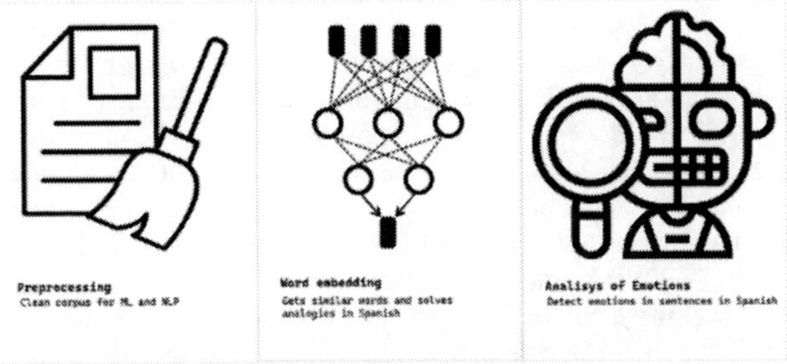

Figure 3. fastText-embedding-viewer application home page (front-end).

This interface offers to users preprocessing, similarities and analogies and analysis of emotions modules.

a) Module for preprocessing: This module allows uploading a corpus in TXT or HTML format with any acceptable coding within the web standard for preprocessing. The functions of Unicode normalization *, cleaning HTML code, segmentation of grammatical sentences, removal of punctuation marks surrounding words, replacement of personalized tokens, normalization of uppercase and lowercase letters are available (see Figure 4).

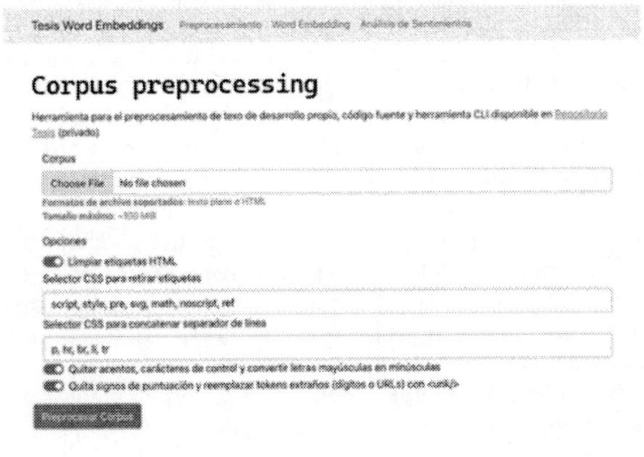

Figure 4. fastText-embedding-viewer preprocessor client module.

Word embedding module for similarities and analogies: This module allows the analysis of words using word embedding (see Figure 5), making it possible to perform similarity and analogy analyses, these functionalities are implemented by the unsupervised model generated from fastText. After entering the data for similarity, the fastText find the most related words a given word. The similarity of a word can support the search for synonyms during the composition of texts, while analogies can allow the discovery of new relationships between words.

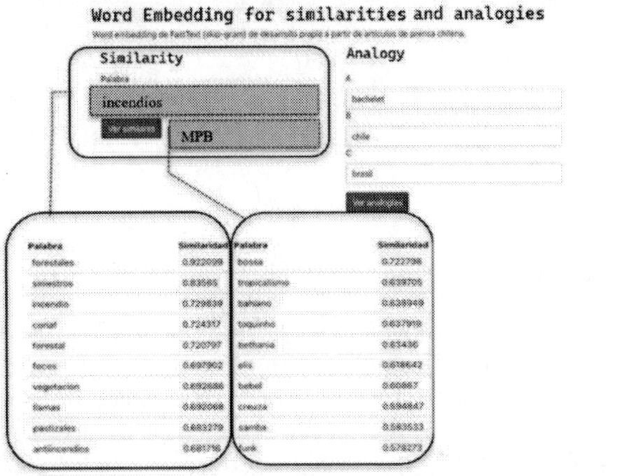

Figure 5. Word embedding module for similarities (Examples 1, 2 and 3).

From the input data of Figure 5, three examples are explained:

Example 1: When entering fires, similar words are obtained, such as forest or sinister, CONAF also arises, which is an organization dedicated to the control of forest fires.

Example 2: With MPB (Brazilian Popular Music), related musical genres such as Bossa Nova and prominent artists of the genre such as Elis Regina are observed.

Example 3: Writing Bachelet shows the name of the former president, the position of president and other presidents chilenos, such as Ricardo Lagos and Eduardo Frei.

In case of analogies, three parameters are entered in the analogy section, called A, B and C, which are read in the rhetorical form: **B** is to **A** as **C** is to ***prediction***. The denomination arises from the vector form used: A - B + C = ***prediction***

From the input data of Figure 6, the following analogies emerge:

Country-Celebrity: Chile is to Bachelet as Brazil is to Rousseff. The most similar word is Dilma, with the second name being Rousseff.

Other outputs obtained were for the country-capital and position-gender analogies:

Country-Capital: Chile is to Santiago as Portugal is to Lisbon. The most similar word is Lisbon, also having a high similarity to the names associated with the population of Portugal.

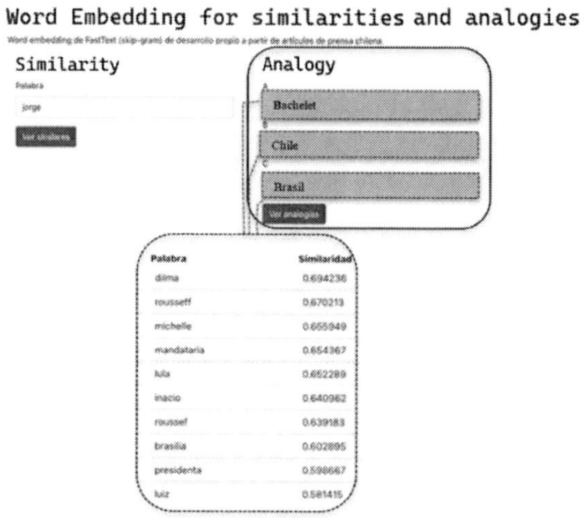

Figure 6. Screenshot with results for Country-Celebrity analogy.

b) Word embedding module for Analisys of emotions using fastText: It is possible to automatically determine the emotions associated with one or more sentences with word embedding. This functionality was implemented by the supervised model generated from fastText. The interface is illustrated in Figure 7. Note that the sentences can be entered by line or as a paragraph because the tool is responsible for separating paragraphs and cleaning the text by calling the preprocessing API to become an appropriate input to the fastText model. The output obtained corresponds to each sentence preprocessed, accompanied by a graph with the profile of predicted emotions and their percentage distribution.

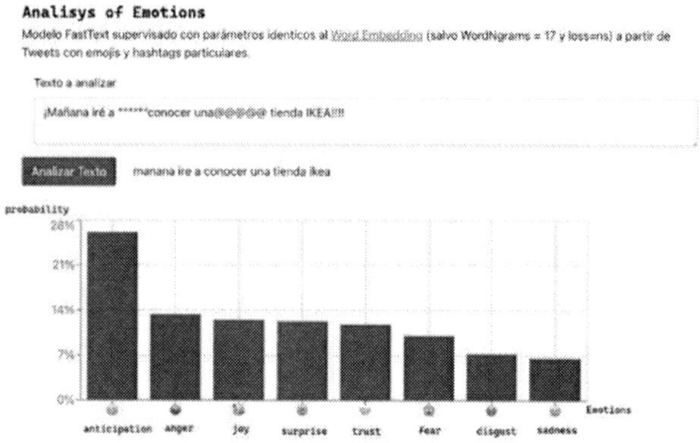

Figure 7. Module for the detection of emotions.

The output obtained corresponds to each sentence preprocessed, accompanied by a graph with the profile of predicted emotions and their percentage distribution.

V. EVALUATION

The evaluation of the tool involved the determination of the quality of the web application by considering aspects of performance, accessibility, good practices, and Search Engine Optimization (SEO). For this, Google lighthouse tool was used, which produced the results (1-100 score) shown in Table III.

TABLE III. EVALUATION OF WEB APPLICATION

Module	Perfor mance	Accessibili ty	Best Practices	SEO
Preprocessing	93	87	100	92
Word embedding for Similarities and Analogies	96	89	100	100
Word embedding for Analysis of emotions	96	90	100	100

Metrics shown in Table III include Performance related to first content paint, speed index, first idle CPU, estimated input latency, blocking time; Accessibility related to universal design; Best practices are related to the security of the web application and its documentation and SEO related to how optimized the site is for search engines.

Table III shows that the best results of the quality assessment were obtained for the word embedding similarity and analogies and analysis of emotions modules, which were slightly lower in the preprocessing module.

Making a comparison between our tool and those included in Table I, in addition to being oriented to the analysis of emotions for the Spanish language, it is based on the embedding of words through the fastText algorithm and integrates the functionality to identify synonyms and analogies through the similarity detection features offered by the algorithm.

VI. CONCLUSION AND FUTURE WORK

The tools that we have developed are useful for the tasks of researchers in the area of subjectivity analysis, specifically in the analysis of emotions in written texts. It is necessary to highlight the functionality of determining similarities and analogies as a novel aspect of our work.

The first module of the web application supports the area of subjectivity analysis by integrating a broad list of preprocessing tasks and considering input from HTML, Twitter or another source. The second, with the option of obtaining similarities, can support the search for synonyms during the process composition of texts, while analogies can allow the discovery of new relationships between words, all this through based on word embedding and unsupervised fastText model. Finally, the analysis of emotions module predicts an emotional profile of a written text, which could guide a commercial strategy based on the opinions of buyers or regulate the intensity of the statements on social networks, among other applications in the current world, all this through based on word embedding and supervised fastText model.

Both the API for text preprocessing corpus-preproc and the web application for analysis of emotions based on fastText are available from [22] and [23]. It is intended to add experimentation with users, since the tool is aimed at them. A benchmarking against other tools could be added.

It would be of interest to create a web browser extension to provide feedback on the predominant emotions in the text that a user writes or to hide comments or news articles in which negative emotions predominate. The incorporation of polysemy within the model will also be explored, such as that which appears in the representation of contextualized words to enhance the tool. Another aspect that could be incorporated into future work would be how a recommendation system [24] could be nourished from the results of the similarity module and analogies such as the analysis of emotions.

ACKNOWLEDGMENT

The authors thank the Department of Information Systems at the University of BioBío and the Research Directorate at the Universidad Católica dela Santísima Concepción.

REFERENCES

[1] M. Lepe-Faúndez, A. Segura Navarrete, C. Vidal-Castro, C. Martínez-Araneda, and C. Rubio-Manzano, "Detecting aggressiveness in tweets: A hybrid model for detecting cyberbullying in the Spanish language," Applied Sciences, 11(22), 10706, 2021.

[2] A. Joulin, E. Grave, P. Bojanowski, and T. Mikolov, "Bag of tricks for efficient text classification," arXiv preprint arXiv:1607.01759, 2016.

[3] P. Bojanowski, P. Grave, A. Joulin, and T. Mikolov, "Enriching word vectors with subword information," Transactions of the Association for Computational Linguistics, 5, pp. 135–146, 2017, doi: https://doi.org/10.1162/tacl_a_00051

[4] M. Bekoff. "Animal Emotions: Exploring Passionate NaturesCurrent interdisciplinary research provides compelling evidence that many animals experience such emotions as joy, fear, love, despair, and grief—we are not alone". BioScience 50(10), pp. 861–870, 2000.

[5] R. C. Solomon, and B. Duignan. Emotion [Encyclopedia]. Encyclopædia Britannica, Available from https://www.britannica.com/science/emotion, last accessed March 2023.

[6] A. Yadollahi, A. G. Shahraki, and O. R. Zaiane, "Current state of text sentiment analysis from opinion to emotion mining," ACM Computing Surveys (CSUR) 50(2), pp. 1–33, 2017.

[7] P.J. Stone, D.C. Dunphy, and M. S. Smith. "The general inquirer: A computer approach to content analysis," M.I.T Press.

[8] S. Mohammad, and P. Turney. "Crowdsourcing a word–emotion association lexicon". Computational intelligence 29(3), pp. 436–465, 2013.

[9] R. Plutchik. "A general psychoevolutionary theory of emotion". In Theories of emotion, pp. 3–33. Academic Press, 1980.

[10] R. Varela. Affective Lexical Resource to Spanish Language (Recurso Léxico Afectivo para idioma Español: REDPAL). Master Thesis. Universidad del Bío-Bío. [Online]. Available from http://mcc.ubiobio.cl/docs/tesis/roberto_varela_medina-2020_varela_roberto.pdf, last accessed March 2023.

[11] E. Öhman, M. Pàmies, K. Kajava, and J. Tiedemann, "XED: A Multilingual Dataset for Sentiment Analysis and Emotion Detection," In Proceedings of the 28th International Conference on Computational Linguistics, pp. 6542–6552, 2020. https://doi.org/https://doi.org/10.18653/v1/2020.coling-main.575

[12] S. Wang, A. Maoliniyazi, X. Wu, and X. Meng, "Emo2Vec: Learning emotional embeddings via multi-emotion category," ACM Transactions on Internet Technology (TOIT) 20(2), pp. 1–17, 2020.

[13] E. Cambria, A. Livingstone, and A. Hussain, "The hourglass of emotions," In Cognitive behavioural systems, pp. 144-157. Springer, Berlin, Heidelberg, 2012, doi: https://doi.org/10.1007/978-3-642-34584-5_11

[14] P. Gupta, R. Inika, B. Gunnika, and A. K. Dubey, "Decoding emotions in text Using GloVe embeddings," In International Conference on Computing, Communication, and Intelligent Systems (ICCCIS), pp. 36–40. IEEE, 2021, doi: https://doi.org/10.1109/ICCCIS51004.2021.9397132

[15] B. Saju, J. Siji, and A. Amal, "Comprehensive Study on Sentiment Analysis: Types, Approaches, Recent Applications, Tools and APIs," In Advanced Computing and Communication Technologies for High Performance Applications (ACCTHPA 2020), pp. 186–193. IEEE, 2020.

[16] U. Krcadinac , P. Pasquier, J. Jovanovic, and V. Devedzic, "Synesketch: An open-source library for sentence-based emotion recognition," IEEE Transactions on Affective Computing 4(3), pp. 312–325, 2013.

[17] Reciptiviti, Inc. Receptiviti's Emotions engine. [Online]. Available from https://docs.receptiviti.com/frameworks/emotions, last accessed March 2023.

[18] F. Calefato, F. Lanubile, and N. Novielli, "EmoTxt: A toolkit for emotion recognition from text," In 2017 seventh International Conference on Affective Computing and Intelligent Interaction Workshops and Demos (ACIIW), pp. 79–80. IEEE, 2017.

[19] F. Calefato, F. Lanubile, N. Novielli, and L. Quaranta, "EMTk: The Emotion Mining Toolkit," SEmotion'19, pp. 34–37, 2019, doi: https://dl.acm.org/doi/10.1109/SEmotion.2019.00014

[20] IBM. IBM Watson Natural Language Understanding Text Analysis. [Online]. Available from https://www.ibm.com/demos/live/natural-language-understanding/self-service/home, last accessed December 2022.

[21] A. Band. Text2emotion: Python package to detect emotions from textual data. [Online]. Available from https://pypi.org/project/text2emotion/, last accessed March 2023.

[22] J. Silva. Corpus-preproc v0.1.0: A preprocessor for text and HTML corpora. [Online]. Available from https://crates.io/crates/corpus-preproc, last accessed March 2023.

[23] J. Silva, A. Segura Navarrete. FastText-embedding-viewer: An emotion detect tool based on fastText [Online]. Available from http://tesis.cuac.dev, last accessed March 2023.

[24] A.M.J. Skulimowski, "Cognitive Content Recommendation in Digital Knowledge Repositories – A Survey of Recent Trends," In: L. Rutkowski, M. Korytkowski, R. Scherer, R. Tadeusiewicz, L. Zadeh, J. Zurada (eds) Artificial Intelligence and Soft Computing. ICAISC 2017. Lecture Notes in Computer Science, vol 10246. Springer, Cham, 2017. https://doi.org/10.1007/978-3-319-59060-8_52

The Treatment of Errors Made by French Second Language Learners in The Use of Object Clitic Pronouns through The Use of a Fine-Tuned Deep Learning Model

Adel Jebali
Département d'études françaises
Concordia University
Montreal, Canada
Email: adel.jebali@concordia.ca

***Abstract*— Object clitic pronouns (particularly third person pronouns) in French are problematic for second and foreign language learners. As a result, several researchers, such as [1], have observed that French second language (L2) learners frequently use avoidance strategies to avoid using these forms, even when doing so allows them to lighten their discourse (written or oral) by avoiding repetition. This is one of the reasons we were interested in technological tools that could assist these learners in comprehending these clitics. We therefore conducted a study with a tripartite goal: to uncover a corpus of L2 French productions focusing on clitics, to use this corpus to train a state-of-the-art deep learning model (CamemBERT), and to implement the trained model to detect learners' errors when producing the forms under study. This model was found to be over 99% reliable when tested. Furthermore, when evaluated on sentences with different turns of phrase than those encountered during training, the model detects errors with the same degree of reliability. This model constitutes a significant advancement in the automatic processing of interlanguage and can be used to develop tools for French L2 learners.**

Keywords— French L2; Object pronoun clitics; deep learning; CamemBERT; model.

I. Introduction

The French Object Clitics (OCs) are primarily personal or oblique pronouns found in contexts, such as in sentence (1b):

(1) a. *Marie a lu la lettre.*
b. *Marie l'a lue.*

In sentence (1b), the OC pronoun *la* (elided as *l'*) is a prosodically weak element that precedes and attaches to the verb while having a syntactic function as the verb's object. This differs from the behavior of equivalent pronouns in English, for example. In the example (2b), the pronoun *it* is placed after the verb, in the same position occupied by the Nominal Phrase (NP) which it replaces, *the letter*.

(2) a. Mary read the letter.
b. Mary read it.

This peculiar behavior of OCs in French, along with other particularities of these elements, causes confusion among the learners of this language. These learners, therefore, resort to several strategies to compensate for their lack of mastery of these forms. Some authors, such as [1], have raised the issue of omission and avoidance, while [2] also highlights other strategies, such as the repetition of the NP. In addition, these learners generally make errors in positioning the OC relative to the verb and the auxiliary, or make false agreements in gender, number or person with the antecedent; in addition to the grammatical case errors discussed in [3]: using the accusative instead of the dative and vice versa.

All these strategies and errors are well represented in the authentic corpus that we used to fine-tune a deep learning model aimed at classifying French L2 learner's productions into three categories, as explained in the following sections.

In Section II of this paper, The data and corpus used in this research are presented. The third Section will present the CamemBERT model as well as the fine-tuned version that we derived from it in order to classify the productions of L2 French learners. Section IV will be devoted to a discussion of the results.

II. Dataset

The dataset used to fine-tune the model comes from a previous research project on new technologies and their quantitative and qualitative effects on the production of French L2 OCs. The corpus in question is described in [2]. The transcription of this corpus was used as a basis to isolate both the OC and a relevant context of its use. Because of the interview-like nature of this corpus, this resulted in pairs containing a question and the answer to it, constructed as follows:

(3) What have I done/ am I doing with X? You are/were Y it.

Where X is an object, Y is a French verb and *it* is the OC (whose position is mostly preverbal in French). In (4), we have an example where the OC produced by the learner is correct (label 1 in my dataset):

(4) *Qu'est-ce que j'ai fait avec mes crayons? Tu les as rangés.*
English: What did I do with my pencils? You put them away.

In (5), we have an example where the learner uses the repetition of the noun phrase (NP) to avoid using the OC (label 2 in the dataset):

(5) *Que fait la fille avec cette pomme? La fille épluche la pomme.*
English: What is the girl doing with this apple? The girl is peeling the apple.

Finally, in (6), we have several examples of errors in the selection of the OC or in its placement in relation to the verb (label 0):

(6)

a. A misplaced OC: *Qu'est-ce que j'ai fait avec mon crayon? *Tu as l'aiguisé.*
English: What did I do with my pencil? *You have sharpened it.

b. Gender error: *Que font les enfants avec la salade? *Ils le mangent.*
English: What are the children doing with the salad? *They eat it.

c. Number error: *Qu'est-ce que j'ai fait avec les lunettes? *Tu l'as pris dans tes mains.*
English: What did I do with the glasses? *You took it in your hands.

d. d. Grammatical case error: *Que fait le père avec ses enfants? *Il les donne un câlin.*
English: What does the father do with his children? *He gives they a hug.

e. e. Object omission: *Que fait la mère avec son bébé? *Elle regarde.*
English: What is the mother doing with her baby? *She is watching.

As is frequently the case when working with interlanguage, as highlighted by [4], the majority of the examples containing OCs errors are riddled with other errors (lexical spelling, grammatical spelling, or others). As a result, some pairs are labeled 1 despite the fact that there are other errors in the answer, and others are labeled 2 (for repetition) even though the repeated NP is misspelled (e.g., *carte* spelled *cart* or even *card*). We will see that this will not prevent the fine-tuned CamemBERT model from making correct predictions on the submitted data.

The resulting dataset contains 899 question/answer pairs annotated in three categories: 0 for pairs containing errors on OCs, 1 for pairs where the use of OCs is correct, and 2 for pairs where there was a repetition of the NP in the answer. Tab. 1 summarizes the dataset statistics:

TABLE I. DATASET STATISTICS

	N	%
0	126	14.01
1	336	37.37
2	437	48.60

Thus, the distribution of the three categories is unbalanced, as shown in Figure 1.

And since we are dealing with unbalanced categories, the Weighted Random Sampler from the Pytorch library was used to give the less represented data a weight based on their size.

To fine-tune the deep learning model, 80% of the dataset was used for training and the remaining 20% for validation. The next section will be devoted to the description of the model.

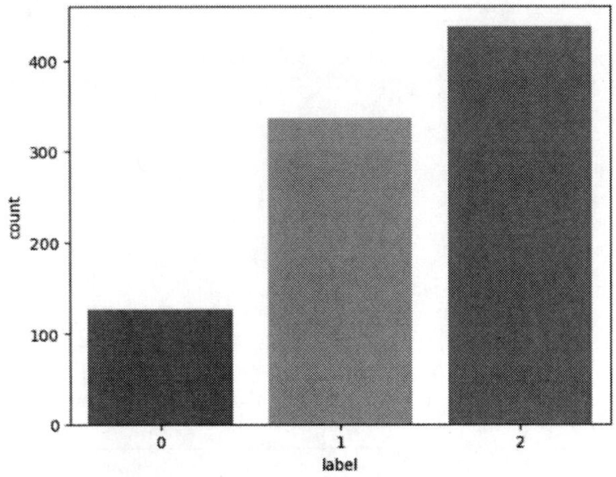

Figure 1. Unbalanced categories in the dataset.

III. CAMEMBERT-BASED MODEL

In this section, the deep learning model that will be used to process object clitics in French is presented. The base model, CamemBERT, will be introduced, as well as the fine-tuned version and its evaluation.

A. *CamemBERT*

Transformer-based [5], CamemBERT, described in [6], is a deep-learning language model for French, based on Bidirectional Encoder Representations from Transformers (BERT), see [7], and more specifically on RoBERTa [8], which "removes BERT's next-sentence pretraining objective, and trains with much larger mini-batches and learning rates". CamemBERT has 110 million parameters and was pretrained on the French subcorpus of the multilingual corpus OSCAR (138 GB of text) as part of a collaboration between INRIA Paris (ALMANACH team) and Facebook/Meta AI.

CamemBERT is suitable for a wide range of NLP tasks, such NER, POS tagging, dependency parsing and natural language inference. Sentiment analysis (see, for instance [9]) through CamemBERT For Sequence Classification python class is another suitable task that led to other applications, such grammaticality judgements. Thus, a fine-tuned version of CamemBERT has been used for coordination error detection in French in [10]. The study by Cheng et al. [11], among many others, used a fine-tuned version of BERT to check the grammaticality of Chinese sentences. Therefore, the goal of this paper is to propose a deep learning model capable of making grammatical judgments by classifying submitted sequences as correct, error-prone, or repetition-prone in order to help French second language learners in better mastering OCs.

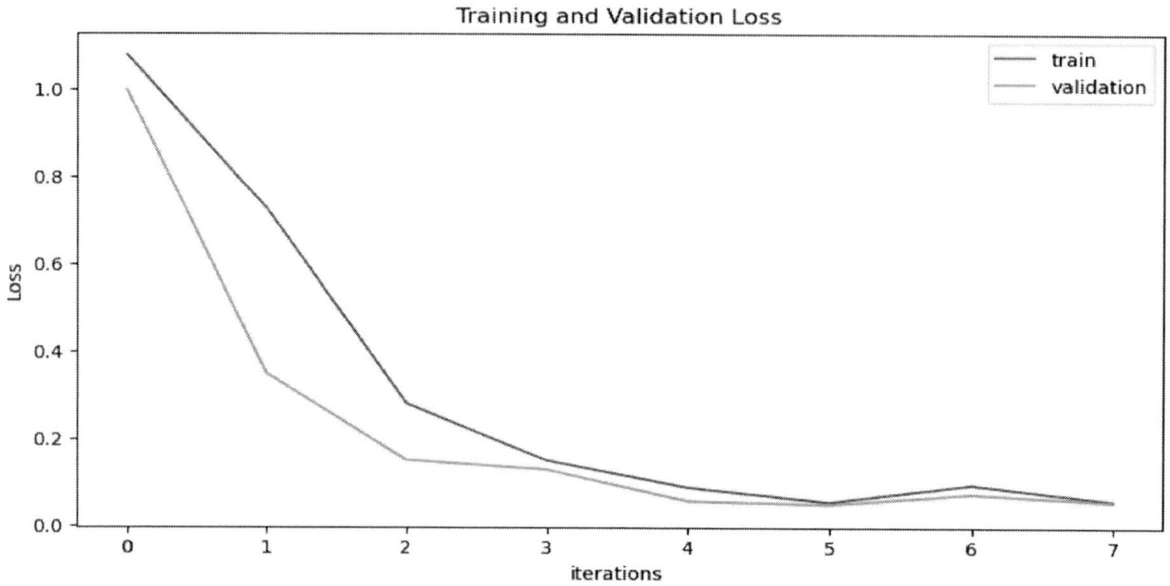

Figure 2. Training and Validation Loss.

B. The fine-tuned model and its evaluation

Using the dataset described in Section II, CamemBERT was trained for 10 epochs on an Nvidia consumer GPU with AdamW as the optimizer. The early stop technique was used, which stopped the training at epoch 7, with the Training and Validation Loss that can be seen in Figure 2.

The fine-tuned model obtained an f-score of 0.99. The classification report is shown in Tab. 2.

TABLE II. CLASSIFICATION REPORT

	PRECISION	RECALL	F1-SCORE	SUPPORT
0	1.00	0.98	0.99	126
1	0.99	1.00	1.00	336
2	1.00	1.00	1.00	437

Figure 3 shows the Confusion Matrix.

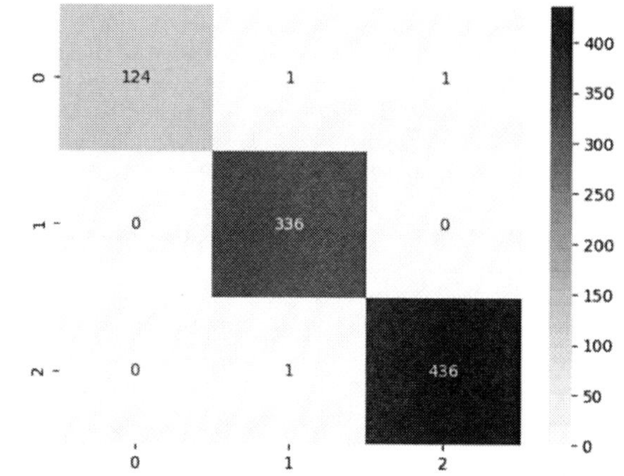

Figure 3. Confusion Matrix.

The model, thus, performed very well on the validation data, with only three pairs misclassified:

(7) *Qu'est-ce que j'ai fait avec le livre? *Vous avez le consulté le livre.*
English: *What did I do with the book? You consulted it the book.
➔ Was classified as 2 (repetition) by the model, but it was labelled 0 (error) in the dataset.

(8) *Que fait l'enfant avec la balle? *L'enfant lance la à son père.*
English: What is the child doing with the ball? *The child it throws to his father.
➔ Was classified as 1 (correct) by the model, but it was labelled 0 (error) in the dataset.

(9) *Que fait la mère avec son bébé? Elle berce son bébé en le regardant.*
English: What is the mother doing with her baby? She rocks her baby while watching him.
➔ Was classified as 1 (correct) by the model, but it was labelled 2 (repetition) in the dataset.

These data will be discussed in Section IV.

IV. Discussion

The model trained on our dataset was able to predict the appropriate grammatical judgment for pairs that it had never seen before but appeared similar to the training data. Here are some examples:

(10) *Qu'est-ce que j'ai fait avec l'échelle? *Tu as la cassée.*
English: What did I do with the ladder? You broke it.
Correct prediction: 0.

(11) *Qu'est-ce que j'ai fait avec le téléphone? Tu l'as donné.*
English: What did I do with the phone? You gave it away.
Correct prediction: 1.

(12) *Qu'est-ce que j'ai fait avec la carte? Tu as sorti la carte.*
English: What did I do with the card? You took the card out.
Correct prediction: 2.

It was also able to correctly make predictions in different contexts of OCs usage. Here are some examples:

(13) *J'ai rencontré Marie et *j'ai lui dit mon secret.*
English: I met Marie and I told her my secret.
Correct prediction: 0.

(14) **Mes amies, je ne peux que l'aimer.*
English: My friends, *I can only love it. Correct prediction: 0.

(15) *Est-ce que les étudiantes aiment la soupe? *Oui, elles aiment.*
English: Do the students like the soup? *Yes, they like.
Correct prediction: 0.

(16) **Je lui aide.*
English: I help him/her.
Correct prediction: 0.

(17) *Je l'observe depuis ce matin.*
English: I have been observing him/her since this morning.
Correct prediction: 1.

(18) *Que mange Marie? *Marie mange.*
English: What is Mary eating? *Mary eats.
Correct prediction: 0.

(19) *Combien de personnes vois-tu? J'en vois trois.*
English: How many people do you see? I see three.
Correct prediction: 1.

(20) *As-tu vu Isabelle? Oui, *je le vois.*
English: Did you see Isabelle? Yes, *I see him.
Correct prediction: 0.

(21) **Elle a le vu.*
English: She saw it/him.
Correct prediction: 0.

The misclassified three pairs (7), (8) and (9) need some explanation. The pair (7), for instance, contains both an error (in the position of the OC) and a repetition of the NP. In this case, the error is more significant and should normally be reported to the user, which was done in the dataset. Pair (8) illustrates the case where the OC is inserted in a postverbal position when it should be in a preverbal position. This error is under-represented in the dataset used for training and accounts for the incorrect label predicted by the model. Finally, pair (9) contains a repetition of the NP and a well-used OC to refer to this phrase. As this repetition here is less troublesome than when the OC is absent, these examples should be annotated differently (as 1) in a future version of the dataset. Therefore, the plan is to conduct a second phase of this research with a completer and more balanced dataset. Regarding the first point, more errors should be represented, such as the one where the OC is postverbal or where the OC is replaced by a strong or tonic pronoun. And in terms of balance, the plan is to create a dataset in which all three classes are equally represented.

V. Conclusion

This paper presented a two-part project: the first one consists of setting up an authentic corpus of written productions of learners of French as a second language regarding their use of OCs. This part aims to provide a dataset from the interlanguage in order to carry out the second part. The latter consists of fine-tuning a deep learning model capable of detecting the most frequent errors, but also repetitions and correct sentences.

The main novelty of this approach is to set up a corpus representing interlanguage, which is a glaring lack in research of this type. Moreover, to our knowledge, there have been no previous research projects that aimed to propose a deep learning model to process this interlanguage.

The deep learning model fine-tuned on the described dataset and derived from CamemBERT is robust enough to correctly predict whether a sentence containing an OC in French is correct, incorrect or contains a repetition. This allowed us to develop a graphical interface in Python and PyQT6 to interact with this model. For the time being, this interface only provides a label and a recommendation, but in a future version, we plan to improve the predictive capabilities of the model as well as the feedback refined by error type.

This study, even though it is based on a corpus of only 899 sequences, demonstrates that it is possible to obtain a reliable classifier without resorting to large-scale data, as is the case for current trends in deep learning and generative artificial intelligence, such as the GPT system. In addition, the resulting tool can be an important ally for learners of French as a second language in their quest to master object clitic pronouns, which is one of the difficult aspects of French for these learners. A didactic study is also planned to establish the pedagogical integration of this digital tool for learners at the B1 and B2 levels.

ACKNOWLEDGMENT

This research was made possible by a grant from SSHRC, through the Insight Development Grants Program (2021-2023).

REFERENCES

[1] V. Wust. "The dictogloss as a measure of the comprehension of y and en by L2 learners of French", The Canadian Modern Language Review, Volume 65, Number 3, pp. pp. 471-499, March 2009.

[2] A. Jebali, "Language anxiety, technology-mediated communication, and elicitation of object clitics in L2 French.", Alsic 21, 2018. Online. URL : http://journals.openedition.org/alsic/3164, DOI : https://doi.org/10.4000/alsic.3164

[3] L. Emirkanian, L. Redmond, and A. Jebali, "Mastery of dative clitics in ditransitive structures in L2 French by English-speaking learners: influence of argument structure in L1.", Canadian Journal of Applied Linguistics, Volume 24, Number 3, pp. 30-60, autumn 2021.

[4] A. Affes, I. Biskri, and A. Jebali, "French Object Clitics in the Interlanguage: A Linguistic Description and a Formal Analysis in the ACCG Framework", in N. T. Nguyen et al. (Eds.): ICCCI 2022, LNAI 13501, pp. 220–231, 2022.

[5] A. Vaswani et al., "Attention Is All You Need", NIPS'17: Proceedings of the 31st International Conference on Neural Information Processing Systems, pp. 6000–6010, december 2017.

[6] L. Martin et al., "CamemBERT: a Tasty French Language Model", Proceedings of the 58th Annual Meeting of the Association for Computational Linguistics, pp. 7203–7219, July 2020.

[7] J. Devlin, M.-W. Chang, K. Lee, and K. Toutanova, "BERT: Pre-training of Deep Bidirectional Transformers for Language Understanding", Proceedings of the 2019 Conference of the North American Chapter of the Association for Computational Linguistics: Human Language Technologies, Volume 1 (Long and Short Papers), pp. 4171–4186, june 2019.

[8] Y. Liu et al., "RoBERTa: A Robustly Optimized BERT Pretraining Approach", ArXiv, abs/1907.11692, 2019.

[9] G. Guerdoux, T. Tiffet, and C. Bousquet, "Inference Time of a CamemBERT Deep Learning Model for Sentiment Analysis of COVID Vaccines on Twitter", in J. Mantas et al. (Eds.): Advances in Informatics, Management and Technology in Healthcare, pp. 269-270, 2022.

[10] L. Noreskal, I. Eshkol-Taravella, and M. Desmets, "Erroneous Coordinated Sentences Detection in French Students' Writings", in K. Wojtkiewicz et al. (Eds.): ICCCI 2021, CCIS 1463, pp. 586–596, 2021.

[11] Y. Cheng and M. Duan, "Chinese Grammatical Error Detection Based on BERT Model", Proceedings of the 6th Workshop on Natural Language Processing Techniques for Educational Applications, pp. 108–113, December 2020.

Sentiment Analysis of Movie Reviews Using BERT

Gibson Nkhata
Department of Computer Science & Computer Engineering
University of Arkansas
Fayetteville, AR 72701, USA
Email: gnkhata@uark.edu

Usman Anjum, Justin Zhan
Department of Computer Science
University of Cincinnati
Cincinnati, OH 45221, USA
Email: anjumun@ucmail.uc.edu, zhanjt@ucmail.uc.edu

***Abstract*—Sentiment Analysis (SA) or opinion mining is analysis of emotions and opinions from any kind of text. SA helps in tracking people's viewpoints, and it is an important factor when it comes to social media monitoring, product and brand recognition, customer satisfaction, customer loyalty, advertising and promotion's success, and product acceptance. That is why SA is one of the active research areas in Natural Language Processing (NLP). SA is applied on data sourced from various media platforms to mine sentiment knowledge from them. Various approaches have been deployed in the literature to solve the problem. Most techniques devise complex and sophisticated frameworks in order to attain optimal accuracy. This work aims to fine-tune Bidirectional Encoder Representations from Transformers (BERT) with Bidirectional Long Short-Term Memory (BiLSTM) for movie reviews sentiment analysis and still provide better accuracy than the State-of-The-Art (SOTA) methods. The paper also shows how sentiment analysis can be applied, if someone wants to recommend a certain movie, for example, by computing overall polarity of its sentiments predicted by the model. That is, our proposed method serves as an upper-bound baseline in prediction of a predominant reaction to a movie. To compute overall polarity, a heuristic algorithm is applied to BERT-BiLSTM output vector. Our model can be extended to three-class, four-class, or any fine-grained classification, and apply overall polarity computation again. This is intended to be exploited in future work.**

***Index Terms*—Sentiment analysis; movie reviews; BERT, bidirectional LSTM; overall polarity.**

I. Introduction

Sentiment analysis aims to determine the polarity of emotions like happiness, sorrow, grief, hatred, anger and affection and opinions from text, reviews, and posts which are available in media platforms [1]. With the emergence of various social media platforms, vast amount of data are contained and various information, e.g., education, health, entertainment, etc, is shared in these online forums everyday across the globe. Therefore, there have been advances in many Natural Language Processing (NLP) tasks in conjunction with machine or deep learning techniques that automatically mine knowledge from the data sourced from these repositories [2]. As an NLP task, sentiment analysis helps in tracking people's viewpoints. For example, it is a powerful marketing tool that enables product managers to understand customer emotions in their various marketing campaigns. It is an important factor when it comes to social media monitoring, product and brand recognition, customer satisfaction, customer loyalty, advertising and promotion's success, and product acceptance. Sentiment analysis is among the most popular and valuable tasks in the field of NLP [3].

Movie reviews is an important approach to gauge the performance of a particular movie. Whereas providing a numerical or stars rating to a movie quantitatively tells us about the success or failure of a movie, a collection of movie reviews is what gives us a deeper qualitative insight on different aspects of the movie. A textual movie review tells us about the strengths and weaknesses of the movie and deeper analysis of a movie review tells if the movie generally satisfies the reviewer.

Movie Reviews Sentiment Analysis is being worked on in this study because movie reviews have standard benchmark datasets, where salient and qualitative works have been published on. In fact, most of these reviews are crawled from the social media platforms [4].

Bidirectional Encoder Representations from Transformers (BERT) is a popular pre-trained language representation model and has proven to perform well on many NLP tasks like question answering, named entity recognition, and text classification [5]. BERT has been used in many works for sentiment analysis, like in [6]. However, regarding the capabilities of BERT, the performance is not satisfactory.

In this paper, BERT is fine-tuned for sentiment analysis on movie reviews and provide optimal accuracy that surpass accuracy of State-Of-The Art (SOTA) models. Our focus is on polarity classification on a 2-point scale. Polarity classification classifies a text as containing either a negative or positive sentiment.

BERT has proven to be satisfactory in many NLP downstream tasks. BERT has been used in information retrieval in [7] to build an efficient ranking model for industry use cases. The pre-trained language model was also successfully utilised in [8] for extractive summarization of text and used for question answering with satisfactory results in [9]. Yang et al. [10] efficiently applied the model in data augmentation resulting in optimal results.

Fine-tuning is a common technique for transfer learning. The target model copies all model designs with their parameters from the source model except the output layer and fine-tunes these parameters based on the target dataset.

The main benefit of fine-tuning is no need of training the entire model from scratch, and only the output layer of the target model needs to be trained. Hence, BERT is being fine-tuned in this work by coupling with Bidirectional Long Short-Term Memory (BiLSTM) and train the resulting model on movie reviews sentiment analysis benchmark datasets. BiLSTM processes input features bidirectionally [5], which helps in improving target model generalisation. Therefore, our fine-tuning approach is called BERT+BiLSTM-SA, where SA stands for Sentiment Analysis.

Finally, how results of sentiment analysis can be applied is shown. If someone wants to recommend a certain movie, for example, by computing overall polarity of its reviews sentiments predicted by the model. That is, the proposed method serves as an upper-bound baseline in prediction of the polarity of predominant reaction to a movie. To compute overall polarity, a heuristic algorithm adopted from [11] is applied to BERT-BiLSTM+SA output vector. The algorithm in their paper is applied on the output vector of three class classification on twitter dataset by LSTM, whereas our approach customises the algorithm for binary classification output vector from BERT+BiLSTM-SA.

This work is divided into two main components. First, fine-tuning BERT with BiLSTM and use the resulting model on binary sentiment polarity classification. Second, using the results of sentiment classification in computation of a predominant sentiment polarity.

1) Our contributions: Our contributions in this work are:

- Fine-tuning BERT by coupling with BiLSTM for polarity classification on well known benchmark datasets and achieve accuracy that beats SOTA models.
- Computing overall polarity of predicted reviews from BERT+LSTM-SA output vector.
- Comparing our experimental outcomes with results obtained from other studies, including SOTA models, on benchmark datasets.

This paper is organised as follows. Section II describes related work, Section III describes the methodology, Section IV discusses experiments and results, and last, Section V gives conclusion and talks about future work. The code for this project is available [12] to enable wider adoption.

II. Related Work

A lot of work has been conducted in literature on movie reviews sentiment analysis. Starting with traditional machine learning, a step-by-step lexicon-based sentiment analysis using the R open-source software is presented in [13]. In [1], the authors implemented and compared traditional machine learning techniques like Naive Bayes (NB), K-Nearest Neighbours (KNN), and Random Forests (RF) for sentiment analysis. Their results showed that Naive Bayes was the best classifier on the task. An ensemble generative approach for various machine learning approaches on sentiment analysis is used in [3]. KNN with the help of information gain technique was also used in [14] on the task. In [15], the authors proposed training document embeddings using cosine similarity, feature combination, and NB. KNN outperforms all other models in these works.

Deep learning approaches have also been implemented in movie reviews sentiment analysis. Recurrent Neural Network (RNN) and Convolutional Neural Network (CNN) architectures performances were explored for semantic analysis of movie reviews in [16]. RNNs give satisfactory results, but they suffer from the problem of vanishing or exploding gradients when used with long sentences. Nonetheless, CNNs provide non-optimal accuracy on text classification. Coupled Oscillatory RNN (CoRNN), which is a time-discretization of a system of second-order ordinary differential equations, was proposed in [17] to mitigate the exploding and vanishing gradient problem, though the performance was still not convincing. Bodapati et al. [18] used LSTM on movie reviews sentiment analysis by investigating the impact of different hyper parameters like dropout, number of layers, and activation functions. Additionally, BiLSTM network for the task of text classification has also been applied via mixed objective function in [19]. BiLSTM achieved better results but at the expense of a very sophisticated architecture.

BERT has also been previously applied to sentiment analysis. BERT was used on SST-2 movie reviews benchmark for sentiment analysis in [6]. In [20], the authors used BERT for stock market sentiment analysis. BERT was also applied on target-dependent sentiment classification in [21]. However, there is still room for improvement considering their results.

Therefore, in this work, BERT is fine-tuned by coupling with BiLSTM for sentiment analysis on a 2-point scale. Afterwards, an application of sentiment analysis is shown by computing overall polarity of movie reviews, which can also be utilised in recommending a movie.

III. Methodology

Different techniques used in our work starting with description of sentiment analysis and BERT are covered in this section. Afterwards, the section explains how BERT is fine-tuned with BiLSTM, elucidates how classification is applied in our work, describes overall polarity computation, and talks about the overview of the whole work.

A. Sentiment analysis

Sentiment analysis is a sub-domain of opinion mining, which aims at the extraction of emotions and opinions of people towards a particular topic from a structured, semi-structured, or unstructured textual data [22]. In our context, the primary objective is to classify a review as carrying either a positive or negative sentiment on a 2-point scale.

B. BERT

BERT was introduced by researchers from Google [5] and focuses on pre-training deep bidirectional representations from unlabeled text by jointly conditioning on both left and right contexts in all layers of the model. As a result, BERT can be fine-tuned with an extra component on a downstream task like question answering and sentiment analysis.

There are two primary models of BERT, namely, $BERT_{BASE}$ and $BERT_{LARGE}$. $BERT_{BASE}$, which has 12 layers, 768 hidden states, 12 attention heads, and 110M parameters is used in this work, whereas $BERT_{LARGE}$ has almost 2 times of each of these specifications. Actually, the uncased version of $BERT_{BASE}$ known as *bert-base-uncased*, which accepts tokens as lowercase, is adapted in this work. Because of multiple attention heads, BERT processes a sequence of input tokens in parallel, thereby improving the model generalization on the input sequence.

BERT has its own format for the input tokens. The first token of every sequence is denoted as [CLS]. The token corresponds to the last hidden layer, aggregates all the information in the input sequence, and is used for classification tasks. Sentences are packed into a single input sequence and differentiated in two ways: using a special token [SEP] to separate them and adding a learned embedding to every token identifying a sentence where it belongs to.

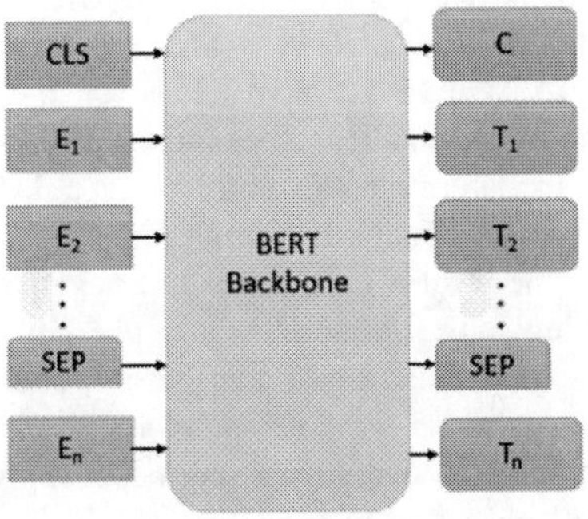

Fig. 1. Simplified diagram of BERT

Figure 1 shows a simplified diagram of BERT. E_n is an input representation of a single token constructed by summing the corresponding token, segment, and position embeddings; BERT Backbone represents main processing performed by BERT; T_n is a hidden state corresponding to token E_n; and C is a hidden state corresponding to aggregate token CLS.

C. Fine-tuning BERT with BiLSTM

Since BERT is pretrained, there is no need of training the entire model from scratch. Hence, information is just needed to be transferred from BERT to the fine-tuning component and train the model for sentiment analysis. This saves training time of the resulting model.

Fine-tuning in this work is conducted as follows. After data preprocessing, two input layers to BERT are built, where names of the layers need to match the input values. These input values are attention masks and input ids, as shown in Figure 2. In other words, attention masks and input ids are input embeddings to the model.

The input embeddings are propagated through BERT afterwards. Dimensionality of the embeddings depends on the input sequence length, batch-size and number of units in a layer. BiLSTM is then concatenated at the very end of BERT, and it includes a dense layer. Therefore, BiLSTM receives information from BERT and feeds it into its dense layer, which then predicts respective sentiments for the input features. BERT and BiLSTM shared same hyperparameters, and all hyperparameters are specified in Section IV under experimental settings.

The fine-tuning part of our model is illustrated in Figure 2. In the figure, *input features* are tokens in a review text, *input ids* identify a sentence that a token belongs to, and *attention masks* are binary tensors indicating the position of the padded indices to a particular sequence so that the model does not attend to them. For the attention mask, 1 is used to indicate a value that should be attended to, while 0 is used to indicate a padded value. Padding helps in making sequences have same length when sentences have variable lengths, which is common in NLP. Therefore, padded information is not part of the input and should rarely be used in model generalization.

The output from BERT has the same dimension as the input to BiLSTM. E_i and T_i mean similar items as E_n and T_n, respectively, in Figure 1. BiLSTM has only one hidden component. Finally, there is a fully connected layer (dense layer) at the end, which has output dimension of batch-size by 1, since binary classification is being worked on here. The dense layer predicts a sentiment polarity.

Weights from first layers of BERT are frozen so that our focus dwells on the last layers close to the fine-tuning component. These layers contain trainable weights, which are updated to minimize the loss during training of the model on the downstream task of sentiment analysis.

D. Classification

In this work, BERT is fine-tuned on polarity classification or binary classification of sentiment analysis. Hence, classification in this context is defined as follows. Given a movie review *R*, classify it as carrying either a positive sentiment or a negative sentiment.

E. Overall polarity

Overall polarity is defined as follows. Given an output vector from BERT+BiLSTM-SA containing sentiment labels of *N* reviews, find the dominating sentiment polarity in the vector. To compute the overall polarity of reviews, the output vector of BERT+BiLSTM-SA is fed into the heuristic algorithm. First, number of labels for each class is counted in the output vector. Then, the computation is conducted as shown in Algorithm 2. While Arasteh et al. [11] used Algorithm 1 to compute overall polarity from the results of three-class classification on twitter replies by LSTM for twitter sentiment analysis, this work adapts the algorithm to compute overall polarity from output vector of binary classification by BERT+BiLSTM-SA.

Algorithm 1 shows how overall polarity is computed from output vector of three-class classification. The overall polarity is first considered to be neutral if the proportion of neutral samples is at least higher than an empirically set threshold, which was set to be 85% of the total predictions. The reason being that most samples are generally expected to be neutral,

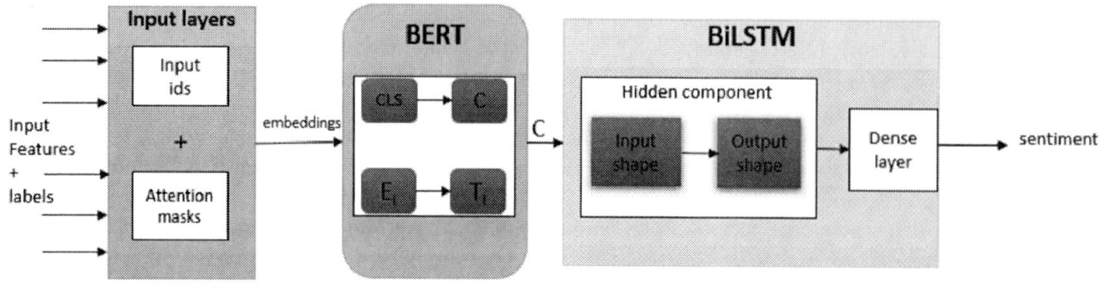

Fig. 2. Fine-tuning of the model

Algorithm 1: Computing overall polarity from three-class classification output vector as done in [11].

Result: Dominating sentiment for all reviews.
if *#total neutral reviews* $>$ *85% of the total reviews* **then**
  overall polarity ← *neutral*;
else
  if *#total positive reviews* $>$*1.5* × *# of total negative reviews* **then**
    overall polarity ← *positive*;
  else if *#total negative reviews* $>$*1.5* × *# of total positive reviews* **then**
    overall polarity ← *negative*;
  else
    overall polarity ← *neutral*;

for not every text can be expected to carry a positive or a negative polarity. Then, negative and positive sentiments are considered in the output vector. Again, there is usually no exclusively positive or negative text sample, that is why a positive overall sentiment is assigned if there is at least 1.5 times as many negative reviews as positive reviews, and vice versa. Meaning that the size of the dominating class must be at least higher for all the reviews to carry its polarity. Lastly, a neutral sentiment is given when the total numbers of positive and negative reviews are close to each other, implying nonexistence of dominance between the two sentiments in the reviews. All constant values in the algorithm were set depending on the various empirical observations in the experiments.

Algorithm 2 is derived from Algorithm 1 by us. Depending on various empirical observations in our experiments, a different threshold coefficient is used when multiplying. Additionally, only proportions of two sentiments are being compared here. Although there is not a neutral sentiment polarity in the output vector of our model, it is introduced for the overall polarity computation if the output of the first two conditions in Algorithm 2 is false, implying a tie between positive and negative reviews.

A naive approach to computing the overall polarity would be just counting the number of labels for each class in BERT+BiLSTM-SA output vector and assign the overall polarity depending on majority class. However, the overall polarity computed from this approach cannot represent a good dominating majority class. For example, assume there is 102 predictions of movie reviews for one movie, and the output vector has 50 positive reviews and 52 negative reviews, the overall polarity will be negative. However, if this is applied in recommending a movie, for example, a difference of 2 is not optimal to determine the dominating polarity of all the movie reviews and conclude that the movie is not interesting. Additionally, the level of positiveness or negativity is different for every review in the datasets. As a result, the formulations in Algorithm 2 are used so that either class in the output vector must contain a bigger proportion to assign its label as the output, otherwise the overall polarity becomes neutral.

The overall polarity computation technique can be used to recommend a movie to a person disregarding subjectivity factors. First, all the reviews pertaining to the movie in question must be gathered, followed by using BERT+BiLSTM-SA to predict the associated sentiments polarities for the reviews. Then, the algorithm can be used to compute the dominating sentiment polarity to see if most people are in favor of the movie or not. Last, the movie can be recommended if the overall polarity is positive.

Algorithm 2: Computing overall polarity from binary classification output vector

Result: Dominating sentiment for all reviews.
if *#total positive reviews* $>$*1.2* × *# of total negative reviews* **then**
  overall polarity ← *positive*
else if *#total negative reviews* $>$*1.2* × *# of total positive reviews* **then**
  overall polarity ← *negative*
else
  overall polarity ← *neutral*

F. Overview of our work

Figure 3 portrays the overview of our work. In a nutshell, the work starts with preprocessing raw text data into features

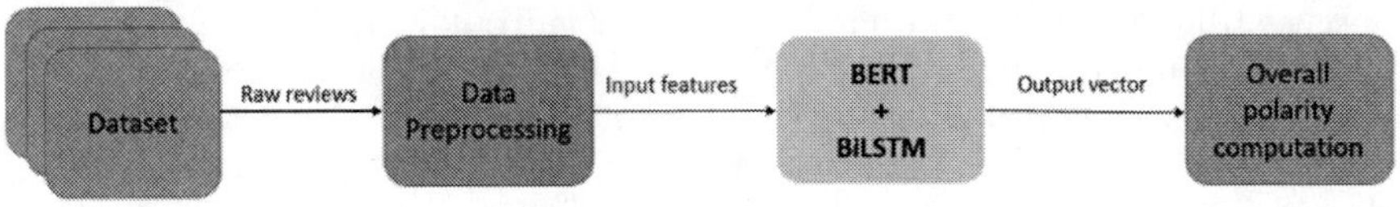

Fig. 3. Overview of our work

that can be understood by BERT and feed the features into BERT ($BERT_{BASE}$ is the same as BERT in the diagram) and BiLSTM through the fine-tuning layer, which specifies the hyperparameters that BERT+BiLSTM should use. Lastly, an output vector from BERT+BiLSTM predictions is used to compute overall polarity.

IV. Experiments

This section starts with an explanation of datasets that are used in the experiments followed by data preprocessing. Afterwards, it describes experimental settings, explains evaluation metrics used in experiments, and discusses experimental results.

A. Datasets

Datasets used in the experiments consist of reviews annotated for sentiment analysis on a 2-point scale. Following is the description of the datasets used and how some of them were changed to suit experimental settings. Table I shows statistics of the datasets used in the experiments.

TABLE I
Statistics of the datasets divided into training and test sets

Dataset	Train samples		Test samples	
	POSITIVE	NEGATIVE	POSITIVE	NEGATIVE
IMDb	12500	12500	12500	12500
MR	4264	4265	1067	1066
SST-2	4300	4244	886	1116
Amazon	239660	37056	59949	9231

1) IMDb movie reviews: Introduced in [23], IMDb movie reviews dataset is a binary sentiment analysis dataset consisting of 50,000 reviews from the Internet Movie Database (IMDb), where the name comes from. It comprises equal number of negative and positive reviews.

2) SST-2: The SST (Stanford Sentiment Treebank) is a corpus with fully labeled parse trees that allows for a complete analysis of the compositional effects of sentiment in language. The corpus is based on the dataset introduced in [2], and it consists of 11,855 single sentences extracted from movie reviews. It was parsed with the Stanford parser and includes a total of 215,154 unique phrases from those parse trees, each annotated by three human judges. In our work, SST-2 version of the dataset is used. SST-2 is designed for binary classification and consists of 11855 movie reviews.

3) MR Movie Reviews: MR Movie Reviews dataset comprises collections of movie review documents labeled with respect to their overall sentiment polarity, positive or negative, or subjective rating, for example two and a half stars, and sentences labeled with respect to their subjectivity status, subjective or objective, or polarity. In this paper, the version introduced in [24], which consists of 5331 positive and 5331 negative processed reviews is used.

4) Amazon Product Data dataset: This dataset contains product reviews and metadata from Amazon, including 142.8 million reviews spanning May, 1996 through July, 2014. The dataset includes reviews, product metadata, and links. It was introduced in [4] for sentiment analysis using product review data, and in [25] to build a recommender system in collaborative filtering setting on amazon products. In our work, only video reviews are focused on. There is a total of 345896 video reviews samples. The dataset originally contained labels with scores from 1 to 5 corresponding to polarity strength variation from negative to positive. The dataset was then prepared for binary classification by replacing 1 and 2 scores with a negative label and 4 and 5 scores with a positive label, and score 3, which represents a neutral class, was discarded as in SST-2 [2].

B. Data preprocessing

The needed data preprocessing steps require to transform the input data into a format that BERT can understand. This involves carrying out two primary data preprocessing steps.

First, creating input examples using the constructor provided in the BERT library. The constructor accepts three main parameters, which are *text_a*, *text_b*, and *label*. *text_a* is the text that the model must classify, which in this case, is the collection of movie reviews without their associated labels. *text_b* is used if a model is being trained to understand the relationship between sentences, for example sentence translation and question answering. The previous scenario hardly applies in our work, so *text_b* is just left blank. *label* has labels of input features. In our case, *label* implies sentiment polarity of every movie review, which can be negative or positive. Refer to BERT original paper [5] for more details about this step and even the next step.

Last, the following preprocessing steps are conducted.

- Lowercase text, since the lowercase version of $BERT_{BASE}$ is being used.
- Tokenize all sentences in the reviews. For example, "this is a very fantastic movie" to "this", "is", "a", "very", "fantastic", "movie".
- Break words into word pieces. That is "interesting" to "interest" and "##ing".
- Map words to indexes using a vocab file that is provided by BERT.

- Adding special tokens: [CLS] and [SEP], which are used for aggregating information of the entire review through the model and separating sentences respectively.
- Append index and segment tokens to each input to track a sentence which a specific token belongs to.

The output of the tokenizer after these steps are *input ids* and *attention masks*. These are then taken as inputs to our model in addition to the reviews labels.

C. Experimental settings

Many simulations were carried on the datasets to find optimal hyperparameters for the model. As a result, optimal results from the experiments were obtained by the following settings. 256 input sequence length (K), adam optimizer, 3e-5 learning rate, 1e-08 epsilon, and sparse categorical cross entropy loss. The model was trained for 10 epochs and repeated steps for each batch. These hyperparameters were cordially fine-tuned regarding both BERT and BiLSTM, and overfitting was noticed when increasing the number of epochs for the model.

D. Evaluation metrics

Accuracy was used to evaluate the performance of our model and compare it with other models. Accuracy metric is adopted because it is greatly applied in most works [6], [26]–[29]. Therefore, this adoption makes our work to be consistent with other works that are being compared against. Accuracy is defined as follows:

$$accuracy = \frac{number\ of\ correct\ predictions}{total\ number\ of\ predictions} \times 100 \quad (1)$$

E. Results

Table II presents accuracy comparisons between our model, BERT+BiLSTM-SA, and other models on all datasets. BERT+BiLSTM-SA outperforms other models on all the datasets, thereby achieving new SOTA accuracy on these benchmark datasets. The best accuracy of 98.76% accuracy is obtained on Amazon dataset.

TABLE II
ACCURACY (%) COMPARISONS OF MODELS ON BENCHMARK DATASETS FOR BINARY CLASSIFICATION

Model name	Dataset			
	IMDb-2	*MR*	*SST-2*	*amazon-2*
RNN-Capsule [30]	84.12	83.80	82.77	82.68
coRNN [31]	87.4	87.11	88.97	89.32
TL-CNN [31]	87.70	81.5	87.70	88.12
Modified LMU [29]	93.20	93.15	93.10	93.67
DualCL [28]	-	94.31	94.91	94.98
L Mixed [32]	95.68	95.72	-	95.81
EFL [26]	96.10	96.90	96.90	96.91
NB-weighted-BON [15] +dv-cosine	97.40	-	96.55	97.55
SMART-RoBERTa [27] Large	96.34	97.5	96.61	-
Ours	**97.67**	**97.88**	**97.62**	**98.76**

Table III shows results of ablation studies to see the impact of each component in the model. It can be seen that both BERT and BiILSTM separately give lower accuracy on the predictions compared against BERT+BiLSTM-SA. Therefore, the coupling of the two tools enhances model generalization.

TABLE III
RESULTS OF ABLATION STUDY

Model name	Dataset			
	IMDb-2	*MR*	*SST-2*	*amazon-2*
BiLSTM	90.42	90.5	91.12	92.18
BERT	93.81	94.29	93.55.97	94.78
BERT+BiLSTM-SA	**97.67**	**97.88**	**97.62**	**98.76**

The discussion of results is finished by talking about the overall polarity computation on all datasets by BERT+BiLSTM-SA. Table IV presents the overall polarity computed from all the datasets. **Original overall polarity** is known before input embeddings are fed into BERT+BiLSTM-SA for prediction, while **Computed overall polarity** is computed and known after BERT+BiLSTM-SA has made predictions on the reviews. The table shows that the **Computed overall polarity** is the same as the **Original overall polarity** for all the datasets. The **Original overall polarity** is calculated by counting the number of samples of each label in the input and use the result in the heuristic algorithm. That is, using original proportion of each class in the input before the model has made predictions on the reviews. The output was then used to verify the **Computed overall polarity**. The **Computed overall polarity** is computed similarly, but predictions are considered. Therefore, without loss of generality, there is confidence that the model predicts the expected sentiment on a given review and the heuristic algorithm computes accurate overall polarity from the model, regarding each dataset.

TABLE IV
OVERALL POLARITY COMPUTATION ON ALL DATASETS

Dataset	Original overall polarity	Computed overall polarity
IMDb	Neutral	Neutral
MR reviews	Neutral	Neutral
SST-2	Neutral	Neutral
Amazon	Positive	Positive

V. CONCLUSION

Sentiment analysis is an active research domain in NLP. In this work, the existing domain knowledge of sentiment analysis is extended by providing another effective way of fine-tuning BERT to improve accuracy measure on movie reviews sentiment analysis and show how to compute an overall polarity of a collection of movie reviews sentiments predicted by a model, BERT+BiLSTM-SA, for example. To fine-tune BERT, the technique of transfer learning was employed by coupling BERT with BiLSTM. BiLSTM, which had a dense layer, acted as a classifier on BERT final hidden states. The model was used for polarity classification and was experimented on

IMDb, MR, SST-2, and Amazon datasets. It was also shown that sentiment analysis can be applied, if someone wants to recommend a certain movie, for example, by computing overall polarity of its sentiments predicted by the model. That is, the proposed method serves as an upper-bound baseline in prediction of a predominant reaction to a movie. Ablation studies also show that BERT and BiLSTM seperately provide non-optimal accuracy compared against BERT+BiLSTM-SA, implying coupling of the two tools is stronger for the model generalization.

To compute overall polarity, a heuristic algorithm is applied to BERT-BiLSTM+SA predictions. For all the datasets, it have been demonstrated that the original overall polarity is the same as the computed overall polarity. To the best of our knowledge, this is the first work to couple BERT with BiLSTM for sentiment classification task and use the model output vector to compute overall sentiment polarity. Our model is robust whereby it can be extended to three-class, four-class, or any fine-grained classification. This is intended to be explored in future work to prove the robustness of the model.

Future work will additionally dwell on how to effectively apply accuracy improvement techniques to transformed BERT features despite loss of semantic information in them, exploring other pre-trained language models, and how different components of a sentence contribute to its sentiment prediction since this is information that is not generally explored by current works.

REFERENCES

[1] P. Baid, A. Gupta, and N. Chaplot, "Sentiment analysis of movie reviews using machine learning techniques," *International Journal of Computer Applications*, vol. 179, no. 7, pp. 45–49, 2017.

[2] R. Socher, A. Perelygin, J. Wu, J. Chuang, and C. D. Manning, "Recursive deep models for semantic compositionality over a sentiment treebank," in *Proceedings of the 2013 conference on empirical methods in natural language processing*, 2013, pp. 1631–1642.

[3] G. Mesnil, T. Mikolov, M. Ranzato, and Y. Bengio, "Ensemble of generative and discriminative techniques for sentiment analysis of movie reviews," *arXiv preprint arXiv:1412.5335*, 2014.

[4] X. Fang and J. Zhan, "Sentiment analysis using product review data," *Journal of Big Data*, vol. 2, no. 1, pp. 1–14, 2015.

[5] J. Devlin, M.-W. Chang, K. Lee, and K. Toutanova, "Bert: Pre-training of deep bidirectional transformers for language understanding," *arXiv preprint arXiv:1810.04805*, 2018.

[6] M. Munikar, S. Shakya, and A. Shrestha, "Fine-grained sentiment classification using bert," in *2019 Artificial Intelligence for Transforming Business and Society (AITB)*, vol. 1. IEEE, 2019, pp. 1–5.

[7] W. Guo, X. Liu, S. Wang, H. Gao, and A. Sankar, "Detext: A deep text ranking framework with bert," in *Proceedings of the 29th ACM International Conference on Information & Knowledge Management*, 2020, pp. 2509–2516.

[8] Y. Liu, "Fine-tune bert for extractive summarization," *arXiv preprint arXiv:1903.10318*, 2019.

[9] Y. He, Z. Zhu, Y. Zhang, Q. Chen, and J. Caverlee, "Infusing disease knowledge into bert for health question answering, medical inference and disease name recognition," *arXiv preprint arXiv:2010.03746*, 2020.

[10] W. Yang, Y. Xie, L. Tan, K. Xiong, and M. Li, "Data augmentation for bert fine-tuning in open-domain question answering," *arXiv preprint arXiv:1904.06652*, 2019.

[11] S. T. Arasteh, M. Monajem, V. Christlein, P. Heinrich, and A. Nicolaou, "How will your tweet be received? predicting the sentiment polarity of tweet replies," in *2021 IEEE 15th International Conference on Semantic Computing (ICSC)*. IEEE, 2021, pp. 370–373.

[12] https://github.com/gnkhata1/Finetuning-BERT-on-Movie-Reviews-Sentiment-Analysis, 2022, [Online; accessed March-15-2022].

[13] M. Anandarajan, C. Hill, and T. Nolan, "Sentiment analysis of movie reviews using r," in *Practical Text Analytics*. Springer, 2019, pp. 193–220.

[14] N. O. F. Daeli and A. Adiwijaya, "Sentiment analysis on movie reviews using information gain and k-nearest neighbor," *Journal of Data Science and Its Applications*, vol. 3, no. 1, pp. 1–7, 2020.

[15] T. Thongtan and T. Phienthrakul, "Sentiment classification using document embeddings trained with cosine similarity," in *Proceedings of the 57th Annual Meeting of the Association for Computational Linguistics: Student Research Workshop*, 2019, pp. 407–414.

[16] H. Shirani-Mehr, "Applications of deep learning to sentiment analysis of movie reviews," in *Technical report*. Stanford University, 2014.

[17] T. K. Rusch and S. Mishra, "Coupled oscillatory recurrent neural network (cornn): An accurate and (gradient) stable architecture for learning long time dependencies," *arXiv preprint arXiv:2010.00951*, 2020.

[18] J. D. Bodapati, N. Veeranjaneyulu, and S. Shaik, "Sentiment analysis from movie reviews using lstms." *Ingenierie des Systemes d'Information*, vol. 24, no. 1, pp. 1–5, 2019.

[19] D. Singh Sachan, M. Zaheer, and R. Salakhutdinov, "Revisiting lstm networks for semi-supervised text classification via mixed objective function," *arXiv e-prints*, pp. arXiv–2009, 2020.

[20] M. G. Sousa, K. Sakiyama, L. de Souza Rodrigues, P. H. Moraes, and E. R. Fernandes, "Bert for stock market sentiment analysis," in *2019 IEEE 31st International Conference on Tools with Artificial Intelligence (ICTAI)*. IEEE, 2019, pp. 1597–1601.

[21] Z. Gao, A. Feng, X. Song, and X. Wu, "Target-dependent sentiment classification with bert," *Ieee Access*, vol. 7, pp. 154 290–154 299, 2019.

[22] T. Gadekallu, A. Soni, D. Sarkar, and L. Kuruva, "Application of sentiment analysis in movie reviews," in *Sentiment Analysis and Knowledge Discovery in Contemporary Business*. IGI global, 2019, pp. 77–90.

[23] A. Maas, R. E. Daly, P. T. Pham, D. Huang, and A. Y. Ng, "Learning word vectors for sentiment analysis," in *Proceedings of the 49th annual meeting of the association for computational linguistics: Human language technologies*, 2011, pp. 142–150.

[24] B. Pang and L. Lee, "Seeing stars: Exploiting class relationships for sentiment categorization with respect to rating scales," *arXiv preprint cs/0506075*, 2005.

[25] R. He and J. McAuley, "Ups and downs: Modeling the visual evolution of fashion trends with one-class collaborative filtering," in *proceedings of the 25th international conference on world wide web*, 2016, pp. 507–517.

[26] S. Wang, H. Fang, M. Khabsa, H. Mao, and H. Ma, "Entailment as few-shot learner," *arXiv preprint arXiv:2104.14690*, 2021.

[27] H. Jiang, P. He, W. Chen, X. Liu, and J. Gao, "Smart: Robust and efficient fine-tuning for pre-trained natural language models through principled regularized optimization," *arXiv preprint arXiv:1911.03437*, 2019.

[28] Q. Chen, R. Zhang, Y. Zheng, and Y. Mao, "Dual contrastive learning: Text classification via label-aware data augmentation," *arXiv preprint arXiv:2201.08702*, 2022.

[29] N. R. Chilkuri and C. Eliasmith, "Parallelizing legendre memory unit training," in *International Conference on Machine Learning*. PMLR, 2021, pp. 1898–1907.

[30] Y. Wang, A. Sun, J. Han, Y. Liu, and X. Zhu, "Sentiment analysis by capsules," in *Proceedings of the 2018 world wide web conference*, 2018, pp. 1165–1174.

[31] T. Semwal, P. Yenigalla, G. Mathur, and S. B. Nair, "A practitioners' guide to transfer learning for text classification using convolutional neural networks," in *Proceedings of the 2018 SIAM international conference on data mining*. SIAM, 2018, pp. 513–521.

[32] D. S. Sachan, M. Zaheer, and R. Salakhutdinov, "Revisiting lstm networks for semi-supervised text classification via mixed objective function," in *Proceedings of the AAAI Conference on Artificial Intelligence*, vol. 33, no. 01, 2019, pp. 6940–6948.

A Corpus Study with German Data Sets into the Similarity of Irony and Satire

Marisa Schmidt
Faculty of Computer Science
University Koblenz
Universitätsstr. 1, 56070 Koblenz, Germany
marisaschmidt@uni-koblenz.de

Karin Harbusch
Faculty of Computer Science
University Koblenz
Universitätsstr. 1, 56070 Koblenz, Germany
harbusch@uni-koblenz.de

Abstract— **In deception detection, i.e., the falsification of news, satire detection is an import research area. This work strives for high accuracy in satire detection. We want to answer the question whether irony detection can serve the purpose of satire detection as well, or even better than specialized satire classification. The hypothesis underlying this claim follows the definition that satire is a genre that uses irony. Thus, we argue that irony should be indicative in a satire dataset. We contrast the results of runs with irony and satire annotated corpora with *Elmo4Irony,* an existing classifier for irony, and *Adversarial Satire,* an existing system for satire detection. In our evaluation, we use three different German data sets labeled with irony and satire, respectively. Our study corroborates the claim. Irony can indeed be found in a satirical dataset—even with higher accuracy. In order to supplement the finding, both systems are evaluated with typical examples from satire papers for deeper exploration. Unexpectedly, for the examples from the scholarly literature, both systems can hardly distinguish between irony/satire and neutral formulations.**

Keywords-Satire; Irony, Fake News; Deception Detection.

I. INTRODUCTION

Deception detection, i.e., the falsification of news in journalistic articles or social media, has become an increasingly important topic [1]. Another widely used term for false news is *fake news*. According to Zhou and Zafarani [2], it is now viewed as one of the greatest threats to democracy, journalism, and freedom of expression.

One strand of deception-detection research deals with *satire* detection. In the scholarly literature, definitions of satire can vary considerably (see, e.g., [3] and [4]). According to *The Oxford English Dictionary* [5], *satire* is "the use of humor, irony, exaggeration or ridicule to expose and criticize people's stupidity or vices." In other definitions, satire is tried to be demarcated from *irony*. In the comparison of definitions from the literature, Singh states: "Satire and irony are often closely related, but there are important distinctions between the two. As form of criticism, satire uses humor to accomplish its goals. One technique that satire uses is irony. Irony focuses on the discrepancies between what is said or seen and what is actually meant. Simply, satire and irony hardly differ because one, satire, often uses the other, irony." [6].

The Oxford English Dictionary defines *irony* as "the expression of meaning through the use of language signifying the opposite, typically for humorous effect." In the context of opinion analysis [7], Karoui and colleagues characterize irony as follows: "Irony denotes a discrepancy between discourse and reality, between two realities or, more generally, between two perspectives to incongruous effect."

Another term in this context often used as label in data sets is sarcasm. Karoui and colleagues demarcate it from irony as follows: "According to the Oxford English Dictionary, sarcasm is "the use of irony to mock or convey contempt". The utterance is bitter in nature and is intended to hurt the target [29]. Sarcasm is thus characterized by aggression, although not to the exclusion of mockery or teasing. Sarcasm is considered as a combination of the processes involved in both humor and irony, but is hurtful and overtly mocks the target. [...] Sarcasm is thus associated with aggression, insult and nastiness, traits that are not present in irony."

Given the subtle differences between the individual figurative language phenomena (cf. [7]), we want to explore whether comparative runs with the same labeled data sets but specific satire and irony detectors help to identify essential features that can lead to improved satire-classification results. We deploy *Adversarial Satire* [8] and *Elmo4Irony* [9] as prototypical detection components for satire and irony, respectively (see Sections III and IV for details). We run our study with the four German data sets outlined in Section II.

In our corpus study, we want to quantify how much irony can be detected in a satire annotated data set. As outlined above, satire is a genre that uses irony and therefore irony should be found in a satire dataset, i.e., irony detection is highly indicative to satire as well. Our study corroborates the claim. Irony can indeed be found in a satirical dataset—even with higher accuracy. In our comparative runs (cf. Section V), we illustrate that the irony detector Elmo4Irony performs better than the specialized satire classifier Adversarial Satire. As supporting evidence, we collected a small number of typical examples underpinning the different irony definitions. In order to make up a corpus, we add neutral facts (28.57% irony). However, for the examples from the scholarly literature, both systems can hardly distinguish between irony and neutral formulations. The implications from this unexpected finding require deeper inspection that is subject to further research (cf. Section VI).

The paper is organized as follows. In the next section, we present the four corpora used in our study. Sections III and IV elaborate on satire and irony detection, respectively. The results of our two experiments are presented in Section V. In the final section, we draw some conclusions.

II. Data sets

From public data collections, we use the three German data sets labelled with satire, irony, and sarcasm, respectively:

- C1: the satire data set by [8] with 329,859 articles from 15 different newspapers (2.82% satirical ones),
- C2: two subsets of a big Reddit corpus labeled for irony [10]: (C2a) *SARC 2.0* with 321,748 entries and (C2b) *SARC 2.0 pol* (17,074 entries), and
- C3: a Twitter data set from SemEval-2018 [11] that is labeled with #irony, #sarcasm and #not. The corpus provides 4,792 tweets, where both, irony and sarcasm, have a percentage of 50%.

In our study, we use only a subset of the satire corpus C1 (dubbed C1SUB) with 125 newspaper articles, 45 of which are satire (36%) to run it on a less powerful system compared to the settings in [8] (according to personal communication, their system has 256 gigabyte (GB) memory). With 60 GB, the classification accuracy with the reduction of the amount of data leads to comparable results with the numbers published in [8]. The other two corpora, i.e., C2a, C2b, and C3, are fully used in the study.

Moreover, we test all models with a newly set up corpus, called C4 here, that aims at a broad collection of prototypical examples from the irony literature used there to illustrate the definition (cf. example (1) in [12]).

(1) *Ich würde dieses Buch Freunden empfehlen, die an Schlaflosigkeit leiden oder die ich absolut verachte.*
'I would recommend this book to friends, who either suffer from insomnia or whom I despise.'

Although, we call C4 a 'corpus', we have to emphasize that it is still in its infancy. Currently, C4 comprises 10 ironic examples from different articles. Moreover, we thought up 5 ironic ones ourselves as a kind of control instance in contrast to the outstanding quality of the literature examples (cf. example (2)) and 6 neutral definitions of facts labelled not-ironic (cf. example (3)). The preliminary size does not create a problem here, for we use it as a kind of litmus test for the models only.

(2) *Oh ja! Du bist definitiv der klügste Mensch, den ich kenne!*
'Oh yes! You are definitively the most clever man I met.'

(3) *Gänseblümchen haben weiße Blüten.*
'Daisies have white blossoms.'

The evaluation with all four data sets is outlined in Section V. In the next two sections, we first sketch the satire and irony detection component, individually, before we employ both system with the four data sets in our study.

III. Satire detection

The challenging task of satire detection has been tackled from various points of view: lexically, syntactically, and semantically. Thu and Aung give an historical overview for systems from the different viewpoints [13].

Additionally, we cite more recent approaches here. McHardy and colleagues extend a satire detector with an adversarial component to control for the confounding variable of publication source [8]. The system, called Adversarial Satire, is based on Tensorflow [14] and uses Word2Vec embeddings [15], [16]. For the evaluation, the German satire corpus (dubbed C1 in Section II), was set up. Li and colleagues [17] propose a multimodal method for satire detection using textual and visual cues. Razali et al. [18] suggest a context-driven satire-detection component deploying Deep Learning.

In our study, we decided to use Adversarial Satire so that the original evaluation results for C1 can directly be compared with our implementation (the code can be found here: https://gitlab.uni-koblenz.de/marisaschmidt/irony-detection) running C1SUB (see Table I). We use the Linux [19] distribution Ubuntu [20]—deploying the CUDA 11— with 50 GB kernel memory plus 500 GB extra; the system runs on 4 CPUs and 1 GPU with 35 GB; this set up requires some smaller adaptions we skip here for reasons of space).

Table I illustrates the results for the smaller corpus C1SUB compared to the original results—for reasons of space, we only outline the results for one setting (confounding variable=0.0). For all settings in the overall evaluation, the quality favorably compares. Thus, we can use the component with the reduced corpus C1SUB in our study.

IV. Irony and Sarcasm detection

For a good overview on satire-detection systems, subdivided into surface and semantic approaches, as well as pragmatic ones, see [7]. Here, we cursorily sum up other approaches.

Ilić and colleagues propose a model that uses character-level vector representations of words, based on Embeddings from Language Model (ELMo [21]). The system is called ElMo4Irony [9]. Kumar and Harish propose to extract five sets of linguistic features fused with features selected using two stages of a feature selection method [22]. Lin and colleagues compare different machine-learning methods for irony detection [23]. Jiang and colleagues present an approach mainly based on fine-tuned BERT models using a Grid-Search and Data Augmentation with MLM (Masked Language Model) substitution [24] based on BERTimbau for smoothing the use of a small data set. Tomás and colleagues propose a transformer-based model for multimodal irony detection [25].

As stated in Section I, sarcasm and irony are closely related, i.e., are often judged to stand in a sub-super relationship. So, we round out our state of the art with a survey article on sarcasm detection: Joshi and colleagues describe various datasets, approaches, trends and issues [26].

TABLE I. EVALUATION OF ADVERSARIAL SATIRE WITH C1SUB

Data	*C1SUB*			*C1*		
	P	R	F1	P	R	F1
dev	0,999	0,667	0,799	0,989	0,526	0,687
test	0,818	0,643	0,719	0,990	0,501	0,665

Concentrating on irony here, we deploy Elmo4Irony in our study. The approach considers a wide variety of features (e.g., capitalizations or emoticons; cf. [7] for a study on the impact of syntactic, semantic and pragmatic features). ElMo4Irony uses PyTorch [27] and GloVe embeddings [28].

For Elmo4Irony, we also skip here the details of our implementation under the above-mentioned system settings. In Table II, we exemplarily sketch the results for dropout = 0.1 to demonstrate that the results favorably compare to the numbers in [9].

V. COMPARATIVE RUNS WITH THE DATA SETS

Two experiments are conducted using the systems deploying the data sets presented in the previous sections. *Experiment 1* is devoted to the research question of whether irony can also be found in a satire dataset. As follow-up question from the positive findings in Experiment 1, *Experiment 2* probes examples of irony given in the literature with the two systems, i.e., tests the models with C4.

As outlined in Section I, satire is defined as a genre that uses irony. This definition leads to the hypothesis that an irony detection system—in our case Elmo4Irony (cf. Section IV) — should find irony in the satire-data set. To test this hypothesis, Elmo4Irony and the satire classifier Adversarial Satire (cf. Section III) both employ the data set C1SUB.

Both methods are trained over 10 epochs with a batch size of 16. Elmo4Irony is trained with dropouts of 0.0, 0.1 and 0.5. For Adversarial Satire, different values for the adversarial weight are used: the confounding variable = 0.0, 0.2, 0.3 and 0.7. For these variable settings, Elmo4Irony performs always better than Adversarial Satire (for two exemplary variable setting, the overall results are outlined in Table III). In fact, the irony classifier provides better results on the satire dataset than the specialized satire classifier. This observation confirms the hypothesis of Experiment 1. Irony is an indicative feature to satire detection.

TABLE II. EVALUATION OF ELMO4IRONY WITH C2 AND C3

Data	*Our implementation*			*Original numbers*		
	P	R	F1	P	R	F1
C2a	0,707	0,704	0,703	0,760	0,760	0,760
C2b	0,687	0,686	0,685	0,720	0,720	0,720
C3	0,685	0,688	0,686	0,696	0,697	0,696

TABLE III. COMPARISON OF IRONY AND SATIRE DETECTION

Data	*Adversarial Satire*			Elmo4Irony		
	Confounding variable = 0.0			Confounding variable = 0.0		
	P	R	F1	P	R	F1
C1SUB	0,622	0,617	0,618	0,895	0,800	0,816
	Confounding variable = 0.7			Confounding variable = 0.1		
	P	R	F1	P	R	F1
C1SUB	0,708	0,617	0,603	0,857	0,867	0,839

In Experiment 2, both systems are evaluated on the new dataset C4 (the training of the models still happens on their regular datasets). C4 is labelled for irony. Based on Experiment 1, we argue that irony can serve as satire feature. However, it is less obvious that a satire classifier will find irony on irony data. It is therefore to be expected that Adversarial Satire will find less satire on this data set with ironic examples. Again, we tested the different values for the dropout in Elmo4Irony and the adversarial weight in Adversarial Satire. Table IV provides the numbers of samples that were correctly classified as irony (TP), wrongly classified as irony (FP), correctly classified as regular (TN) and wrongly classified as regular (FN). The numbers in brackets show the results probing additionally provided neutral text to obtain article length in C4 aiming at improving the quality of Adversarial Satire.

Interestingly, the results show that most models classify all examples as ironic. In the initial scenario, the Elmo4Irony model, which is trained with a dropout of 0.0, finds the least irony. However, it still classifies almost all the non-ironic examples as ironic, while the ironic examples are classified as non-ironic. A second Elmo4Irony model that correctly classifies at least one example as non-ironic is the model trained with a drop rate of 0.5.

Additionally, we tested Adversarial Satire (which was trained on whole articles instead of single sentences) with adding a neutral text to the example sentences. With this extended input, Elmo4Irony classifies everything as non-ironic with most variable settings. The only Adversarial Satire model that classifies one example as non-ironic in the scenario with additional text is the model trained with an adversarial weight of 0.2. This model correctly classifies one of our self-created neutral examples as non-ironic. Under the condition of no additional text, the same model also classifies one example as non-ironic, however, this is actually an ironic one. In essence, additional neutral text does not have a positive impact on the classification of adversarial satire.

In order to sum up the findings of Experiment 2, unexpectedly, the features calculated by both systems are not suitable for this new data set, as almost everything is classified as ironic. The small size of C4 cannot be the reason for failure given that the corpus is only used as test set. Deeper analysis of the features is required here (cf. [7] and [13]).

TABLE IV. EVALUATION OF C4

drop-out	TP	FP	TN	FN	*adv. weight*	TP	FP	TN	FN
0.0	3 (0)	5 (0)	1 (6)	12 (15)	0.0	15 (15)	6 (6)	0 (0)	0 (0)
0.1	15 (0)	6 (0)	0 (6)	0 (15)	0.2	14 (15)	6 (5)	0 (1)	1 (0)
0.5	15 (0)	5 (0)	1 (6)	0 (15)	0.3	15 (15)	6 (6)	0 (0)	0 (0)
					0.7	15 (15)	6 (6)	0 (0)	0 (0)

VI. CONCLUSIONS

We have presented the results of a corpus study into the relationship between satire and irony. Based on the definition that satire uses irony, we could verify that irony detection can serve as satire classification very well. Experiment 2 was designed to better understand the irony features. However, the results were unexpectedly poor. We plan to extend C4 to a full development/test corpus with a larger collection of examples from very divergent sources. The goal is to obtain a richer set of features to classify irony.

REFERENCES

[1] V. L. Rubin, N. J. Conroy, Y. Chen, and S. Cornwell, "Fake news or truth? Using satirical cues to detect potentially misleading news," Proc. NAACL-HLT, pp. 7–17, Jun. 2016.

[2] X. Zhou and R. Zafarani, "A survey of fake news: fundamental theories, detection methods, and opportunities," ACM Computing Surveys, vol. 53, no. 5, art. 109, Sept. 2020. https://dl.acm.org/doi/pdf/10.145/3395046 [retrieved: 23.03.23]

[3] L. Colletta, "Political satire and postmodern irony in the age of Stephen Colbert and Jon Stewart," The Journal of Popular Culture, vol. 42, no. 5, pp. 856-874, 2009. https://doi.org/10.1111/j.1540-5931.2009.00711.x [retrieved: 23.03.23]

[4] C. Condren, "Satire and definition," Humor, vol. 25, no. 4 , 2012, https://doi.org/10.1515/humor-2012-0019 [retrieved: 23.03.23]

[5] OED, Oxford Univ. Press, Oxford. https://www.oed.com/public/freeoed/loginpage [retrieved: 23.3.23]

[6] R. K. Singh, "Humour, irony and satire in literature," IJEL, vol. 3, no. 4, pp. 65-72, 2012. https://www.academia.edu/4541187/Humour_Irony_and_Satire_in_Literature [retrieved: 23.03.23]

[7] J. Karoui, F. Benamara, and V. Moriceau, "Automatic detection of irony: opinion mining in microblogs and social media," London: ISTE, 2019. https://doi.org/10.1002/9781119671183 [retrieved: 23.03.23]

[8] R. McHardy, H. Adel, and R. Klinger, "Adversarial training for satire detection: controlling for confounding variables," Proc. NAACL-HLT, pp. 660–665, Jun. 2019. https://doi.org/10.48550/arXiv.1902.11145 [retrieved: 23.03.23]

[9] S. Ilić, E. Marrese-Taylor, J. A. Balazs, and Y. Matsuo, "Deep contextualized word representations for detecting sarcasm and irony," Proc. 9th WASSA, pp. 2–7, Oct. 2018. https://aclanthology.org/W18-6202 [retrieved: 23.03.23]

[10] M. Khodak, N. Saunshi, and K. Vodrahalli, "A large self-annotated corpus for sarcasm," Proc. 11th LREC, pp. 641-646, May 2018. https://doi.org/10.48550/arXiv.1704.05579 [retrieved: 23.03.23]

[11] C. van Hee, E. Lefever, and V. Hoste, "SemEval-2018 task 3: irony detection in English tweets," Proc. 12th SemEval, pp. 39-50, Jun. 2018. http://dx.doi.org/10.18653/v1/S18-1005 [retrieved: 23.02.23]

[12] J. Ling, and R. Klinger, "An empirical, quantitative analysis of the differences between sarcasm and irony," Proc. *European* Semantic Web Conference, pp. 203-216, Jun. 2016. https://doi.org/10.1007/978-3-319-47602-5_39 [retrieved: 23.02.23]

[13] P. P. Thu and T. N. Aung. "Implementation of emotional features on satire detection," International Journal of Networked and Distributed Computing, Vol. 6, No. 2, pp. 78-87, 2018.

[14] https://www.tensorflow.org [retrieved: 23.02.23]

[15] T. Mikolov, K. Chen, G. Corrado, and J. Dean, "Efficient estimation of word representations in vector space," 2013a. https://doi.org/10.48550/arXiv.1301.3781 [retrieved: 23.02.23]

[16] T. Mikolov, I. Sutskever, K. Chen, G. Corrado, and J. Dean, "Distributed representations of words and phrases and their compositionality," Proc. NeurIPS: Advances in neural information processing systems, vol. 26, pp. 3111-3119, 2013b. https://doi.org/10.48550/arXiv.1310.4546 [retrieved: 23.02.23]

[17] L. Li, O. Levi, P. Hosseini, and D. A. Broniatowski, "A multimodal method for satire detection using textual and visual cues," Proc. 3rd NLP4IF, pp. 33–38, Dec. 2020. https://arxiv.org/abs/2010.06671 [retrieved: 23.02.23]

[18] M. S. Razali, A. Abdul Halin, Y. W. Chow, N. Mohd Norowi, and S. Doraisamy, "Context-driven satire detection with deep learning," IEEE Access, vol. 10, pp. 78780-78787, 2022. https://ieeexplore.ieee.org/document/9841563 [retrieved: 23.02.23]

[19] https://www.linuxfoundation.org/ [retrieved: 23.02.23]

[20] https://ubuntu.com [retrieved: 23.03.23]

[21] M. E. Peters, M. Neumann, M. Iyyer, M. Gardner, C. Clark, K. Lee, L. Zettlemoyer, "Deep contextualized word representations," Proc. NAACL-HLT, vol. 1, pp. 2227–2237, Jun. 2018. https://aclanthology.org/N18-1202.pdf [retrieved: 23.02.23]

[22] H. M. Kumar, and B. S. Harish, "Automatic irony detection using feature fusion and ensemble classifier," International Journal of Interactive Multimedia and Artificial Intelligence, vol. 5, no. 7, pp. 70–79, 2019. https://www.ijimai.org/journal/sites/default/files/files/2019/07/ijimai20195_7_7_pdf_17438.pdf [retrieved: 23.02.23]

[23] C. L. Lin, M. Ptaszynski, and F. Masui, "Exploring machine learning techniques for irony detection," Proc. 33rd JSAI, Jun. 2019. https://www.jstage.jst.go.jp/article/pjsai/JSAI2019/0/JSAI2019_2A4E203/_pdf/-char/en [retrieved: 23.02.23]

[24] S. Jiang, C. Chen, N. Lin, Z. Chen, and J. Chen, "Irony detection in the Portuguese language using BERT," Proc. IberLEF 2021, pp 891-897, Sept. 2021. http://ceur-ws.org/Vol-2943/idpt_paper1.pdf [retrieved: 23.02.23]

[25] D. Tomás, R. Ortega-Bueno, G. Zhang, P. Rosso, and R. Schifanella, "Transformer-based models for multimodal irony detection," Journal of Ambient Intelligence and Humanized Computing, 2022. doi.org/10.1007/s12652-022-04447-y [retrieved: 23.02.23]

[26] A. Joshi, P. Bhattacharyya, and M. J. Carman, "Automatic sarcasm detection: a survey," ACM Computing Surveys, vol. 50. no. 5, art. 73, pp.1–22, 2017. https://doi.org/10.1145/3124420 [retrieved: 23.02.23].

[27] https://pytorch.org [retrieved: 23.02.23]

[28] J. Pennington, R. Socher, and C. D. Manning, "GloVe: global vectors for word representation," Proc. EMNLP, pp. 1532-1543, Oct. 2014. http://dx.doi.org/10.3115/v1/D14-1162 [retrieved: 23.02.23]

[29] V. Simédoh, "Humour and irony in sub-Saharan Francophone literature: from critical issues to a poetics of laughter," Berlin: Peter Lang, 2012.

Prediction Pipeline on Time Series Data Applied for Usage Prediction on Household Devices

1st Raluca Portase
Technical University of Cluj-Napoca
Cluj Napoca, Romania
email: raluca.portase@cs.utcluj.ro

2nd Ramona Tolas
Technical University of Cluj-Napoca
Cluj Napoca, Romania
email: ramona.tolas@cs.utcluj.ro

3rd Camelia Lemnaru
Technical University of Cluj-Napoca
Cluj Napoca, Romania
email: camelia.lemnaru@cs.utcluj.ro

4th Rodica Potolea
Technical University of Cluj-Napoca
Cluj Napoca, Romania
email: rodica.potolea@cs.utcluj.ro

***Abstract*—Processing time series is wildly used for many real-world applications such as financial market prediction, resource demand forecasting, device maintenance prediction, or environmental state prediction. In this work, we propose a general time series prediction pipeline with a hybrid unit for the relevance intervals on the processing part. The granularity unit is separated based on the intermittency level of the time series. We further apply the pipeline to real data from household appliances for non-intrusive usage pattern modeling and multistep-ahead prediction using machine learning methods.**

Keywords*—*Time series; data filtering; processing pipeline; home appliances data; forecasting devices usage.

I. INTRODUCTION

Time series prediction is the subject of multiple studies due to its general applicability to various domains. The existence of null, unrecorded, zero values in time series requires filtering data at different intervals, which still maintains the relevant recordings. The granularity level refers to these intervals of relevance. Changing the granularity could lead to a smaller number of non-relevant entries in the time series but would affect the overall sampling of the result. Depending on the problem, a smaller granularity might enhance the processing step.

Machine learning approaches have various applications in time series processing. One such application is the prediction of future values. Depending on the intermittency level of the dataset, classical regression models, neural networks, or specific ones that target data with multiple zeros are commonly used. Therefore, this work can be classified as an application of machine learning supervised models for knowledge and information extraction and processing.

A substantial percentage of water and energy resources used by a given household comes from household appliance usage [1] [2]. Therefore, extracting and understanding usage patterns would lead to a more accurate prediction of the resources needed in the future.

This work addresses a time series forecasting problem that uses intermittent time series and multistep ahead prediction. First, we propose a sampling rate separation based on the time series' intermittency level. Then, further, we integrate this in a general processing pipeline for prediction, which uses a combination of different sampling rates based on the number of zero entries from the time series. Finally, we apply this for knowledge extraction on real home appliance data from the industry to predict the following usage of given devices for a month. To the best of our knowledge, the previous pipelines used in the literature do not propose a separation of the sampling rate to obtain a better overall combined result. Our proposed pipeline offers a more rigorous approach from the perspective of the sampling rate.

Section 2 presents related work on time series sampling rate and prediction with a focus on forecasting using machine learning methods. Next, we present in Section 3 our proposed strategy for multistep prediction of time series with different intermittency levels. Then, in Section 4, we project the general model to household appliance data to predict the devices' future running time. Finally, we round up this paper in Section 5 with some conclusions and remarks.

II. RELATED WORK

A time series is a sequence of consecutive data points over time and is the most commonly used data type [3]. The sampling rate of a time series gives the maximum resolution of any prediction on that data. However, the best results are only sometimes given by using the smallest granularity of the data [4].

Intermittent time series refers to those series that have values equal to zero on multiple entries without obvious patterns of variation [5]. Prediction of their future values has been a subject of interest for numerous studies since long ago. Most of these studies are concerned with predicting intermittent and irregular sales demands [6] [7]. Non-intermittent data can become intermittent at fine-grained decomposition levels, for example, by using the time granularity of minutes or hours instead of days or months.

Univariate time series regression or forecasting is the simplest version and relies only on historical data of a variable to predict future behavior. On the other hand, multivariate analysis and prediction use the relationship between several variables. Several studies suggest that models with multiple time series perform better than models with a single time series [8] [9].

Machine learning strategies are used to forecast and classify time series. One of the most common methods for multivariate forecasting is Vector Autoregression (VAR), but this has the disadvantage of not capturing non-linearity patterns. Numerous studies are using deep neural networks for prediction due to their capabilities in capturing non-linear interdependencies [10] [11] [12]. On the other hand, more straightforward methods that provide fast results, such as Support Vector Regression (SVR), have been successfully applied in time series forecasting due to their generalization capability in obtaining a unique solution [13] [14] [15].

The random forest regression model can also be used to predict multiple points in the future based on historical data by combining several single-point forecasting [16] [17]. Extreme gradient boosting is a decision tree ensemble learning algorithm similar to the random forest and can be used for classification and regression. Compared to the random forest, it uses a gradient of the data for each tree, which makes the calculation faster and more accurate. XGBoost [18] implementation for extreme gradient boosting method has also been successfully used for time series forecasting [19] [20].

The evaluation metrics are essential to any machine learning linear regression or forecasting problem. The most commonly used ones are Mean Square Error (MSE), Mean Absolute Error (MAE), and Mean Absolute Percentage Error (MAPE) [21]. For regression problems where the output might be zero, percentage error metrics, such as MAPE [22], are not suitable, instead Symmetric Mean Absolute Percentage Error (SMAPE) [23] can be used.

Time series forecasting applied to data from household appliances is a subject of multiple studies. This is done in the context of predicting the resources needed in the near future for a specific household [1] [24], as well as extracting and understanding usage patterns [25]. A specific time series data from home appliances are the running time information of the devices. This subject is particularly interesting in the cases of appliances with running cycles. Extracting runtime information in a non-intrusive manner from already existing data is tackled in [26].

Electrical energy consumption and peak demand forecasting are vital in planning and maintaining power systems. The appliances give part of the variation of the household consumers. Machine learning approaches have shown the best accuracy in forecasting electrical appliance consumption and are the current state-of-the-art solutions [27].

III. STRATEGY FOR DEALING WITH INTERMITTENT DATA

This section covers two dimensions: the data sampling strategy at different granularities on data sets with different levels of intermittency and a general processing pipeline. This pipeline decomposes the processing part in two, based on the number of empty values in the input data. Our strategy proposes the usage of a model selector to decide the model used for the prediction and its corresponding granularity level. Due to the different granularity levels, the prediction result will have a hybrid time series unit.

Time series data from multiple sources can have zero values which could be caused by the nature of the data or the sampling rate used. When data does not offer sufficient initial information, projecting it onto a different subspace could lead to better results.

When applying multivariate forecasting or predicting values based on multiple time series, zero values negatively impact performance. Several strategies could be used to overcome this, such as handling missing data in forecasting or regression, cutting off data portions with multiple zero values, or reducing the overall sampling rate. Removing parts of time series data would lead to a loss of information regarding time dimension and misalignment. Simultaneously, setting the overall sampling rate to a higher value for all time series to overcome the prediction issues of the ones with multiple zeros would impose a prediction with a higher granularity regardless of the level of intermittency of the data series. More than that, it would reduce the dimension of the data set, which might lead to insufficient data in some cases.

To maintain the granularity as small as possible where it does not affect the identification of the objectives in hand and to have proper outcomes over the entire dataset, we propose a hybrid sampling rate based on the time series intermittency level as follows: time series with the number of zero values on initial sampling rate smaller than a given threshold - granularity level set to time series unit. The granularity should be composed of several time units for the other time series. For example, for time series data with a granularity level of a second, if the data has a high level of intermittency, a minute can be used as a time unit in the prediction pipeline. Using a hybrid sampling rate could partially overcome the disadvantages that arise from the sampling rate for portions of the dataset.

The general pipeline is comprised of three main steps: pre-processing, processing, and post-processing. Our method introduces new steps in the processing part.

We propose a multistep-ahead time series prediction pipeline that divides the problem into two parts. A regression problem in the first part predicts the usage of time series with a smaller intermittency level and outputs the prediction for a given period by using the initial time series unit of time. The second model gives the prediction with a higher granularity level for the sampling rate for time series with a smaller number of non-zeros per day. This method is illustrated in Figure 1. Depending on a threshold, the newly added selector component will choose the appropriate model and granularity for the time series. This way, we would achieve the best prediction results in the most suitable unit given a time series used as input in the pipeline.

The threshold used for the decision can vary depending on the nature of the data and the problem at hand. Depending on the initial time series unit, the higher level granularity should be chosen based on the problem to be solved while maintaining

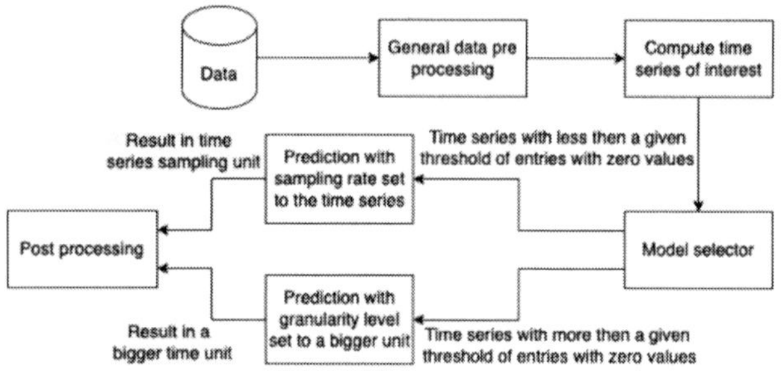

Fig. 1. Proposed pipeline for prediction based on time series intermittency level

a logical predefined time scale such as second, minute, hour, day, week, month, and so on. The post-processing part, as well as the pre-processing, depends on the problem to be solved and the data and is not the subject of this work.

A possible application of this pipeline could be estimating resources - such as the energy or water consumption in our examples. Having an accurate prediction of the future needed resources could lead to better management of the resources.

IV. Method instantiation on home appliances data

The strategies presented in Section III are applicable in the general context of time series prediction with intermittent demand or missing data. We further applied them in the context of home appliances and present the results in this section. We evaluated three machine learning strategies for prediction: decision trees, extreme gradient boosting, and support vector regression. We particularised the general time series pipeline presented for home appliances running time data based on the results.

A. Context and dataset description

Several types of household appliances have functioning cycles, such as washing machines, tumble dryers, dishwashers, ovens, or microwaves. Given the data's nature, reducing the intermittency in forecasting the sampling period is crucial.

The best-suited granularity from the perspective of the possibility of making an accurate prediction would be of one day because a smaller one would lead to a massive number of samples with values equal to zero. As a consequence, the prediction would be less accurate. According to [25], appliances tend to be used based on a general pattern on the temporal dimension. Therefore, undersampling the devices not so used by cutting off extensive intervals with no usage would lead to a loss of information that arises from the time dimension.

When projecting the appliance usage forecasting into the energy consumption estimation, having a daily prediction could lead to a better estimation of the resources per day. A smaller granularity could be used for a more detailed analysis of the variation of the energy needed for a day.

The methods presented in Section III for data sampling and the pipeline for the prediction can be applied to any type of data. We projected them in our experiments on real operational data from household appliances. More specifically, we used data logs from washing machines recorded over one year. Due to copyright reasons, we will further maintain the data's anonymity. We used a time series unit of one day of usage, pre-processed the data, and computed each device's run time in seconds per day. The result is a time series where one point represents each device's runtime per that day of the year. The proportion of zero values is computed taking into account the entire interval of data samples. Since we are interested in predicting the duration a device would be used during a time interval of a given granularity, we have chosen seconds as the unit of measurement for appliance usage.

Figure 2 presents the usage patterns of appliances investigated - the histogram with the number of days an appliance was used computed for all devices from the initial data set. As can be seen, most of the devices are used for a few days. Thus, we removed them from the investigation.

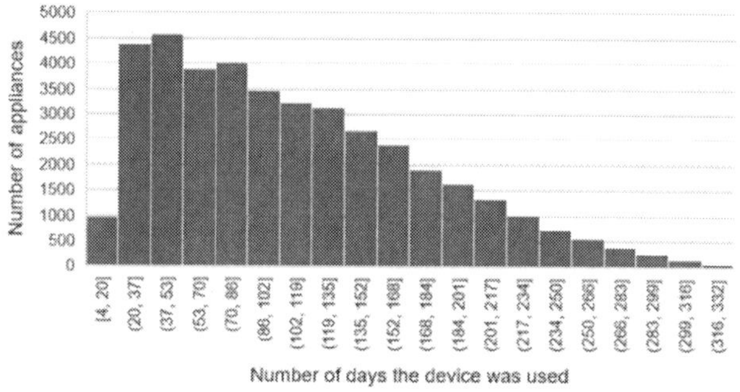

Fig. 2. Histogram of the number of appliances and their numbers of days with running cycles over a year

We removed from the initial data set the devices that have more the 50% of days with no usage since their lack of usage adds a question mark regarding the correctness of their utilization and if it is the usual one. Furthermore, the remaining appliances were sufficient to create a meaningful sample. We separated the remaining entries into two groups based on the average usage of the machines. From the initial dataset of tens of thousands of devices, we obtained a dataset formed of 1.2k devices used at least 70% of the days and a total of 6.3k devices operated at least 50% of the days. The dimensions of the initial dataset compared to the one after selecting instances are presented in Table I.

TABLE I
DIMENSIONS OF THE INITIAL DATASET VERSUS SELECTED INSTANCES OVER ONE YEAR

Dataset	Size	No of devices	Time period
Raw data	8.1mil	49k	1 year
Selected instances	2.4mil	6.3k	1 year

For our evaluations, we have selected several different appliances. Among the investigated ones, we present the results for six appliances representative of their categories out of the

6.3k selected devices. Their characteristics are summarised in Table II, which we refer to further. All of these appliances have a different number of days without usage per year and different average runtime per day.

TABLE II
NUMERICAL CHARACTERISTICS OF APPLIANCES USED FOR EXPERIMENTS

Appliance	Average usage/ day (s)	No of days without usage/ year
App 1	36.718	39
App 2	7.233	46
App 3	6.976	67
App 4	7.848	120
App 5	5.926	141
App 6	6.483	156

The first three appliances have a lower level of intermittency, while the last 3 have a higher number of zero values. Moreover, they all have a different average usage number of seconds per day. We will further refer to these appliances in the experiments from the next section.

B. Daily prediction of future appliance usage

We designed and implemented several preliminary experiments on our dataset to reduce the search area. From the available tools commonly used for prediction, we selected Random Forest, Support Vector Regression, as well as XGBoost [18] implementation for gradient-boosted trees. We split the dataset and used it for training data from 11 months, while for evaluation, 1-month data.

The purpose of the first set of experiments is included in the multiple-step-ahead prediction category. More specifically, to predict the appliances' daily usage for a month's time window. For each strategy, we investigated the best suited parameters for our dataset. As a result, we identified 125 trees for the random forest as the best configuration, 100 trees for XGBoost, and a linear kernel for SVR.

We made several preliminary investigations to identify the number of zeros from raw data by using levels 10%, 15%, 20%, 30%, 40%, and 50%. We filtered the data and ran several experiments where we varied the dataset used for the model based on the percentage of zeros from the time series. The comparison of the mean average error and symmetric mean absolute percentage error obtained on several appliances using random forest on the three most significant levels from our dataset is presented in Table III. Table II summarizes the appliance characteristics from this experiment. From there, we selected the first three devices due to their low level of intermittency.

In the first experiment, we only used for training the appliances that have less than 15% of days with no usage. Then we added the devices that had up to 30% of days zero runtime seconds. Finally, we added appliances in training set up until half of the entry points were zeros and evaluated the model's performance.

The best results without modifying the granularity of the prediction were obtained for daily prediction of devices for models based on learning data with up to 30% of the days

TABLE III
MEAN AVERAGE ERROR AND SYMMETRIC MEAN ABSOLUTE PERCENTAGE ERROR FOR DAILY PREDICTION OF APPLIANCES BASED ON THE PERCENTAGE OF ZEROS ENTRIES APPLIANCES IN THE TRAINING SET

	15% zeros		30% zeros		50% zeros	
Appliance	MAE	SMAPE	MAE	SMAPE	MAE	SMAPE
App 1	8365	10.92	**7871**	**10.28**	7886	10.32
App 2	3345	25.07	**2913**	**22.69**	3134	23.95
App 3	**4292**	27.25	4374	**27.23**	4494	28.01

of a year. However, the prediction was less accurate when we used the appliances with a higher number of zeros for the model. Therefore, further on, we are using the 30% threshold for the daily prediction.

We implemented and compared the results for daily prediction by using random forest, XGBoost, and SVR on the best size for the dataset for training previously found. The results are presented in Table IV. For measuring the prediction, we have used mean average error in seconds and symmetric mean absolute percentage error normalized on [0,100] interval.

TABLE IV
RESULTS OF DAILY PREDICTION OF APPLIANCES USAGE AFTER USING THREE DIFFERENT METHODS

	Classifier					
	Random forest		XGBoost		SVR	
Metrics	MAE	SMAPE	MAE	SMAPE	MAE	SMAPE
App 1	**7871**	**10.28%**	8771	11.38%	9148	12.44%
App 2	**2913**	**22.69%**	3573	26.22%	3810	27.39%
App 3	4374	27.23%	**4321**	**26.61%**	4613	41.81%

In our experiments, XGBoost and Random Forest had similar results, while SVR performed worse for daily usage prediction regardless of the set size.

C. Impact of variation of the granularity level

Generally, predicting time series with a more significant intermittency level using classical forecasting methods does not perform well. For these, several other methods could be used. These scaled on our experiments too, where the average SMAPE was over 50% for daily prediction of devices with more the 30% of the data having values equal to zero when using random forest, SVR, and XGBoost.

According to our previous experiments from Table III, in the case of appliance data, using an upper threshold of 30% for the number of zero values where the daily usage can be predicted would be appropriate. Further, we propose the usage of the next logical time unit as a granularity level. This gives us the time unit of a week instead of a day for devices with a more significant number of missing data or zero values.

We used a granularity level of a week and recomputed the time series for the devices with a higher percentage of zero data. Then, we applied the machine learning strategies from above and recorded the results in Table V. The mean average error represents the number of seconds per week. Although there was no general winner as the best tool for all the appliances, XGBoost and SVR performed well on a subset of devices.

TABLE V
RESULTS OF WEEKLY PREDICTION OF APPLIANCES USAGE AFTER USING THREE DIFFERENT METHODS

	Classifier					
	Random forest		XGBoost		SVR	
Metrics	MAE	SMAPE	MAE	SMAP	MAE	SMAPE
App 4	11339	15.52 %	13760	17.98%	**9148**	**13.89%**
App 5	29483	30.64%	**22435**	**22.65%**	28623	30.70%
App 6	16571	19.65%	**15637**	**17.93%**	16207	19.79%

The initial SMAPE values obtained when using daily prediction on appliances 4-6 were over 50%. However, by changing the granularity of the time series to a week, on all of our experiments, symmetric mean absolute percentage error became under 25%, which means that SMAPE was reduced by at least 50% for devices with a higher number of zeros.

D. Processing pipeline particularized on home appliances data

According to the results for time series data from appliances with running cycles, a daily sampling rate performs well for highly used devices. In our experiments, the machines used at least 70% of the days are part of this category. In the case of the other appliances, using a granularity level of a week gives good results while maintaining a logical time unit, making the results valuable and keeping the dataset size to a reasonable amount.

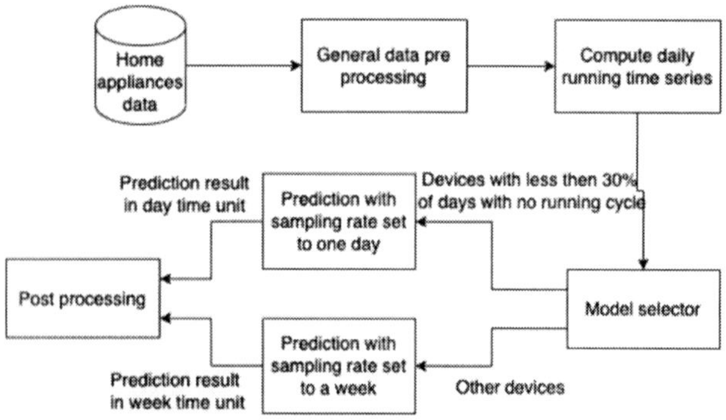

Fig. 3. Proposed pipeline instantiated on home appliances data

Figure 3 presents the corresponding instantiation in the context of home appliances data of the pipeline presented in Section III. The purpose of this pipeline is the non-intrusive usage pattern prediction with a hybrid granularity level.

V. CONCLUSION AND FUTURE WORK

The major contributions of this work consist in the granularity level separation on time series data and the general processing pipeline for time series having different levels of intermittency. We applied these strategies to running time information from real household appliance data. Further on, we instantiated the general pipeline for this particular use case based on our threshold determination experiments to predict the future running cycles of a given appliance in the next month using machine learning. Applying the presented strategies to other types of time series is the subject of future work.

REFERENCES

[1] S. Koop, A. Van Dorssen, and S. Brouwer, "Enhancing domestic water conservation behaviour: A review of empirical studies on influencing tactics," vol. 247. Elsevier, 2019, pp. 867–876.

[2] W. Kong, Z. Y. Dong, Y. Jia, D. J. Hill, Y. Xu, and Y. Zhang, "Short-term residential load forecasting based on lstm recurrent neural network," vol. 10, no. 1. IEEE, 2017, pp. 841–851.

[3] J. Lin, S. Williamson, K. Borne, and D. DeBarr, "Pattern recognition in time series," vol. 1, no. 617-645. Citeseer, 2012, p. 3.

[4] R. J. Frank, N. Davey, and S. P. Hunt, "Time series prediction and neural networks," vol. 31. Springer, 2001, pp. 91–103.

[5] J. D. Croston, "Forecasting and stock control for intermittent demands," vol. 23, no. 3. Springer, 1972, pp. 289–303.

[6] M. W. Seeger, D. Salinas, and V. Flunkert, "Bayesian intermittent demand forecasting for large inventories," vol. 29, 2016.

[7] X. Zhuang, Y. Yu, and A. Chen, "A combined forecasting method for intermittent demand using the automotive aftermarket data." Elsevier, 2022.

[8] D. Salinas, V. Flunkert, J. Gasthaus, and T. Januschowski, "Deepar: Probabilistic forecasting with autoregressive recurrent networks," vol. 36, no. 3. Elsevier, 2020, pp. 1181–1191.

[9] K. Bandara, C. Bergmeir, and S. Smyl, "Forecasting across time series databases using recurrent neural networks on groups of similar series: A clustering approach," vol. 140. Elsevier, 2020, p. 112896.

[10] S.-Y. Shih, F.-K. Sun, and H.-y. Lee, "Temporal pattern attention for multivariate time series forecasting," vol. 108. Springer, 2019, pp. 1421–1441.

[11] M. Sousa, A. M. Tomé, and J. Moreira, "Long-term forecasting of hourly retail customer flow on intermittent time series with multiple seasonality," vol. 5, no. 3, 2022, pp. 137–148. [Online]. Available: https://www.sciencedirect.com/science/article/pii/S2666764922000273

[12] Y. Jeon and S. Seong, "Robust recurrent network model for intermittent time-series forecasting," vol. 38, no. 4, 2022, pp. 1415–1425, special Issue: M5 competition. [Online]. Available: https://www.sciencedirect.com/science/article/pii/S0169207021001151

[13] K. Lau and Q. Wu, "Local prediction of non-linear time series using support vector regression," vol. 41, no. 5. Elsevier, 2008, pp. 1539–1547.

[14] C.-J. Lu, T.-S. Lee, and C.-C. Chiu, "Financial time series forecasting using independent component analysis and support vector regression," vol. 47, no. 2. Elsevier, 2009, pp. 115–125.

[15] N. I. Sapankevych and R. Sankar, "Time series prediction using support vector machines: a survey," vol. 4, no. 2. IEEE, 2009, pp. 24–38.

[16] A. González-Vidal, V. Moreno-Cano, F. Terroso-Sáenz, and A. F. Skarmeta, "Towards energy efficiency smart buildings models based on intelligent data analytics," vol. 83. Elsevier, 2016, pp. 994–999.

[17] E. Mussumeci and F. C. Coelho, "Large-scale multivariate forecasting models for dengue-lstm versus random forest regression," vol. 35. Elsevier, 2020, p. 100372.

[18] T. Chen, T. He, M. Benesty, V. Khotilovich, Y. Tang, H. Cho, K. Chen *et al.*, "Xgboost: extreme gradient boosting," vol. 1, no. 4, 2015, pp. 1–4.

[19] N. Zhai, P. Yao, and X. Zhou, "Multivariate time series forecast in industrial process based on xgboost and gru," in *2020 IEEE 9th Joint International Information Technology and Artificial Intelligence Conference (ITAIC)*, vol. 9. IEEE, 2020, pp. 1397–1400.

[20] R. A. Abbasi, N. Javaid, M. N. J. Ghuman, Z. A. Khan, and S. Ur Rehman, "Short term load forecasting using xgboost," in *Web, Artificial Intelligence and Network Applications: Proceedings of the Workshops of the 33rd International Conference on Advanced Information Networking and Applications (WAINA-2019) 33*. Springer, 2019, pp. 1120–1131.

[21] A. Botchkarev, "Performance metrics (error measures) in machine learning regression, forecasting and prognostics: Properties and typology," 2018.

[22] A. De Myttenaere, B. Golden, B. Le Grand, and F. Rossi, "Mean absolute percentage error for regression models," vol. 192. Elsevier, 2016, pp. 38–48.

[23] S. Makridakis, "Accuracy measures: theoretical and practical concerns," vol. 9, no. 4. Elsevier, 1993, pp. 527–529.
[24] M. Razghandi, H. Zhou, M. Erol-Kantarci, and D. Turgut, "Short-term load forecasting for smart home appliances with sequence to sequence learning," in *ICC 2021-IEEE International Conference on Communications*. IEEE, 2021, pp. 1–6.
[25] C. Firte, L. Iamnitchi, R. Portase, R. Tolas, R. Potolea, M. Dinsoreanu, and C. Lemnaru, "Knowledge inference from home appliances data," in *2022 IEEE 18th International Conference on Intelligent Computer Communication and Processing (ICCP)*, 2022, pp. 237–243.
[26] E. M. Olariu, R. Tolas, R. Portase, M. Dinsoreanu, and R. Potolea, "Modern approaches to preprocessing industrial data," in *2020 IEEE 16th International Conference on Intelligent Computer Communication and Processing (ICCP)*, 2020, pp. 221–226.
[27] E. U. Haq, X. Lyu, Y. Jia, M. Hua, and F. Ahmad, "Forecasting household electric appliances consumption and peak demand based on hybrid machine learning approach," vol. 6, 2020, pp. 1099–1105, 2020 The 7th International Conference on Power and Energy Systems Engineering. [Online]. Available: https://www.sciencedirect.com/science/article/pii/S2352484720314967

Mining User Behavior: Inference of Time-boxed Usage Patterns from Household Generated Data

1st Ramona Tolas
Computer Science Department
Technical University
Cluj-Napoca, Romania
ramona.tolas@cs.utcluj.ro

2nd Raluca Portase
Computer Science Department
Technical University
Cluj-Napoca, Romania
raluca.portase@cs.utcluj.ro

3nd Mihaela Dinsoreanu
Computer Science Department
Technical University
Cluj-Napoca, Romania
mihaela.dinsoreanu@cs.utcluj.ro

4rd Rodica Potolea
Computer Science Department
Technical University
Cluj-Napoca, Romania
rodica.potolea@cs.utcluj.ro

***Abstract*—The growth of technology and the reduced cost of data storage are enablers for producing and storing a large amount of data. Smart household devices are a category of data producers due to the monitoring sensors equipping the device. These sensors monitor the device's state and user interaction with the device. Besides the initial reason for planting the monitoring equipment, further valuable information can be extracted from this data, such as user behavior. Mining usage patterns can further be used in forecasting user presence, data-driven decisions, or service personalization. A processing pipeline for mining usage patterns is proposed in this paper. The problem is theoretically formulated and a method of mining usage patterns is proposed. The method is developed and tested on synthetic data and interesting insights are extracted from real data by deploying the pipeline in a data lake containing real interactions of users with smart home appliances. Similarities between real usages of household appliances are found as a result of this step and sevaral categories of users are defined based on them.**

***Index Terms*—knowledge inference; clustering; event-based signal processing; pattern mining; household-generated data; usage mining**

I. Introduction

The last years are considered to be one of the periods of the greatest growth of technology. This expansion of technology together with the invention of smart devices has as effect a constantly growing trend of creation and consumption of data. The reduced cost of data storage is also a powerful enabler.

A smart device is an electronic device that is usually connected with the Internet or with other devices via different communication protocols. Smart devices are equipped with sensors that measure various characteristics of both the appliance and the surroundings where the appliance is deployed. Events generated from the interaction of the user with the appliance are also captured and recorded. Most of the time, these measurements are transmitted via the Internet in data lakes [1] owned by smart appliance producers. These data lakes contain a large number of such measurements and events.

In this context, a research goal of processing this type of data and extracting useful information from it is defined in both academic and industrial worlds. Knowledge inference has many other pragmatic sub-tasks such as predictive maintenance, identification of usage patterns and user profiling.

The profile of a smart device user is a summary of the user's behavior and preferences. Mining user profiles is often used for service personalization as users differ in their interests and goals when using the same device. Mining the usage of a smart device can also be a powerful source of insights. Inference of usage patterns can be used in forecasting user presence [2]. These insights can be used further in management systems like those proposed in [2] and [3].

In this paper, we propose a formalization of the usage mining task. A processing pipeline to tackle the formalized problem is presented. The method is tested on synthetic data and deployed in production with the goal of discovering interesting real insights.

The rest of the paper is organized as follows: First, we give an overview of the related work. Section III is establishing the required theoretical background needed for formalizing the problem statement of mining user behavior in Section IV. In Section V the processing pipeline is presented and its evaluation on both synthetic and real data is described in Section VI. Conclusions, presented method limitations and future work are tackled in the last section of this work.

II. Related work

The topic of mining usage patterns is strongly represented in the literature as applied in the business domain of software services, such as web usage mining [4] [5], network usage mining [6] or API usage [7] [8]. The concept of user profiling, collecting relevant information about the user, is also frequently referring to the users of software applications [9] [10] [11].

However, in the current technological-driven context, the need of analysing the user has bypassed the software domain. A special type of user profiling, profiling the user presence, is presented by Barbato et al. [2], where the business domain is home automation systems. The authors tackle the topic of energy saving by proposing a system of energy management. This home automation system is proposed as part of the smart home concept. The goal is to reduce the overall energy consumption and reduce the energy peaks with intelligent management of the appliances.

The authors use context awareness as part of the management system and user presence plays an important role. For example, the heating and cooling systems, which are big consumers of energy can be pragmatically managed to function in the time frames when the user is not present in the room to avoid having multiple energy consumers. The presence monitoring is done with a system of sensors dedicated to this task - multiple infrared sensors deployed in all the rooms. The user presence is recorded and the system is forecasting future values.

Identifying user presence can also be done without planting a special monitoring system in the house, using non-intrusive systems. The smart household appliances that are already in the house and are recording the interactions of the users can be a powerful source of such insights.

Another use case of analyzing user behaviors in a non-software context is presented by Wang et al. [12]. The authors study routine in the business concept of water consumption.

Household domain and mining patterns are studied by Rahim et. al [13], where an advanced household profiling based on digital water meters are proposed. In [14], machine learning is applied to the same business concept. Gaussian Mixture Model is used to represent the water demand measurements in low dimensional feature space with the goal of pattern classification.

Data produced by smart home appliances are intensively studied by Olariu et al. [15] and Chira et al. [16], where pre-processing techniques and other associated challenges are presented in the context of data produced by smart ovens and refrigerators. Home appliance-produced data is the source of knowledge in the studies of Firte et al. [17], where data generated by washing machines and refrigerators are used for profiling their users.

As the data produced by these types of appliances is represented by large volumes, Big Data processing techniques need to be used. Portase et al. [18] present a methodology for bypassing Big Data challenges while Tolas et al. [19] is tackling transmission-related topics in the context of home appliance-generated data.

III. Theoretical Background

This section is covering basic theoretical aspects relevant to the defined goal of this paper: mining usage patterns from data produced by smart home appliances regarding user interaction.

A. Time series

The literature contains important findings and many developed libraries for pattern finding and signal processing [20] [21] [22], but for signals that are in the syntactic form of time series. This implies that the property of interest (or in this case the value of the recorded state) is measured at successive equally spaced points in time [23].

Time series are classified by the authors of [24] as the most commonly encountered data type. Given the popularity of this data type, approaches for pattern recognition applied to this type of data are in the attention of many researchers.

In order to benefit from all the research done in the time series domain, the representation of one day in the form of events unequally spaced in time needs to be transformed in time series syntactically form.

B. Taxonomy of transforming event based signal to time series

The available community and the powerful representation in the literature are making time series a preferred form of syntactical representation for the input data. However, the interaction of the user with the appliances is most of the time represented using events. Usually, the events are not equally spaced in time.

To benefit from the entire research and tooling development made in the time series domain, a transformation to this syntactical form is required. The strategy for performing this transformation is strongly connected with the business domain. Available practical mechanism of the transformation and their possible configuration and mixture are studied for realizing this taxonomy [20].

Possible methods for this transformation are:

- **Lower the frequency methods**: establishing a lower level frequency and filling the indexes which have no correspondence in the sequences of the events.
  The filling can also be done in several ways:
  - **SVP**: simple value propagation.
    The value which is propagated can also be selected:
    * **Forward-filling**: propagation of last recorded value
    * **Backward-filling**: propagation of the next recorded value
  - **ANV**: aggregation of the neighbor values (values corresponding to indexes placed in the immediate neighborhood of the index for which the value computation is made)
- **Upscaling the frequency methods**: aggregating multiple values to a higher level frequency

The frequency is dependent on the nature of the problem. The values of the observed state is also encoded in a numerical form for ease of processing.

C. Feature extraction from time series

The problem of pattern recognition in time series can be reduced to a shape-based similarity problem. Having a mechanism for determining if two time series are similar in shape is a basic tool for finding patterns in time series. For computing the similarity between time series, extraction of representative features is a required step. While contributing to dimensionality reduction, this step also has a major effect on the overall performance of the data mining algorithm.

In [25] , the feature extraction methods from time-series are identified to be spread across temporal, statistical and spectral domains.

In the research [24], the authors identify several methods of determining shape similarity. One solution is using the euclidean distance, but this solution comes with associated disadvantages: sensitive to distortions and has strict requirements about the lengths of the compared time series. Dynamic Time Warping (DTW) and Longest Common SubSequence are solutions to these limitations but are computationally expensive. DTW is used in [26] to extract discriminative features and the authors report competitive results in a real-world application setup compared with other state-of-the-art methods such as InceptionTime and Convolutional Neural Network.

In [24], it is shown that shape-based similarity strategies have good results when comparing short time series. For long time series comparison, other methods such as structural similarity need to be tackled.

The shape similarity is also tackled by Zheng et al. [27], where a set of 14 shape-related features are extracted for describing financial time series. In [28], the authors use the temporal domain for feature extraction in the task of supervising artificial forest plantation trends using Google Earth Engine.

Using the frequency domain is also intensively used in the literature as a method of extracting features that describe time series.

1) Frequency domain: Projecting the signal into the frequency domain is shown to be an efficient descriptor of the time series in the literature. Schneider et al. [29] use it in the classification of cyclically recorded time series.

Nedelcu et al. [30] use the Fourier transform as a feature extraction method in the task of classifying portions of the EEG signal which are artifacts. For the same task, extracting EEG artifacts, Fast Fourier Transform and Wavelet Transform are used by Al-Fahoum et. al [31] and by Wen et al. [32].

There are also various practical implementations for frequency domain feature extraction methods such as TSFEL framework [25].

2) Discrete Fourier Transform: Discrete Fourier Transform is one method in which the frequency indicators can be included in this representation by converting a signal into individual spectral components, providing frequency information. The Fourier transform maps a signal into two vectors representing the influence of the corresponding basis function in the original signal.

A signal containing N points is represented by N complex numbers after Fourier Transform is applied. For a reduction in feature space, not all the coefficients need to be further considered. First X coefficients describe, in the form of a rough sketch, the original signal. X is determined by the business domain. In [33], an alternative strategy of selecting the coefficients which represent the signal is presented. The authors claim that selecting the largest coefficients increases the level of representation of the original signal.

D. Clustering in pattern mining

The goal of pattern mining methods is to extract interesting patterns from large data sets and use the extracted information for a better understanding of the domain or decision-making.

Clustering techniques refer to the task of partitioning a set of objects into groups with the constraints of maximizing the similarity between objects inside a group and minimizing the similarity between clusters [34]. Clustering was and still is a hot topic in computer science literature. Multiple algorithms and libraries are already developed. The authors of [34] categorize the clustering techniques into six types: partitioning (groping the objects into N groups and N is given as input parameter), hierarchical (building a dendogram), grid-based (based on space segmentation), model-based (fitting the data to a mathematical defined model) and constraint-based (clustering is based on user-defined constraints) and density-based (clusters are considered high density areas).

One advantage of density-based clustering techniques is the non-parametric approach. The number of clusters is not an input paramter of the algorithm, making it suitable for unsupervised learning models.

In a context of large databases, the research made in [35] identify DBSCAN [36], GDBSCAN [37] and DENCLUE [38] as popular density based algorithms which were developed with a focus on efficient compatibility.

Density Based Spatial Clustering of Applications with Noise (DBSCAN) is one of the most popular popular density based algorithms. The algorithm is intensively referred in the literature (at the moment of writing it has more than 27k citations in the literature). Multiple intensive used frameworks implement the DBSCAN algorithm [39], increasing the confidence of usage.

IV. MINING USER BEHAVIORAL PATTERNS - PROBLEM STATEMENT

The goal of this paper is to present a method of mining time-boxed usage patterns from data generated by smart home appliances.

A. Input data: user interactions with smart home appliances

This paper is defining a method of inferring usage profiles from data generated by home appliances capable of sensing and transmitting user interactions with the appliance.

Data generated by such appliances consist of a series of user interaction events. For the rest of this paper, the input for the defined knowledge extraction method is identified as user interaction events series (UIES), formally defined in Definition 1.

Definition 1 (User interaction events series): A user interaction event series UIES is a sequence of n events ordered in time.

$$UIES = (e_{t_1}, e_{t_2}, ...e_{t_n})$$

Each event is containing the timestamp of the event occurrence and the value of the observed state as defined in Definition 2. The timestamps are not necessary to be equally spaced in time.

Definition 2 (Observed state): The value of the recorded state can be one of the values of the state space S.

$$S = (S_1, S_2, ...S_m)$$

An example of input for the usage profiling method which is also used in the Experiments section of this paper is represented by the events transmitted by a smart refrigerator, having sensors that are capable of sensing when the door of the appliance is open or closed. In this case, the event is represented by the action of opening or closing the door of the smart refrigerator by the user. The recorded state is the state of the door, having the state space equal to $OPEN, CLOSED$. Another example of UIES is the interaction of the user with a smart washing machine having the capability of recording the start and end of a certain washing cycle. The events series in this case are the sequences of starting the washing cycle by the user. The observed state can be represented in this case by the type of washing cycle used by the user or the parameters of the washing cycles with which the user started the washing program.

B. Time-boxed usage representation

Part of the defined goal of this paper is to identify patterns in user behavior. This implies a certain level of recurrence of a behavior which is shifting attention to a time granularity.

Definition 3 (Time-boxed usage): Given a UIES of length n, a time interval T defined by timestamp boundaries T_{start} and T_{end} a time-boxed user interaction event series $TBES^T$ is a subset of m consecutive events of the UIES i.e.

$$TBES^T = (e_{t_{p1}}, e_{t_{p2}}, ...e_{p_m})$$

where $T_{start} \leq t_{pi} \leq T_{end}$

Definition 4 (Similar time-boxed usage): Given two time-boxed usage representations $TBES_1^T$ and $TBES_2^T$ with the same time interval T, if the distance between them is not greater than a defined threshold R, the two usage representations are similar.

Definition 5 (Time series): The time series representation of the observed state in a day is represented by sequences indexed in time with a frequency f.

$$TS.TBES = (x_{t_1}, x_{t_2}, ...x_{t_n})$$

where t_i - t_{i+1} = f

C. Behavioral pattern

Definition 6 (Behavior pattern): Given a defined time frame T, a behavior pattern is a sequence of probabilities representing the probability of the user interacting with the appliance.

$$B = (p_{t1}, p_{t2}, ...p_{tn})$$

The previously exemplified UIES, consisting of events of opening the door of a smart refrigerator, can be taken as an example. A user of a smart refrigerator could have the routine of preparing breakfast before going to work in the time interval 8 AM and 9 AM and interacting with the smart device during dinner time, between 18:30 and 20:30. This is an example of a behavioral pattern occurring every day from the week. During weekend days, the behavioral pattern might not match as the user has a different schedule. With a time granularity of one hour, the above pattern can be expressed with 24 probability values representing the probability that the user will open the door during the considered hour. The probability of the user opening the door between 8 AM and 9 AM will be close to 1 while the probability of the user opening the door between 2 AM and 1 AM will be close to zero.

D. Mining behavioral patterns - problem statement

With the defined formalism, the problem of user behavioral patterns inference is reduced to finding behavior patterns as formalized in Definition 6 given the input in form of UIES as defined in Definition 1.

V. PROPOSED PROCESSING PIPELINE FOR USAGE PATTERN MINING

The proposed solution for inferring usage patterns from events generated by user interaction is described in Figure 1. Input in the pipeline is considered data in the syntactic form of UIES and a parameter representing the time granularity, identified by T. The syntactic form of the data is referring in this case to the data structure: events, time series, arrays of features. The T parameter is influencing the type of patterns that are extracted. For T equal to 24 hours, the effect on the processing pipeline is that daily patterns are going to be discovered. This parameter is strongly influencing the computational complexity of the overall solution as it is directly impacting the number of time-boxed usage events (TBES) which are going to be further processed.

The input is syntactically processed by a fragmentation step: user events are split into multiple time-boxed events. Following the taxonomy defined in Section III, the time-boxed events are transformed into time series, as a next step. These processes are defined as Syntactic transformations because input data is successively migrated to a different syntactic form: from UIES and TBES (events) to time-series (TS.TBES).

Applying Fast Fourier Transform [40] and selecting the first N coefficients is transposing the time-boxed events to a new representational state - spectral domain is now used to represent the user interaction events. For a given N, the number of features used to represent time-boxed events is 2*N because the Fast Fourier Transform is producing coefficients having real and imaginary parts. The time-boxed usage representation at this point is the 2*N coefficients resulting from the Transition to the spectral domain.

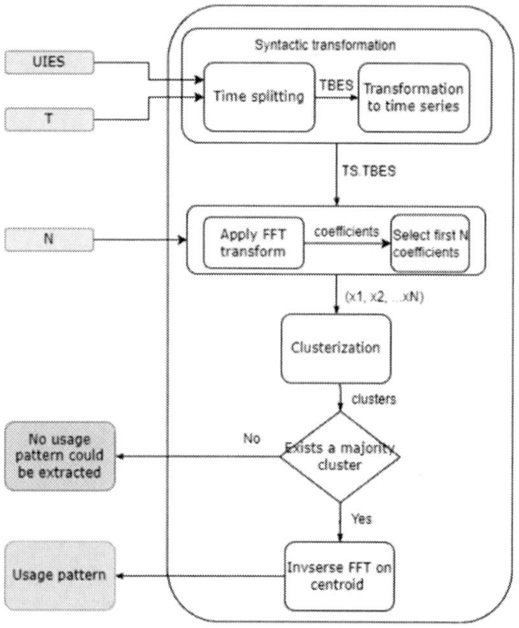

Fig. 1. Usage pattern inference pipeline

The problem of finding daily usage patterns can, at this stage, be translated to finding groups of similar usages. This step is done with clustering.

After clustering, if there is a predominant pattern in the usage of the device, the description of the usage is identified by the cluster which is holding the largest number of instances.

VI. Experiments and Results

The proposed usage profiling method is tested on Door open events series, a type of UIES as mentioned in previous sections. For the rest of this paper, this type of data is referred to as Door Open Events (DOE). The time parameter for the evaluation of the processing pipeline is one day. This means that daily usage patterns are extracted from the DOE data.

A. *DOE characterisation*

In model development, synthetic data is utilized. The processing pipeline is also deployed in an environment containing real recordings of user interactions with refrigerator home appliances.

In TABLE I, a snapshot from a synthetic data set representing the syntactic form of DOE is shown.

TABLE I
Example of door open events from one smart refrigerator.

Timestamp	Door State
2023-01-04 08:04:35	OPEN
2023-01-04 08:05:35	CLOSED
2023-01-04 08:15:02	OPEN
2023-01-04 08:15:58	CLOSED
2023-01-04 20:11:00	OPEN
2023-01-04 20:11:35	CLOSED

For ease of processing, a numerical encoding is given to each state, as proposed in TABLE II.

TABLE II
Numerical encoding of door state

Door state	Encoding
OPEN	1
CLOSED	0

Pre-processing operations such as duplicates elimination are performed on the input data. Both the synthetically generated data and the real data are pre-preprocessed in order to reach the syntactic form described in this section (events consisting of opening and closing the door with door state encoded with numerical values of 0 and 1).

1) Synthetic data set: The synthetic data is used mainly in the development phase of the pattern mining pipeline.

A number of 6 appliances are used for the evaluation of the model. The monitored period differs from one month to years of recording. The data is configured to include certain usage patterns and noise is parametrically added to the synthetic data.

Behavioral patterns are planted in the synthetically generated data in order to provide a ground truth for the evaluation phase. In this section a briefly description of the data simulation process is provided as the focus of this paper is not the simulation strategy.

The planted behavioral patterns are based on the following concepts which are combined to obtain a behavior:

a) ***N-AP:*** N active periods in user daily interaction.

This means that in N time frames during the day the user is interacting actively with the home appliance. Outside the active period the user might also use the home appliance but with a lower frequency.

In Figure 2, a sample of DOE represented by 2-AP is shown. The snapshot contains 4 days of user interactions and there are 2 active periods.

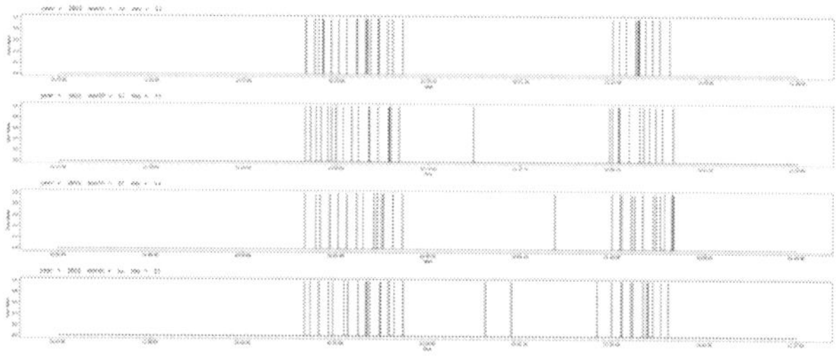

Fig. 2. Door open time series for multiple days

b) ***N-NIP:*** - This parameter represents N consecutive days with no interaction of the user with the appliance.

c) ***Noise*** : is introduced in the data for emulating real conditions. Having realistic data in the development phase is an important aspect in producing good results when the model is deployed in a real data context. The noise is introduced in the data simulation by configuring the probability to miss one active period from that day. For example, a probability of 0.1

of missing one active period for the data shown in Figure 2 means that in 1 of 10 cases, the day might not be characterized by two active periods, one of them missing.

d) $\boldsymbol{p{*}R_{InterOpeningDurationBound}}$*:* : percentage of planted random behavior. This parameter contains the number of random behaviors inserted in the data. Randomm daily behavior is represented by simulating the event of opening the door and holding the door open for a duration of time expressed in seconds and upper bounded by a threshold. The strategy is to make the duration of keeping the door open to follow the same probability distribution as the real user interactions. The number of seconds between two consecutive opening events is randomly chosen from the range [0, InterOpeningDurationBound] with equal probability for any value from the range. The InterOpeningDurationBound is simplified to IODB in the rest of the paper, hence the percentage of plated random behavior is identified by $p{*}R_{IODP}$.

Multiple concepts from above are combined in order to obtain the synthetic data. In TABLE III, a characterization of the appliances included in the synthetic data used for developing and evaluating the behavior mining pipeline is presented. **App id** represents the identifier of the appliance. **RP** represents the recorded period measured in days. A value of 30 for RP means that there are usage events spread over a time frame of 30 days for that appliance. **PBP** represents planted behavioral patterns and describes what behavioral models are planted in the dataset when the synthetic data is generated. For the behavior description, the parameters defined above are used. **NP** represents the noise percentage added in the synthetic data.

TABLE III
CHARACTERISATION OF THE APPLIANCES INCLUDED IN SYNTHETIC DATA

App id	**RP** [days]	**PBP** [N-AP & $p{*}R_{IOPB}$ & N-NIP]	**NP** [%]
2-AP_1	30	2AP & 0.28R_{1000}	20
3-AP_1	60	3AP & 0.28R_{1000}	20
2-AP_2	365	2AP & 0.42R_{1000}	40
1-AP_1	730	2AP & 0.42R_{1000}	20
2-AP_3	365	2AP & 0.28R_{1000} & 15-NIP	20
RB	60	Random behavior	-

2) Real data use-case - usage patterns identified in smart refrigerators: The developed processing pipeline is deployed in a data lake which contains a collection of more than 12k appliances of type smart refrigerator. The raw data is unstructured: all events generated by the interaction with the user and all recordings of the sensor deployed on the appliances generate new entry in the same general storage structure. The appliances have recorded user activity for a period which varies from one day to more than 4 years.

Pre-processing operations such as duplicates elimination, selection of events of interest, numerical encoding of door state in case of door opening events are preformed. As the pipeline is designed to process events generated from one appliance, a device selection step is performed in the real data in order to select the most meaningful devices which are feed to the processing pipeline. Analysis consisting of probability distribution of opening the door and duration of keeping the door open are used for the device selection.

The experiments are performed in a DataBricks environment [41] using Databricks Workflows (lakehouse orchestration service provided by the framework).

B. Event based signal to time series

The initial syntactic structure of the data is in the form of events, as presented in TABLE I. In Figure 3, we can see a visual representation of the events presented in the snapshot data from Figure I.

Fig. 3. Visual representation of the door open events from TABLE I

From the defined taxonomy of transforming the events into time series, a forward-filling method is used. This is practically implemented with indexation mechanisms offered by Python libraries [20].

The same data as presented in TABLE I and in Figure 3 is visually represented in Figure 4. The numerical encoding from TABLE II is used for representing the states.

Fig. 4. Door open events from Figure 3 represented as time series having sampling frequency of one second and state of the door numerically represented by 0 and 1

A resampling to one hour time granularity is made, as searched patterns are daily patterns and the same information about user interaction can be modeled with fewer data. To preserve all the interactions of the user with the home appliance the aggregation method of the resampling phase is the sum of the composing aggregates. This means that the new signal represents the number of seconds the door was open in the corresponding hour. In Figure 5, it is presented a visualization of the snapshot data after this resampling phase is done.

Fig. 5. Door open events from 4 after resampling the signal to hourly time granularity by summing all the seconds in which the door of the appliance was open

The result of this step is the representation of the smart refrigerator daily door state as time series indexed in time, with a frequency of one hour and value range from 0 (during that hour the door was never opened) to 3600 (the entire hour the door was open).

C. Feature extraction and clustering

In order to group together days with similar user behavior a clustering algorithm is used. Before applying the clustering algorithm, a feature extraction step is needed. Fast Fourier Transform is applied. After empirical research, the number of considered coefficients from the FFT method that are selected to be included in the clustering algorithm as feature is first 10 coefficients.

After this step, the events from one day of the user interaction with the appliance are represented by 20 real numbers (a coefficient from FFT has real and imaginary parts). A normalization operation is applied on all the features using a min-max scaler [42].

For clustering step, the Python implementation of the DBSCAN algorithm [43] is used, configured with euclidian distance and auto algorithm. The leaf size parameter is 30 while eps parameter and minimum samples parameter (minimum number of points to form a dense region) are empirically discovered.

Because the goal is the mining of a usage pattern which is the most frecvent behavior of the user, a cluster containing a majority of points is searched in the resulting clusters. The centroid of this cluster is the behavioral pattern.

D. User behavior pattern extraction

The centroid is used to characterize the daily usages which are grouped together. The features composing the centroid are de-normalized with the goal of using again the value space before the normalization step. Using the de-normalized centroid features, the IFFT (inverse fourier transform) is applied on those features. This step of reconstructing the time-series represents the modeling of the appliance daily usage.

In Figure 6, the usage behavior is reconstructed for the centroid of the cluster which grouped the behaviors of the data sampled in Figure 2. The pattern with 2 active periods is clearly seen from the samples and the centroid reconstruction is correctly identifying the two active periods (higher values for the hours where the user is frequently opening the door).

Fig. 6. Usage behavior reconstructed from the centroid of the cluster containing the usage represented by the sample represented in Figure 2

In order to obtain a usage behavior as described in Definition 6 the values are normalized to [0, 1] interval.

Figure 7 shows a numerical description of a usage pattern which is visually represented in Figure 8. As we can see, the active periods identified in the pattern are in the morning and in the evening.

E. Evaluation on synthetic data

Discovering the pattern is based on grouping similar days in the same cluster. As a consequence, F1-score measure is used after the clustering phase for evaluating the overall performance.

Time interval	Probability of user opening the door	Time interval	Probability of user opening the door
0-1	0.187580	12-13	0.102323
1-2	0.097206	13-14	0.160298
2-3	0.147478	14-15	0.169510
3-4	0.157930	15-16	0.134724
4-5	0.071992	16-17	0.212702
5-6	0.237944	17-18	0.135447
6-7	0.000000	18-19	0.682228
7-8	0.289808	19-20	0.897410
8-9	1.000000	20-21	0.178503
9-10	0.457822	21-22	0.086722
10-11	0.026312	22-23	0.189280
11-12	0.234447	23-24	0.078350

Fig. 7. Example of representing a behavioral pattern: the pattern is describing the interaction of a user with a smart refrigerator in 2 periods of the day

Fig. 8. Visual representation of user behavior. The user interacts with the smart appliance with a higher probability during hours 8 and 9 and also during 18 and 20.

In TABLE IV, the experiments performed for choosing the EPS parameter and MS parameter (min samples - minimum number of points to form a dense region) are described.

TABLE IV
EXPERIMENTS PERFORMED IN THE CLUSTERING PHASE WITH DBSCAN CLUSTERING ALGORITHMS

App id	EPS	MS	F1-score
2-AP_1	0.2	2	0.965
	0.75	2	0.930
	0.2	5	1.0
	0.75	5	0.904
3-AP_1	0.2	2	0.775
	0.75	2	1.0
	0.2	5	1.0
	0.75	5	1.0
2-AP_2	0.2	2	0.959
	0.75	2	0.532
	0.2	5	0.959
	0.75	5	0.566
1-AP_1	0.2	2	0.998
	0.75	2	0.596
	0.2	5	0.998
	0.75	5	0.642
2-AP_3	0.2	2	0.899
	0.75	2	0.746
	0.2	5	0.897
	0.75	5	0.833
RB	0.2	2	1.0
	0.75	2	0.666
	0.2	5	1.0
	0.75	5	0.909

F. Discovered usage behaviors in real data

As the combination of EPS = 0.2 and MS = 5 report the best performance in the synthetic data, this configuration is used when the processing pipeline is deployed in the data lake storing real data.

Data recorded from 16 devices deployed all over the world is utilized. Similar behaviors of using the smart device mainly in two periods of the day are found for 37.5% of the devices. Patterns of using the appliance in mainly 3 periods of the day are found for 18.75%. Using the device in four time intervals is found in 12.5% of the analyzed devices. No behavioral pattern could be extracted from 31.25% of the devices.

VII. Conclusions And Future Work

This paper presents a processing pipeline for discovering usage patterns in the data generated by smart home appliances. The proposed method can easily be extended to any type of event-based data. A taxonomy of transforming event-based data to a more approachable syntactic form is presented.

The proposed mining method is evaluated on synthetic data which is generated with a strategy that maximizes the similarity with the real data by closely following real data characteristics. The processing pipeline is deployed in a data lake environment containing real interactions of users with smart refrigerators and interesting insights are presented.

The presented method certainly merits further investigation, especially in problems involving multiple unknowns, such as the mining of composed patterns. The experiments conducted in this study can be continued with variations in the time window which leads to mining different behaviors from the time perspective: weekly patterns, monthly patterns and even yearly patterns.

References

[1] "Data lake," https://en.wikipedia.org/wiki/Data_lake, [Online; accessed 29-March-2023].

[2] A. Barbato, L. Borsani, and A. Capone, "Home energy saving through a user profiling system based on wireless sensors," pp. 49–54, 2009.

[3] H. Abu-Bakar, L. Williams, and S. H. Hallett, "A review of household water demand management and consumption measurement," *Journal of Cleaner Production*, vol. 292, p. 125872, 2021. [Online]. Available: https://www.sciencedirect.com/science/article/pii/S0959652621000925

[4] J. Srivastava, R. Cooley, M. Deshpande, and P.-N. Tan, "Web usage mining: Discovery and applications of usage patterns from web data," *Acm Sigkdd Explorations Newsletter*, vol. 1, no. 2, pp. 12–23, 2000.

[5] B. S. Kumar and K. Rukmani, "Implementation of web usage mining using apriori and fp growth algorithms," *Int. J. of Advanced networking and Applications*, vol. 1, no. 06, pp. 400–404, 2010.

[6] S.-T. Li, L.-Y. Shue, and S.-F. Lee, "Enabling customer relationship management in isp services through mining usage patterns," *Expert Systems with Applications*, vol. 30, no. 4, pp. 621–632, 2006.

[7] M. Linares-Vásquez, G. Bavota, C. Bernal-Cárdenas, R. Oliveto, M. Di Penta, and D. Poshyvanyk, "Mining energy-greedy api usage patterns in android apps: an empirical study," in *Proceedings of the 11th working conference on mining software repositories*, 2014, pp. 2–11.

[8] M. A. Saied, O. Benomar, H. Abdeen, and H. Sahraoui, "Mining multi-level api usage patterns," in *2015 IEEE 22nd international conference on software analysis, evolution, and reengineering (SANER)*. IEEE, 2015, pp. 23–32.

[9] S. Schiaffino and A. Amandi, "Intelligent user profiling," in *Artificial intelligence an international perspective*. Springer, 2009, pp. 193–216.

[10] C. I. Eke, A. A. Norman, L. Shuib, and H. F. Nweke, "A survey of user profiling: State-of-the-art, challenges, and solutions," *IEEE Access*, vol. 7, pp. 144 907–144 924, 2019.

[11] J. Peng, K.-K. R. Choo, and H. Ashman, "User profiling in intrusion detection: A review," *Journal of Network and Computer Applications*, vol. 72, pp. 14–27, 2016.

[12] J. Wang, R. Cardell-Oliver, and W. Liu, "An incremental algorithm for discovering routine behaviours from smart meter data," *Knowledge-Based Systems*, vol. 113, pp. 61–74, 2016. [Online]. Available: https://www.sciencedirect.com/science/article/pii/S095070511630332X

[13] M. S. Rahim, K. A. Nguyen, R. A. Stewart, D. Giurco, and M. Blumenstein, "Advanced household profiling using digital water meters," *Journal of Environmental Management*, vol. 288, p. 112377, 2021. [Online]. Available: https://www.sciencedirect.com/science/article/pii/S0301479721004394

[14] S. McKenna, F. Fusco, and B. Eck, "Water demand pattern classification from smart meter data," *Procedia Engineering*, vol. 70, pp. 1121–1130, 2014, 12th International Conference on Computing and Control for the Water Industry, CCWI2013. [Online]. Available: https://www.sciencedirect.com/science/article/pii/S187770581400126X

[15] E. M. Olariu, R. Tolas, R. Portase, M. Dinsoreanu, and R. Potolea, "Modern approaches to preprocessing industrial data," in *2020 IEEE 16th International Conference on Intelligent Computer Communication and Processing (ICCP)*, 2020, pp. 221–226.

[16] C.-M. Chira, R. Portase, R. Tolas, C. Lemnaru, and R. Potolea, "A system for managing and processing industrial sensor data: Sms," in *2020 IEEE 16th International Conference on Intelligent Computer Communication and Processing (ICCP)*, 2020, pp. 213–220.

[17] C. Firte, L. Iamnitchi, R. Portase, R. Tolas, R. Potolea, M. Dinsoreanu, and C. Lemnaru, "Knowledge inference from home appliances data," in *2022 IEEE International Conference on Intelligent Computer Communication and Processing (ICCP)*, 2022.

[18] R. Portase, R. Tolas, and R. Potolea, "MEDIS: analysis methodology for data with multiple complexities," in *Proceedings of the 13th International Joint Conference on Knowledge Discovery, Knowledge Engineering and Knowledge Management, IC3K 2021, Volume 1: KDIR, Online Streaming, October 25-27, 2021*, R. Cucchiara, A. L. N. Fred, and J. Filipe, Eds. SCITEPRESS, 2021, pp. 191–198. [Online]. Available: https://doi.org/10.5220/0010655100003064

[19] R. Tolas, R. Portase, A. Iosif, and R. Potolea, "Periodicity detection algorithm and applications on iot data," in *2021 20th International Symposium on Parallel and Distributed Computing (ISPDC)*, 2021, pp. 81–88.

[20] "Pandas," https://pandas.pydata.org/, 2022, [Online; accessed 2-Jan-2022].

[21] "Numpy," https://numpy.org/, 2022, [Online; accessed 2-Jan-2022].

[22] F. Pedregosa, G. Varoquaux, A. Gramfort, V. Michel, B. Thirion, O. Grisel, M. Blondel, P. Prettenhofer, R. Weiss, V. Dubourg, J. Vanderplas, A. Passos, D. Cournapeau, M. Brucher, M. Perrot, and E. Duchesnay, "Scikit-learn: Machine learning in Python," *Journal of Machine Learning Research*, vol. 12, pp. 2825–2830, 2011.

[23] Wikipedia, "Time series," https://en.wikipedia.org/wiki/Time_series, [Online; accessed 24-Jan-2023].

[24] J. Lin, S. Williamson, K. Borne, and D. DeBarr, "Pattern recognition in time series," *Advances in Machine Learning and Data Mining for Astronomy*, vol. 1, no. 617-645, p. 3, 2012.

[25] M. Barandas, D. Folgado, L. Fernandes, S. Santos, M. Abreu, P. Bota, H. Liu, T. Schultz, and H. Gamboa, "Tsfel: Time series feature extraction library," *SoftwareX*, vol. 11, p. 100456, 2020. [Online]. Available: https://www.sciencedirect.com/science/article/pii/S2352711020300017

[26] W. Nikolai, T. SCHLEGL, and J. DEUSE, "Feature extraction for time series classification using univariate descriptive statistics and dynamic time warping in a manufacturing environment," in *2021 IEEE 2nd International Conference on Big Data, Artificial Intelligence and Internet of Things Engineering (ICBAIE)*. IEEE, 2021, pp. 762–768.

[27] Y. Zheng, Y.-W. Si, and R. Wong, "Feature extraction for chart pattern classification in financial time series," *Knowledge and Information Systems*, vol. 63, no. 7, pp. 1807–1848, 2021.

[28] H. Fu, W. Zhao, Q. Zhan, M. Yang, D. Xiong, and D. Yu, "Temporal information extraction for afforestation in the middle section of the yarlung zangbo river using time-series landsat images based on google earth engine," *Remote Sensing*, vol. 13, no. 23, p. 4785, 2021.

[29] T. Schneider, N. Helwig, and A. Schütze, "Automatic feature extraction and selection for classification of cyclical time series data," *tm-Technisches Messen*, vol. 84, no. 3, pp. 198–206, 2017.

[30] E. Nedelcu, R. Portase, R. Tolas, R. Muresan, M. Dinsoreanu, and R. Potolea, "Artifact detection in eeg using machine learning," in *2017 13th IEEE International Conference on Intelligent Computer Communication and Processing (ICCP)*, 2017, pp. 77–83.

[31] A. S. Al-Fahoum and A. A. Al-Fraihat, "Methods of eeg signal features extraction using linear analysis in frequency and time-frequency domains," *International Scholarly Research Notices*, vol. 2014, 2014.

[32] T. Wen and Z. Zhang, "Effective and extensible feature extraction method using genetic algorithm-based frequency-domain feature search for epileptic eeg multiclassification," *Medicine*, vol. 96, no. 19, 2017.

[33] F. Mörchen, "Time series feature extraction for data mining using dwt and dft," 2003.

[34] K. Khan, S. U. Rehman, K. Aziz, S. Fong, and S. Sarasvady, "Dbscan: Past, present and future," in *The Fifth International Conference on the Applications of Digital Information and Web Technologies (ICADIWT 2014)*, 2014, pp. 232–238.

[35] R. J. G. B. Campello, P. Kröger, J. Sander, and A. Zimek, "Density-based clustering," *WIREs Data Mining and Knowledge Discovery*, vol. 10, no. 2, p. e1343, 2020. [Online]. Available: https://wires.onlinelibrary.wiley.com/doi/abs/10.1002/widm.1343

[36] M. Ester, H.-P. Kriegel, J. Sander, and X. Xu, "A density-based algorithm for discovering clusters in large spatial databases with noise," in *Proceedings of the Second International Conference on Knowledge Discovery and Data Mining*, ser. KDD'96. AAAI Press, 1996, p. 226–231.

[37] J. Sander, M. Ester, H.-P. Kriegel, and X. Xu, "Density-based clustering in spatial databases: The algorithm gdbscan and its applications," *Data Min. Knowl. Discov.*, vol. 2, no. 2, pp. 169–194, 1998. [Online]. Available: https://link.springer.com/article/10.1023/A:1009745219419

[38] A. Hinneburg and D. A. Keim, "An efficient approach to clustering in large multimedia databases with noise," in *Proceedings of the Fourth International Conference on Knowledge Discovery and Data Mining*, ser. KDD'98. AAAI Press, 1998, p. 58–65.

[39] Scikit-learn, "DBSCAN," https://scikit-learn.org/stable/modules/generated/sklearn.cluster.DBSCAN.html, [Online; accessed 19-Jan-2023].

[40] Wikipedia, "Fast fourier transform," https://en.wikipedia.org/wiki/Fast_Fourier_transform, [Online; accessed 29-March-2023].

[41] "Databricks," https://www.databricks.com/, [Online; accessed 29-March-2023].

[42] "Scikit-learn minmaxscaler," https://scikit-learn.org/stable/modules/generated/sklearn.preprocessing.MinMaxScaler.html, [Online; accessed 29-March-2023].

[43] "Scikit-learn dbscan," https://scikit-learn.org/stable/modules/generated/sklearn.cluster.DBSCAN.html, [Online; accessed 19-July-2022].

Commenter Behavior Characterization on YouTube Channels

Shadi Shajari
COSMOS Research Center
University of Arkansas at Little Rock
Little Rock, USA
Email: sshajari@ualr.edu

Nitin Agarwal
COSMOS Research Center
University of Arkansas at Little Rock
Little Rock, USA
Email: nxagarwal@ualr.edu

Mustafa Alassad
COSMOS Research Center
University of Arkansas at Little Rock
Little Rock, USA
Email: mmalassad@ualr.edu

***Abstract*—YouTube is the second most visited website in the world and receives comments from millions of commenters daily. The comments section acts as a space for discussions among commenters, but it could also be a breeding ground for problematic behavior. In particular, the presence of suspicious commenters who engage in activities that deviate from the norms of constructive and respectful discourse can negatively impact the community and the quality of the online experience. This paper presents a social network analysis-based methodology for detecting commenter mobs on YouTube. These mobs of commenters collaborate to boost engagement on certain videos. The method provides a way to characterize channels based on the level of suspicious commenter behavior and detect coordination among channels. To evaluate our model, we analyzed 20 YouTube channels, 7,782 videos, 294,199 commenters, and 596,982 comments that propagated false views about the U.S. Military. The analysis concluded with evidence of commenter mob activities, possible coordinated suspicious behavior on the channels, and an explanation of the behavior of co-commenter communities.**

***Keywords*-*Social Network Analysis*; *YouTube*; *Commenter Network Analysis*; *Principal Component Analysis*; *Suspicious Behaviors*;**

I. INTRODUCTION

YouTube is a popular online platform for sharing and discussing videos, which allows millions of users to upload content and comment on videos daily. While YouTube has many benevolent uses, it has also been used to spread misinformation, propaganda, and other inappropriate or malicious content [1]. In addition, the comments section on YouTube has been used as a breeding ground for suspicious commenter behavior. For example, adversarial information actors deployed an information tactic known as commenter mobs, a strategy of random group of commenters collectively comment on a video (or a set of videos) to boost the video's engagement (hence, fabricate virality), as investigated by Hussain et al. [2].

Moreover, such mobs of commenters could comment on videos on one or multiple channels, where these comments may or may not be relevant to the videos. This behavior can harm the quality of the YouTube community and shape public perceptions of important issues.

Prior studies on this issue have mostly focused on identifying certain keywords and phrases that may indicate suspicious behavior. Researchers applied methods to analyze the behavior of the key sets of commenters in co-commenter networks on YouTube [3]. However, we discovered some limitations in these methods as well as shortcomings in the final analysis, in which the authors did not count the suspicious behavior of commenters at the channel level.

This paper proposes a social network analysis based methodology to detect commenter mobs, which helps to develop a channel-level characterization from highly suspicious to least suspicious level. In addition, the methodology helps assess the similarity between channels based on commenter behaviors, which allows the detection of varying degrees of collusion (or coordination) among channels. This systematic analysis was implemented to investigate suspicious commenter behavior on 20 YouTube channels promoting false views of the U.S. military and claiming to report official news and information about the U.S. Department of Defense. Likewise, mob activities were detected in this collection of channels. For example, the method found activities in standalone channels that shared similar organizational structures (mob leaders and affiliates), comment posting styles, and languages. Further analysis was done on the commenter mobs of the three most suspicious channels to describe their similarities and the nature of the content they posted. This study has contributed significantly and generated new insights into analyzing inorganic behaviors in YouTube platform, as presented below:

- Conducted an analysis of co-commenter networks on 20 YouTube channels to identify similarities using clustering methods and Principal Component Analysis (PCA) for dimensionality reduction.
- Detected the commenter mobs of the three most suspicious channels.
- Investigated cross-channel activities among the three most suspicious channels.

The rest of the paper is organized as follows: Section II reviews the suspicious behavior on YouTube, commenter network analysis, and the current understanding of the topic. Section III details the methods used for data collection, including the techniques and tools utilized to collect data. Section IV explains the methodology used in the study, which involves a combination of PCA, k-means, and hierarchical clustering methods. Section V presents the results of the study, including a detailed analysis of the data, commenters behavior, and the YouTube channels analysis. Finally, Section VI provides a conclusion and recommendations for further research.

II. RELATED WORK

In this section, we review the relevant literature related to suspicious behaviors on YouTube. Since this area is vastly understudied, we expand our literature survey to include approaches that are methodologically relevant to ours, even if they are studying a different research problem.

A. Suspicious Behavior on YouTube

Several approaches have been proposed to study suspicious behaviors on YouTube. A study by Alassad et al. [1] discovered intensive groups on YouTube, and identified content-user networks that responsible for disseminating conspiracy theories using a two-level decomposition optimization method. Likewise, Alassad et al. [3] applied the bi-level max-max optimization approach to identify key sets of individuals on social media who have the power to mobilize crowds and regulate the flow of information. Research by Kaushal et al. [4] focused on detecting child unsafe content on YouTube, using supervised classification and a convolutional neural network with an accuracy of 85.7%. Furthermore, Hussain et al. [2] analyzed metadata, such as engagement scores to identify inorganic behaviors on YouTube.

Kirdemir et al. [5] presented an unsupervised model for coordinated inauthentic behavior assessment on YouTube using a methodology that combines multiple layers of analysis, including rolling window correlation analysis, anomaly detection, peak detection, rule-based supervised classification, network feature engineering, and unsupervised clustering approaches. These studies come close to analyzing suspicious behaviors on YouTube. There is still a gap in the literature on examining suspicious commenter behaviors on YouTube that may lead to engagement boosting or fabricating the virality of the content. We focus on addressing this knowledge gap at the channel level through the research presented in this paper.

B. Commenter Network Analysis

An extensive body of literature applies social network analysis methods to reduce the complexity of social media data structures. Reviewing all those studies would be outside the scope of this research. Therefore, we narrow our focus on the studies that utilize social network analysis to analyze networks on YouTube only. Shapiro et al. [6] analyzed the video-commenter discussion on YouTube. They presented a comprehensive network analysis for the 20 most popular climate change-related YouTube videos to understand the role of elites and small groups of frequent commenters in shaping the discussion.

More recently, studies have focused on exponential random graph modeling [7]. Another study by Ferreira et al. [8] examined the mechanisms of imitation, intergroup interaction, and communities of co-commenters. In this research, the model focused on groups of users who frequently interact by commenting on the same posts. Coppola et al. [9] found that machine learning can detect maximal cliques within larger networks by implementing the Bron-Kerbosch algorithm to detect communities and central nodes. Likewise, the study presented by Cascavilla et al. [10] focused on analyzing commenters' comments and social network graphs to identify censored individuals in news articles. Another study by Wattenhofer et al. [11] analyzed the social and content aspects of YouTube and compared them to traditional online social networks, such as Twitter.

However, there are gaps in the literature related to commenter behavior on YouTube that could be addressed in future research. For example, we noticed a need for more research on the effectiveness of different approaches to detecting and addressing the multi-channel suspicious commenter behavior. In this research, we propose graph theoretic methods to identify mobs of commenters who post comments together on one or a set of videos and exhibit similar behaviors on different Youtube channels, in an attempt to discover collusion (or coordination) among channels.

III. Data Collection

In this study, we used a Python-based multi-thread script [12] to collect data related to the U.S. Military on YouTube channels. For this purpose, subject matter experts identified a list of 20 YouTube channels that promoted false views of the U.S. military.

TABLE I. YOUTUBE DATASET STATISTICS

Channels	***Videos***	***Comments***	***Commenters***
20	7782	596,982	294,199

The YouTube Data API is utilized to retrieve huge amounts of data about the number of videos, the number of comments, the details of the comments, and the commenter's IDs as presented in Table I.

IV. Methodology

This section describes our model. First, we describe how to create a co-commenter network (Section IV-A) and then discuss the 20 network structural features extracted from the co-commenter network (Section IV-B). Next, the model utilizes k-means and hierarchical clustering methods [13] on the co-commenter networks to determine the level of similarity between all 20 YouTube channels. The network structural features also allow us to rank the suspiciousness of the channels based on their co-commenting behaviors. Next, we explain the model in detail.

A. Creating Co-commenter Network

The process begins by creating a co-commenter network for each channel based on a chosen threshold. This co-commenter network is made up of edges between commenters who have commented on the same video, with the weight of the edge representing the number of the same videos they have commented on. Let's call this number n. To maintain stronger co-commenter relations, a threshold needs to be identified for n. To find the optimal threshold, 10 co-commenter networks were created for each channel using thresholds from 1 to 10. The average clustering coefficient was calculated for each network at each threshold, and the results were analyzed. The optimal threshold for each channel was determined by identifying the point in the plot where the rate of change starts to decrease, which is commonly known as the "elbow point" [14]. This method is often used to determine the optimal number of clusters in a data set. We analyze the co-commenter network with the best threshold that is calculated through the "elbow point" for each channel.

B. Extracting Co-commenter Network Features

Kirdemir et al. [5] have developed a method to detect suspicious clusters and behavior on YouTube channels by analyzing the interactions between commenters. They established a set of network features, including metrics from well-established graph measures to analyze the networks' behavior from different dimensions. In our analysis, we utilized 20 network structural features to study the co-commenter networks, such as number of nodes, number of edges, total number of unique commenters, total number of comments, normalized ratio of co-commenters (nodes / total commenters), average degree, density, average clustering coefficient, modularity, number of maximal cliques that have at least 5 members, number of unique commenters in cliques, number of commenters in cliques / total number of commenters in the channel, number of commenters in cliques / number of nodes, average degree of cliques, average degree of cliques / average degree in the co-commenter network, average clustering coefficient of cliques, average clustering coefficient of cliques / average clustering coefficient in the co-commenter network, mean clique size, median clique size and maximum clique size.

The methodology presented in this paper attempts to discover the similarities between channels across all the features in the dataset using unsupervised methods, such as k-means and hierarchical clustering [15]. In other words, utilizing k-means and hierarchical clustering methods, we gain insights into the similarities of commenter behaviors exhibited in different channels. In addition, the Principal Component Analysis (PCA) is utilized to reduce the high-dimensional co-commenter network feature space, thereby reducing the complexity of the dataset, retaining important links between commenters, increasing the interpretability of the identified patterns, and minimizing information loss [16].

Additionally, channels are ranked on suspiciousness based on the highest number of commenters, comments, and maximal cliques that have at least five members (for having significant number of cliques). The behavior of the commenters across the top suspicious channels is analyzed. While per channel analysis allows us to see commenter mob behaviors on a particular channel, combined-channel analysis shows how commenter mobs span across multiple channels. Such an analysis shows how some influential commenter mobs move from one channel to another in an attempt to amplify/boost the videos' engagement in a highly sophisticated manner, much like a well-choreographed flash mob.

As the next step, social network analysis is conducted on the most suspicious channels. This analysis is done in order to gain insight into the behavior and interactions of those who comment on these three channels. Furthermore, the co-commenter network for each channel is examined separately, and communities are identified based on modularity methods. The influential commenters who posted the most comments within these communities were identified by analyzing the average degree centrality of nodes. The next section discusses our results and findings.

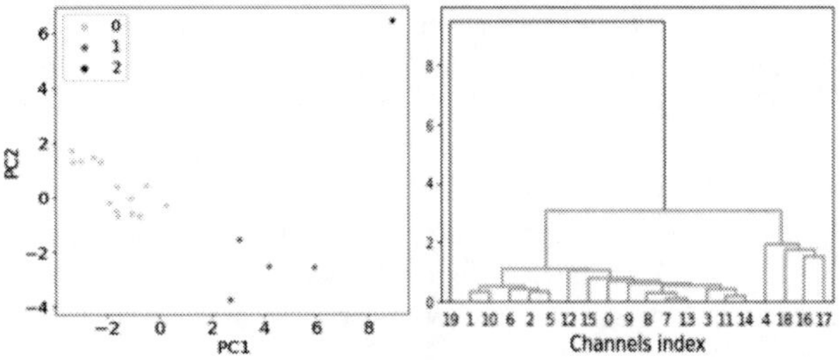

Figure 1. Channel categorization using k-means (left) and hierarchical clustering (right).

V. Results

This section will cover the results of K-Means and Hierarchical Clustering, followed by an examination of the findings from the analysis of commenter mobs on the top three suspicious channels.

A. K-Means and Hierarchical Clustering

This section discusses the results of clustering analyses performed using both the k-means and hierarchical clustering methods [13]. The utilized techniques identified three clusters in both methods. The optimal number of clusters for k-means was found by utilizing the silhouette score as described in [17], where a higher score indicates higher similarity among channels within a cluster. For hierarchical clustering as presented in [18], the single linkage method is used to create a dendrogram (tree-like structure) that shows how close each channel is to other channels.

Moreover, the cut-tree method is used to determine the optimal number of clusters and separate the channels into groups based on their similarity. Likewise, the optimal number of clusters helps to evaluate the quality of clustering by determining how similar an object is to its own cluster compared to other clusters. The visualizations of the clusters, such as scatter plots [19] demonstrated that the clusters were well separated. In other words, such a clustering method offers a better visual representation of how well each data point has been classified within a cluster. The clusters identified by both k-means and hierarchical clustering were distinct and did not overlap, as shown in Figure 1. The PC1 and PC2 correspond to the two principal components identified using the PCA method for dimensionality reduction, as explained in Section IV.B. The channel index is the unique channel ID assigned to each channel in our dataset. Both methods successfully identified the same number of clusters in the data with good separation between them. Finally, we examined the structure of clusters' networks based on three primary characteristics of the co-commenter network. In other words, we measured the average clustering coefficient (ACC), the modularity values, and the density to identify the characteristics of channels within these clusters, as shown in Table II.

In summary, the clustering analysis indicates that three channels require further investigation due to the network structures. Channels like "USA Military Channel" and "USA Military Channel 2" are classified as part of cluster 1, which is logical as they have similar video content and denser co-commentor network structures. On the other hand, "The Military TV" channel is part of cluster 0, which comprises channels with smaller co-commenter networks and distinct content.

B. Commenter Mobs for All Three Channels

As described in Section IV-B, our model can rank channels' suspiciousness based on the highest number of commenters, comments, and maximal cliques that have at least five members. We identified the top three suspicious channels from our model for further analysis. The three most suspicious channels are "USA Military Channel" (1.53M subscribers), "The Military TV" (399K subscribers), and "USA Military Channel 2" (372K subscribers). We created a combined-channel commenter network for the three channels. Figure 2, illustrates groups of commenters across the three most suspicious channels. The structure of each channel is represented by

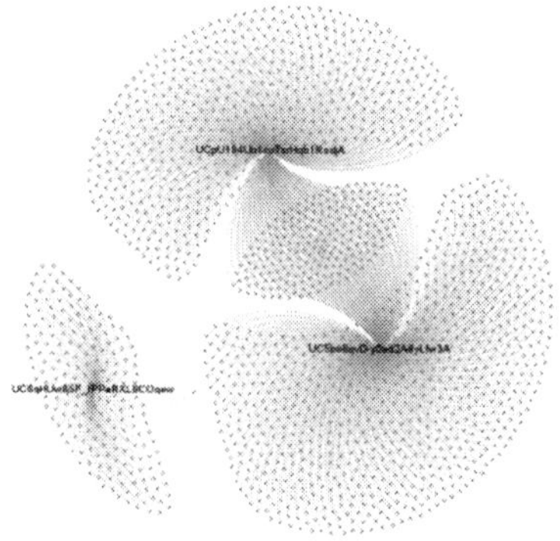

Figure 2. Commenter mobs spanning across the three most suspicious channels.

a central node called the channel's name, and nodes connected to that channel are the commenters who post comments on that channel's videos. Next, we employed the modularity method to identify patterns and communities (different colors) within this network. The green group is "The Military TV" channel with ID "UC6qHUwB5F_fPPaRXL8COqew", the purple group is "USA Military Channel" with ID "UC5bu8qvD-y0eo2A6yLfvr3A", and the orange group is "USA Military Channel 2" with ID "UCpU184Ub1cuTsrHqb1RodjA". The channels' analysis tells us that the most active commenters are those who frequently post comments on both "USA Military Channel" and "USA Military Channel 2".

Moreover, these commenters show interest in channels that primarily post videos related to the United States military and other narratives, such as the Army, Navy, Air Force, and Marine Corps. From our analysis, we identified many Japanese comments posted by these commenters due to possible common interests in Japan's self-defense forces and NATO countries [20]. Moreover, Figure 2 shows the bridge commenters sitting at the intersection of two channels, "USA Military Channel" and "USA Military Channel 2". We could call such behavior "YouTube cross-channel activities" due to the behavior of these commenters. Finally, "The Military TV" channel offers viewers footage from various military branches, including the narrative weapons, aircraft, tanks, ships, guns, artillery, vehicles, military operations, and technologies of the US and other countries [21]. However, it appears that the commenters on this channel are less active than those on the other two suspicious channels. Next, we illustrate each channel's structure and discuss commenters' behavior.

C. Commenter Mobs for USA Military Channel

In Figure 3, the co-commenter network presents 1.53M subscribers, and 41,092 commenters spread information across 1,993 videos. According to the modularity measurements, the

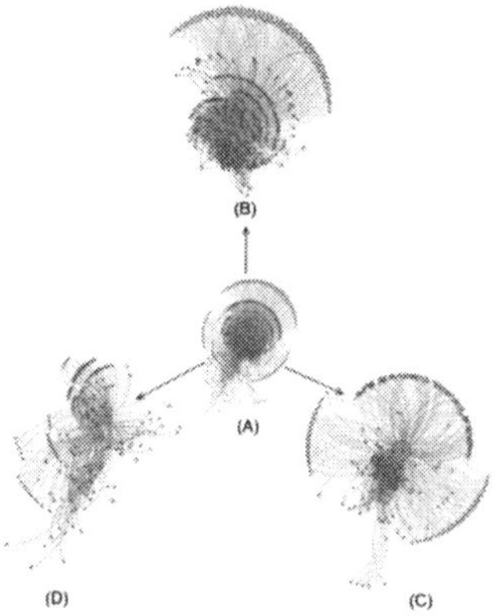

Figure 3. USA Military Channel's co-commenter network (A) and the three largest commenter mobs (B, C, and D).

co-commenter network in the USA Military Channel is divided into four distinct communities. Due to the space limit, the analysis focused on the top three largest communities shown in Figure 3. Moreover, the structures of communities (B), (C), and (D) indicate leaders and followers in organizations based on the degree centrality values. In other words, we observed commenters supporting comments posted by highly central commenters in the channel. For example, the leader-follower case was related to comments on videos related to the United States military, such as the Army, Navy, Air Force, and Marine Corps. In addition, our analysis shows that US allies were involved in many comments with Japanese contexts and videos related to the Japanese Self-Defense Forces and NATO countries.

D. Commenter Mobs for USA Military Channel 2

Figure 4 illustrates the "USA Military Channel 2" which has 372,000 subscribers, and 37,527 commenters across 227 videos. The analysis shows similar behavior from the commenter as we implemented the exact steps explained in Section V-C. From our results, we observed similar context, language, and the same commenters were active on both channels. Likewise, these two channels display a strong resemblance in

TABLE II. CLUSTER STATISTICS AND DESCRIPTION

Cluster	*Acc*	*Density*	*Modularity*	Description
0	0.35	0.06	0.41	Channels in this cluster have fewer network structures than the channels in other clusters. The co-commenter networks do not have many tightly knit groups of commenters and not cohesive structure.
1	0.75	0.07	0.25	Channels' co-commenter networks are well-connected networks with strong internal connections among commenters.
2	0.52	0.002	0.24	The clusters' channels show larger co-commenter network structures than the networks in other clusters.

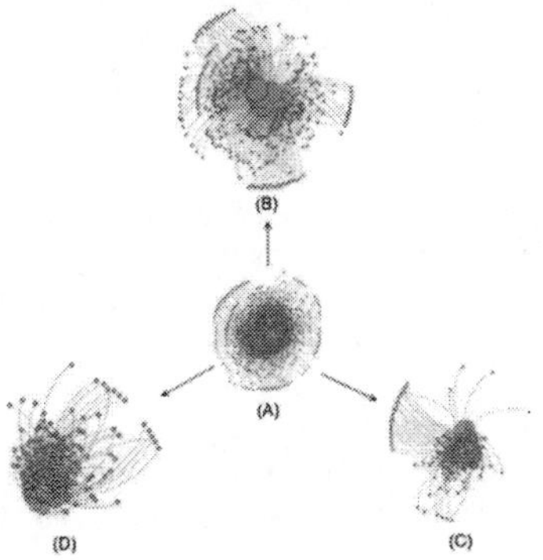

Figure 4. USA Military Channel 2's co-commenter network (A) and the three largest commenter mobs (B, C, and D).

organizational structures on YouTube, indicating a potential level of collusion or coordination among commenters. Moreover, our analysis revealed commenters were active on both channels, "USA Military Channel" and "USA Military Channel 2" which indicates cross-channel activities on YouTube. Furthermore, these two channels were part of cluster 1 using k-means and hierarchical clustering methods, as shown in Figure 1.

E. Commenter Mobs for The Military TV

Figure 5 depicts the last suspicious groups of commenters in the structure of channel "The Military TV" This YouTube channel includes 399,000 subscribers, 54,898 comments, and 29,113 commenters across 582 videos. Our findings indicate

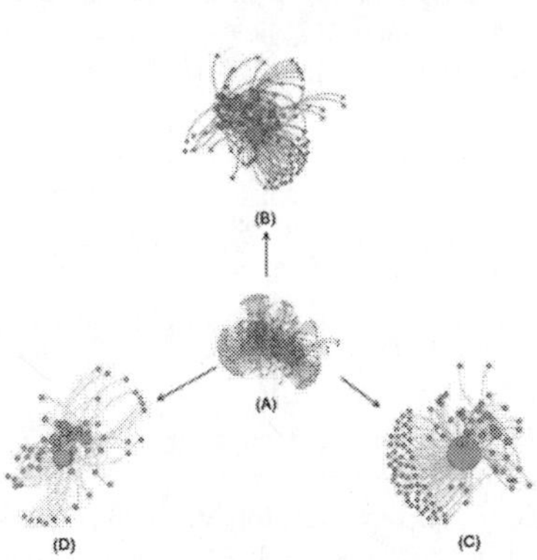

Figure 5. The Military TV channel's co-commenter network (A) and the three largest commenter mobs (B, C, and D).

that the network structure for this channel is smaller in terms of nodes, edges and the number of commenters in comparison to the other two channels. Additionally, the organizational structure of the channel is different from "USA Military Channel" and "USA Military Channel 2" similarly, k-means and hierarchical clustering methods put this channel in cluster 0 as shown in Figure 1. Likewise, our analysis showed different context used by commenters in this channel, where the videos and comments were related to the US and other countries, such as Russia and Ukraine.

To recap, we observed similarities among the 20 YouTube channels with false views about the U.S. Military. These similarities were captured by analyzing the network structural features of co-commenter networks on these channels and applying k-means and hierarchical clustering methods. PCA was used to reduce the dimensionality. The similarities in commenters' behaviors suggested a high level of collusion (or coordination) among the channels. Three most suspicious channels were identified where commenter mobs were detected. Furthermore, cross-channel commenter mobs were identified on two of the three most suspicious channels, meaning the commenter mob moved from one channel to the other.

VI. Conclusion and Future Work

In this study, we present a methodology to identify suspicious commenter behaviors by analyzing co-commenter networks, in particular on YouTube. We developed a network analysis based approach that leverages 20 network structural features to assess suspicious behaviors in commenter networks, which enables channel-level characterization. Furthermore, the proposed methodology helps identifying behavioral similarities among the channels based on commenter network structures, which allows assessment of varying degrees of collusion (or coordination). We evaluated the proposed methodology on a set of 20 YouTube channels that post videos containing untrue and unflattering views of the U.S. Military. Our methodology helped identify the top 3 most suspicious channels. A deeper analysis of these three channels revealed false narratives being pushed in their videos. The methodology also revealed clusters of channels with similar commenter behavioral profiles that range from highly suspicious to semi-suspicious.

To advance our understanding of suspicious commenter behavior on online platforms like YouTube, future research should analyze the motivations, interests, and power of the users willing to participate in suspicious activities. Furthermore, there is a requirement for an extended research study to explore behavior patterns associated with suspicious activities, such as topic modeling, sentiment scoring, and toxicity analysis. Another future study will investigate the potential impact of suspicious commenter behavior on the spread of misinformation and the integrity of online discussions. Utilizing the focal structure analysis models [22] could help to observe mob activities on suspicious YouTube channels, with the importance of identifying any commenters' collusion or coordination.

ACKNOWLEDGMENT

This research is funded in part by the U.S. National Science Foundation (OIA-1946391, OIA-1920920, IIS-1636933, ACI-1429160, and IIS-1110868), U.S. Office of the Under Secretary of Defense for Research and Engineering (FA9550-22-1-0332), U.S. Office of Naval Research (N00014-10-1-0091, N00014-14-1-0489, N00014-15-P-1187, N00014-16-1-2016, N00014-16-1-2412, N00014-17-1-2675, N00014-17-1-2605, N68335-19-C-0359, N00014-19-1-2336, N68335-20-C-0540, N00014-21-1-2121, N00014-21-1-2765, N00014-22-1-2318), U.S. Air Force Research Laboratory, U.S. Army Research Office (W911NF-20-1-0262, W911NF-16-1-0189, W911NF-23-1-0011), U.S. Defense Advanced Research Projects Agency (W31P4Q-17-C-0059), Arkansas Research Alliance, the Jerry L. Maulden/Entergy Endowment at the University of Arkansas at Little Rock, and the Australian Department of Defense Strategic Policy Grants Program (SPGP) (award number: 2020-106-094). Any opinions, findings, and conclusions or recommendations expressed in this material are those of the authors and do not necessarily reflect the views of the funding organizations. The researchers gratefully acknowledge the support.

REFERENCES

[1] M. Alassad, M. N. Hussain, and N. Agarwal, "Finding fake news key spreaders in complex social networks by using bi-level decomposition optimization method," in *Modeling and Simulation of Social-Behavioral Phenomena in Creative Societies*. Springer International Publishing, 2019, vol. 1079, pp. 41–54.

[2] M. N. Hussain, S. Tokdemir, N. Agarwal, and S. Al-Khateeb, "Analyzing disinformation and crowd manipulation tactics on YouTube," in *2018 IEEE/ACM International Conference on Advances in Social Networks Analysis and Mining (ASONAM)*. IEEE, 2018, pp. 1092–1095, Oct. 2018.

[3] M. Alassad, M. N. Hussain, and N. Agarwal, "Comprehensive decomposition optimization method for locating key sets of commenters spreading conspiracy theory in complex social networks," *Central European Journal of Operations Research*, vol. 30, no. 1, pp. 367–394, Feb. 2021.

[4] R. Kaushal, S. Saha, P. Bajaj, and P. Kumaraguru, "KidsTube: Detection, characterization and analysis of child unsafe content & promoters on YouTube," in *2016 14th Annual Conference on Privacy, Security and Trust (PST)*, Dec 2016, pp. 157–164.

[5] B. Kirdemir, O. Adeliyi, and N. Agarwal, "Towards characterizing coordinated inauthentic behaviors on YouTube," in *The 2nd Workshop on Reducing Online Misinformation through Credible Information Retrieval (ROMCIR 2022) held with the 44th European Conference on Information Retrieval (ECIR 2022)*, vol. 3138, Apr 2022, pp. 100–116.

[6] M. A. Shapiro and H. W. Park, "Climate change and YouTube: Deliberation potential in post-video discussions," *Environmental Communication*, vol. 12, no. 1, pp. 115–131, Jan. 2018.

[7] Y. Chen and L. Wang, "Misleading political advertising fuels incivility online: A social network analysis of 2020 u.s. presidential election campaign video comments on YouTube," *Computers in Human Behavior*, vol. 131, p. 107202, Jun. 2022.

[8] C. H. Ferreira et al., "On the dynamics of political discussions on instagram: A network perspective," *Online Social Networks and Media*, vol. 25, p. 100155, Sep. 2021.

[9] C. Coppola and H. Elgazzar, "Novel machine learning algorithms for centrality and cliques detection in youtube social networks," vol. 11, no. 1, p. 65–77, Jan. 2020.

[10] G. Cascavilla, M. Conti, D. G. Schwartz, and I. Yahav, "Revealing censored information through comments and commenters in online social networks," in *Proceedings of the 2015 IEEE/ACM International Conference on Advances in Social Networks Analysis and Mining 2015*, Aug. 2015, pp. 675–680.

[11] M. Wattenhofer, R. Wattenhofer, and Z. Zhu, "The YouTube social network," *Proceedings of the International AAAI Conference on Web and Social Media*, vol. 6, no. 1, pp. 354–361, Aug. 2021.

[12] J. Kready, S. A. Shimray, M. N. Hussain, and N. Agarwal, "YouTube data collection using parallel processing," in *2020 IEEE International Parallel and Distributed Processing Symposium Workshops (IPDPSW)*, Jun. 2020, pp. 1119–1122.

[13] F. Murtagh and P. Contreras, "Algorithms for hierarchical clustering: an overview," *WIREs Data Mining and Knowledge Discovery*, vol. 2, no. 1, pp. 86–97, Jan. 2012.

[14] C. Shi et al., "A quantitative discriminant method of elbow point for the optimal number of clusters in clustering algorithm," *EURASIP Journal on Wireless Communications and Networking*, vol. 2021, no. 1, p. 31, Dec. 2021.

[15] A. Gupta, H. Sharma, and A. Akhtar, "A comparative analysis of k-means and hierarchical clustering," *EPRA International Journal of Multidisciplinary Research (IJMR)*, pp. 412–418, Sep. 2021.

[16] I. T. Jolliffe and J. Cadima, "Principal component analysis: a review and recent developments," *Philosophical Transactions of the Royal Society A: Mathematical, Physical and Engineering Sciences*, vol. 374, no. 2065, p. 20150202, Apr 2016.

[17] K. R. Shahapure and C. Nicholas, "Cluster quality analysis using silhouette score," in *2020 IEEE 7th International Conference on Data Science and Advanced Analytics (DSAA)*, Oct. 2020, pp. 747–748.

[18] F. Nielsen, "Hierarchical clustering," in *Introduction to HPC with MPI for Data Science*. Springer International Publishing, 2016, pp. 195–211.

[19] D. A. Keim, M. C. Hao, U. Dayal, H. Janetzko, and P. Bak, "Generalized scatter plots," *Information Visualization*, vol. 9, no. 4, pp. 301–311, Dec 2010.

[20] USA military channel 2. [retrieved: March, 2023]. [Online]. Available: https://www.youtube.com/@USAMilitaryChannel2

[21] The military TV. [retrieved: March, 2023]. [Online]. Available: https://www.youtube.com/@USAMilitaryChannel

[22] M. Alassad, B. Spann, and N. Agarwal, "Combining advanced computational social science and graph theoretic techniques to reveal adversarial information operations," *Information Processing & Management*, vol. 58, no. 1, p. 102385, Jan. 2021.

Uncovering the Dynamic Interplay of YouTube Co-commenter Connections through Contextual Focal Structure Analysis

Mustafa Alassad
COSMOS Research Center
UA - Little Rock
Little Rock, AR, USA
Email: mmalassad@ualr.edu

Nitin Agarwal
COSMOS Research Center
UA - Little Rock
Little Rock, AR, USA
Email: nxagarwal@ualr.edu

Abstract- Contextual Focal Structure Analysis (CFSA) model aims to improve the discovery and interpretability of focal structure spreaders on social networks. This method can present influential sets of commenters and contexts in terms of specific interaction patterns or narrative structures on YouTube. The CFSA model utilizes multiplex networks, where the data is structured into multiple layers to consider the different activities of the users on social networks. The first layer is the co-commenter network based on two commenters commenting on the same video; then, the second layer is the network between videos and channels that shows to which channel the video belongs. The two layers have interconnections based on the commenters' activities and the participation relations on different YouTube channels. The model's performance was evaluated through the Cheng Ho disinformation narrative within the Indo-Pacific region on YouTube. The dataset includes more than 36,495 commenters and 145,923 videos on YouTube. The model results showed commenters activities with supplementary contexts in the form of co-commenter-Channels activities. Likewise, this study provides the best answer to "How to explain the dynamic interplay between commenters, videos, and YouTube channels in the Indo-Pacific region?" The research model discovered the most impactful contextual focal structure sets for the YouTube co-commenters network. The results involve popular channels such as "Asumsi," "Erwan Tuinesia," "KOMPASTV," and "metrotvnews," which primarily serve the Indonesian community in the Indo-Pacific region. Nevertheless, it is noteworthy that several of these channels are known for spreading misinformation.

Keywords- Indo-Pacific region; Cheng Ho; Multiplex Networks; Complex Network; Entropy; Contextual Focal Structures.

I. INTRODUCTION

The Indo-Pacific region is the world's speediest rising economic region, and its importance to the world's power countries like the United States of America, the Union Europe, and China will continue to expand over time [1]. The Indo-Pacific region is a vast area that encompasses numerous countries with diverse cultural, economic, and geopolitical backgrounds. Some of the countries that fall under the ambit of the Indo-Pacific region include Australia, Bangladesh, China, India, Indonesia, Japan, Malaysia, Pakistan, Philippines, Singapore, Taiwan, Thailand, and Vietnam. The Indo-Pacific region makes up more than one-third of all global economic activity and will account for more than half of the global economy by 2040 [1], 65% of the world's oceans, and 25% of its land [2]. In addition, the Indo-Pacific region's population growth in the next 20 years is driving massive demands for health education, health services, food agriculture and fisheries, natural resources, energy, and advanced manufacturing and green infrastructure [1]. Furthermore, like all great power countries, the European Union, the United States of America, China, Canada, and Japan seek to influence the region to set ways for their own interests [3]. Likewise, the United States is considered an Indo-Pacific power, "the future of each of our nations- and indeed the world- depends on a free and open Indo-Pacific enduring and flourishing in the decades ahead" President Joe Biden underlined this point on September 24, 2021[2]. However, China, the largest trading and economy in the world [3], has chosen the path of challenge and confrontation, where China is taking over and rising power that is viewed with suspicion and challenges for nations in the Indo-Pacific region and beyond [4].

Moreover, Indo-Pacific nations like China, India, Japan, Philippines, and Indonesia are leading the way in terms of active users and growth in the social media consumption [5]. For example, YouTube is a video-sharing site and is considered an integral part of the social media platforms [6] and is one of the famous platforms for sharing news and social activities that cover over 95% of the internet population in 80 different languages [7]. For instance, users within the Indo-Pacific region were split between India (467 million), Indonesia (139 million), and Japan (102 million), respectively [8]. Furthermore, YouTube's channels show a strong presence for the Indo-Pacific people to share content and recommendations on the posted videos, where the top four channels' distribution categorized to people and blogs (24.89%), entertainment (18.63%), gaming (12.66%), and music (11.13%) [9]. In fact, The recommendation system on YouTube is a critical driver and plays a significant role in driving video views on the platform. Its primary function is to provide users with video recommendations based on their viewing history and the content they are currently engaged with [10]. In this research paper, we analyzed the recommendations made by commenters on YouTube regarding a disinformation narrative known as "Cheng Ho" or "Zheng He" within the Indo-Pacific region.

Cheng Ho is a disinformation narrative created to increase regional support for China and its geopolitical interest in the South China Sea, the Belt Road Initiative, and as a response to the accusations of China's oppression of Muslims [11]. The goal of pushing this narrative is to tackle the accusations of China's oppression of the Uyghur Muslims and increase support for China and its strategic pursuits including the aggression in the South China Sea.

Oftentimes, misinformation and disinformation are spread by commenters in a coordinated manner on social networks [12]. Highlighting focal groups of commenters on YouTube is the main contribution of this research, where these commenters could develop unique structures and act to influence individuals/communities to maximize information dissemination between Indo-Pacific region nations. Conventional community detection methods focus on larger communities and are oblivious to these influential groups. Şen et al. [13] proposed the Focal Structure Analysis (FSA) model to identify the smallest possible influential groups of users that can maximize information diffusion in social networks. Likewise, Alassad et al. [14] introduced the FSA 2.0 model to enhance the quality of the focal structure sets discovery and to overcome the limits in the activities of the influential users. The authors developed a bi-level decomposition optimization model to identify groups that could maximize the individual's influence in the first level and measure the network's stability in the second level. Both FSA and FSA 2.0 exclusively exhibit the activities of users in relation to other users. For instance, node i is linked to other nodes like j in the network, where neither model reveals any data on other activities taking place within the network. To improve the analysis of the state-of-the-art FSA model and FSA 2.0 model, this paper introduces the CFSA model to enhance the discovery and interpretability, reveals the context and highlights the interests of commenters in the form of contextual focal structure sets on YouTube.

The rest of the paper is organized as follows: Section II describes the research problem statement. Section III describes the YouTube dataset implemented to evaluate the model's performance and the overall structure of the methodology. The results in Section IV concluded that the CFSA results are interpretable and informative. Likewise, Section IV states the findings and presents the benefits of the proposed CFSA model enhanced the quality and the interpretability of the focal structure sets of commenters on YouTube. Finally, the conclusion, limitations, and future research path are given in Section V.

II. Research Problem Statement

The proposed research aims to highlight the CFSA model in YouTube's recommendation system. Given the raw datasets from the YouTube environment, the research problem statement is to implement a systematic model that utilizes the FSA 2.0 model [15] and the multiplex network approach to reveal the co-commenters' activities, interests and behavior in the form of context that may act in different cultural circumstances [12]. This approach involves different layers, including co-commenters, commenter-video, and video-channel in the form of participation layers.

Moreover, this research presents essential ideas and analysis to study questions like, can traditional community detection methods identify influential commenters and reveal the context on different YouTube channels? How the CFSA model utilizes the multiplex network to fill the gap in the information limitations? Finally, could the CFSA model structure the information to identify activities and explain the actions or interests of influential commenters? The next section discusses the methodology and the overall structure of the CFSA model.

III. Methodology

This section describes the technical intuition in our model; it consists of three main components. The data collection level is to collect all related context from Twitter including different trending hashtags related to events on Twitter network. The multiplex information matrix structure and CFS sets discovery level, where the layers of the multiplex network include co-commenters, commenter-video, and video-channel in the form of co-commenters' adjacency matrix layer and the participation layer network. Finally, the third level to validate and analyze the CFS set. For this level, we measure three Truth (GT) measures to calculate the amount of influence that any CFS set may generate in the entire structure of the network.

A. *Multiplex Matrix Structure*

In general, the adjacency matrix of an unweighted and undirected graph G with N nodes in an $N \times N$ symmetric matrix is $\mathbf{A} = \{a_{ij}\}$, with $a_{ij} = 1$, only if there is an edge between i and j in G, and $a_{ij} = 0$ otherwise. The adjacency matrix of layer graph G_α is $n_\alpha \times n_\alpha$ symmetric matrix $\mathbf{A}^\alpha = a_{ij}^\alpha$, with $a_{ij}^\alpha = 1$ only if there is an edge between (i, α), and (j, α) in G_α.

Likewise, the adjacency matrix of G_β is an $n \times m$ matrix $\rho = p_{i\alpha}$, with $p_{i\alpha} = 1$ only if there is an edge between the node i and the layer α in the participation graph, i.e., only if node i participates in layer α. We call it the participation matrix. The adjacency matrix of the coupling graph G_F is an $N \times N$ matrix $\mathcal{L} = \{c_{ij}\}$, with $c_{ij} = 1$ only if there is an edge between node-layer pair i and j in G_F, i.e., if they are representatives of the same node in different layers. We can arrange rows and columns of $\mathcal{L}$ such that node-layer pairs of the same layer are contiguous, and layers are ordered as shown in the next section. It results that $\mathcal{L}$ is a block matrix with zero diagonal blocks. Thus, $c_{ij} = 1$, with $i, j = 1, \ldots, N$ represents an edge between a node-layer pair in layer 1(co-commenter layer) and node layer pair in layer 2 (video-channel layer) if $i < n_1$ and $n_1 < j < n_2$ as shown in Figure 1. The supra-adjacency matrix is the adjacency matrix of the supra-graph $G_{\mathcal{M}}$. Just as $G_{\mathcal{M}}$, $\bar{A}$ is a synthetic representation of the whole multiplex $\mathcal{M}$. It can be obtained from the intra-layer adjacency matrices and the coupling matrix in the following way:

$$\bar{A} = \mathbf{A}^\alpha \oplus_\alpha \mathcal{L} \tag{1}$$

Where the same consideration as in $\mathcal{L}$ applies for the indices we also define. $\mathbf{A} = \oplus \mathbf{A}^\alpha$, which we call the intra-layer adjacency matrix.

Additionally, Figure 1 shows the Multiplex network, it is the union of the co-commenter layer and the video-channel layer. The participation layer is the interconnections between commenters, videos, and YouTube channels.

The CFSA model was built on a bi-level decomposition optimization problem to maximize the centrality values at the commenter level and maximize the network modularity values at the network level. Equation (2) shows the objective function used at the commenter level to maximize the centrality values in the multiplex network.

$$\max \sum_{i=1}^{n} \sum_{j=1}^{m} (\delta_i^{UU} \oplus \beta_{ij}^{UH} \hbar_j^{HH}) \tag{2}$$

Where n is the number of nodes in the co-commenter layer UU. m is the number of nodes in the video-channel layer HH. δ_i^{UU} is the sphere of influence for commenter i in UU. $\oplus$ is the direct sum. $\hbar_j^{HH}$ is the number of j channels in HH connected by an edge to commenter i in UU. Finally, β_{ij}^{UH} represents the interconnection in the participation layer and the links between commenters and channels, where

$\beta_{ij}^{UH} = 1$ if and only if commenter i in UU has a link with channel j in HH; otherwise 0.

The local clustering coefficient C_u was utilized to measure the level of transitivity and the density of a commenter's direct neighbors as shown in (3).

$$C_u = {}^{t_u}/_{d_u} \quad (3)$$

$$\beta_{ij}^{UH} c_{*,i} \qquad \forall i,j \quad (4)$$

Where t_u is the adjacency matrix of the network A, and d_u is the adjacency matrix of the complete graph G_F with no self-edges as shown in Figure 1. Equation (4) ensures the model considers the commenters to have edges to the participation network $\bar{A}$.

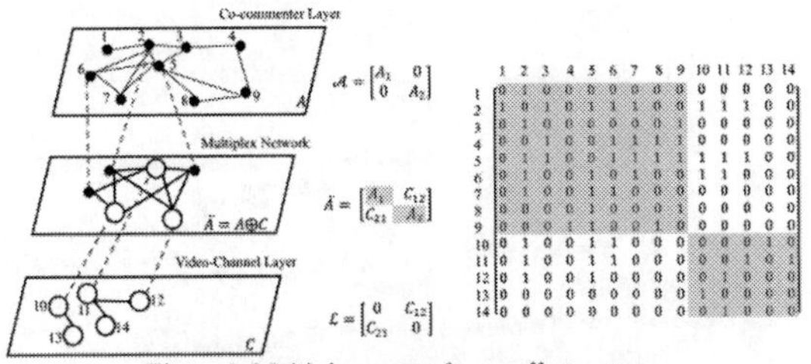

Figure 1. Multiplex network overall structure.

In the network level, the model measures every set of commenters' spheres of influence in the entire $\bar{A}$ network. This level is designed to measure the commenters' impact when they join $\bar{A}$ network. To measure the influence the commenters' identified from the commenter level, we utilize the spectral modularity method proposed in [6]. Furthermore, we utilized a vector parameter $\overline{\vec{c}\delta_{\iota m \times k}}_{k \le m}$ to transfer the commenters' information between the commenter level and the network level. The network level is designed based on the following set of equations.

$$\varrho_{jx} = \frac{1}{2m} Tr(\xi_{jx} \bar{A} \xi_{jx}^T) \qquad \forall j,x \quad (5)$$

$$\xi_{jx} = \{ \overline{\vec{c}\delta_{\iota m \times k}}_{k \le m} \cup \delta_{jx} | \overline{\vec{c}\delta_{\iota m \times k}}_{k \le m}, \neq \delta_{jx} \} \qquad \forall j,x \quad (6)$$

$$\overline{\mu_{jx}^{Q}} = \max\{\varrho_{1x}, \varrho_{2x}, \dots, \varrho_{jx}\} \qquad \forall j,x \quad (7)$$

$$\mathbb{C}\varrho_{jx} = \delta_{jx}(\overline{\mu_{jx}^{Q}}) \qquad \forall j,x \quad (8)$$

The objective in the network-level is to identify sets of commenters that maximize the spectral modularity value ϱ_{jx} in each x iteration as shown in (5). Likewise, the model would search for the active set of commenters that will maximize the network's sparsity as indicated in (6). $\bar{A}$ is the modularity matrix. In constraint (6), $\xi_{jx} \in R^{m \times k}$ is the union between the commenters sets of users from the commenter level, $\overline{\vec{c}\delta_{\iota m \times k}}_{k \le m}$, and the candidate sets of commenters δ_{jx} that presumably will maximize the network's sparsity. Constraint (7) is used to calculate the spectral modularity values $\overline{\mu_{jx}^{Q}}$. In constraint (8), $C\varrho_{jx}$ utilized to transfer back the results to the commenter level, where $\delta_{jx}(\overline{\mu_{jx}^{Q}})$ is the non-dominated solution that maximized the network's modularity. $C\varrho_{jx}^{M}$ is the set of commenters that maximized the modularity values when they joined the network and a vector parameter to interact with the commenter level and transfer the optimal solution from the network level to the commenter level. $C\varrho_{jx}^{M}$ selects the contextual focal structure sets that gather all the criteria from both levels at each iteration x.

B. Data Collection

YouTube's data API was used to collect an initial set of videos on key phrases relating to the Cheng Ho narrative at COSMOS research center, UA Little Rock, USA. The data collected was written to a MySQL database, where special queries were implemented against the database with a full-text search. To prevent personalized recommendations based on the user's history, we didn't log into the account used for collection and the browser instances and all cookies were cleared before a new crawl job. This data API run time was repeated in multiple iterations to get the most recent commenters' recommendations on videos, channels, and posted videos as shown in Table I.

TABLE I. YOUTUBE API DATA COLLECTION

Attempts	Number of Videos	Number of Unique Videos
Seed	50	50
Iterations 1-3	5985	3521
Iteration 4-5	145923	47101

Moreover, the retrieved data was in real-time, stored in different tables, and segmented into columns depending on the content as shown in Table .

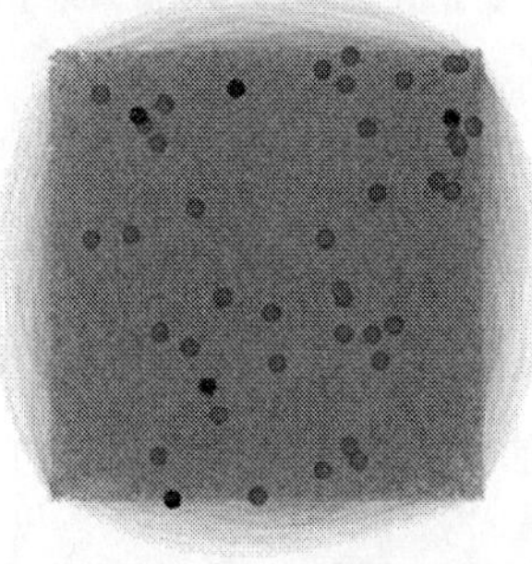

Figure 2. Co-COMMENTER YOUTUBE NETWORK. (COMPLEX NETWORK IN GRAY, CFS 3 (COMMENTERS IN RED, CHANNELS IS BLACK).

TABLE II. DATASET RETRIEVED FROM YOUTUBE. MULTIPLEX NETWORK (UH), CO-COMMENTER LAYER (UU), VIDEO-CHANNEL (HH), NODE (N), EDGES (E)

Network	UH		UU		HH	
	E	N	E	N	E	N
Cheng Ho	68975	36559	68803	36495	87799	57686

C. CFS Sets Validation and Analysis

In this part of the solution procedure, we implemented various steps to validate the outputs of the CFSA model. These steps should quantitatively measure the impacts of the commenters' influence and illustrate their interest on YouTube networks. For this purpose, we implemented three measures to calculate the changes in the network; first, the modularity values [16], [17] we call it (Ground Truth Modularity (GTMOD)); second, the clustering coefficient method [18] (Ground Truth Clustering Coefficient (GTCC)); and lastly, the change in the number of communities (Ground Truth Network Stability (GTNS)).

Moreover, the solution procedure selects the top ten CFS sets from each Ground Truth (GT) measure (GTMOD, GTCC, and GTNS). In other words, the rate of changes in GTMOD, GTCC, and GTNS after suspending all CFS sets from the YouTube co-commenter-channel network is the identifier of the top ten CFS sets. The findings and theoretical and practical implications are presented in the next section.

IV. Results

This research aims to present the benefits of the proposed CFSA model that could enhance the quality and the discovery of the focal structure sets of commenters on YouTube.

The case study shown in Figure 2, implemented in the research was related to the Cheng Ho dataset. The CFSA model identified 30 CFS sets in the multiplex network (co-commenters-channels layer). These sets are different in size, number of commenters, channels, and network structures on YouTube.

Furthermore, Table shows the manual analysis and the activities of the co-commenter - channels identified in one of the CFS sets, witnessing "what is going on between online commenters on YouTube?" in the most straightforward and smallest possible sets. For example, CFS3 set, shown in Figure 3, includes 70 commenters who were active and shared comments on five YouTube channels. The CFS model identified this set as one of the most influential sets hosting live streams on YouTube in the Indo-Pacific reign and spreading information to the maximum number of YouTube accounts. Besides, to describe the structure of the CFS3 set in-depth, Figure 3 shows the spread of commenters (red dots) and the channels (gray dots) in the structure of the co-commenter-channel network. Equally, this set is considered one of the top influential sets, including commenters from different parts of the co-commenter network.

TABLE III. CFS3 SET IN COMPLEX SOCIAL NETWORKS

CFS Set Id	Number of commenters	Number of channels	Number of Edge
CFS3	70	5	129
Contexts	@Asumsi @KOMPASTV, @metrotvnews, @Muhammad Hanif Hasballah, @TRANS7 OFFICIAL		

Likewise, CFS3 includes commenters linked to different channels like "@Asumsi"; 1.27M subscribers; this YoutTube channel is a media-tech institution focusing on various affairs and pop culture that targets the younger Indonesian demographic as shown in Figure 3. This channel is interested in critical angle and telling stories from the unheard point of views, as we study the structure of CFS3 links other influential commenters active on different set of channels [19]. Likewise, CFS3 set shows "@KOMPASTV", 14.3M subscribers, it is another YouTube channel in the Indo-Pacific region, where this channel is the rapid advancement of information technology, has an impact on the behavior of the Indonesian people, especially for television and KompasTV lovers. This channel focuses on free streaming to be at the forefront of various social media [20]. Other channels like "@metrotvnews" [21], 6.31M subscribers, and "@TRANS7 OFFICIAL" [22], 24.3M subscribers.

The advantages of implementing the CFSA model would reveal different desires between commenters in the identified CFS sets. In other words, the results present that commenters have entirely different interests on different YouTube channels. These findings lead to commenters being active and interested increase engagement of the shared videos on different channels.

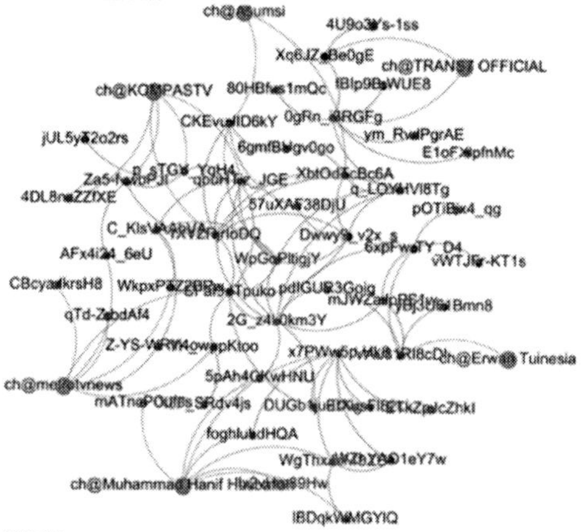

CFS3

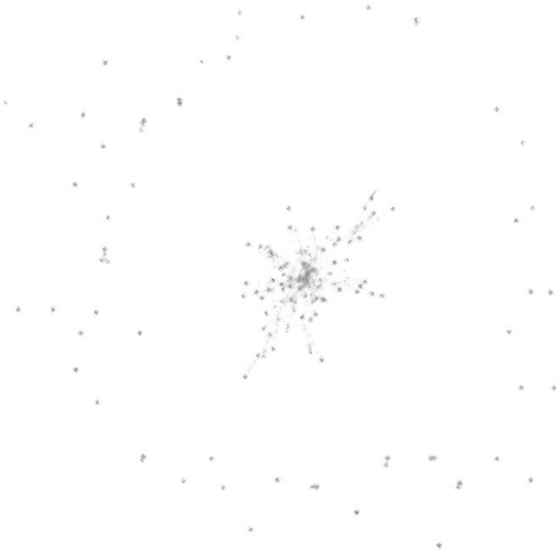

G-CFS3

Figure 3. CFS sets in social networks. These three CFS sets changed the structure of the network as we can observe the changes before and after suspending these three sets from the network.

Moreover, to evaluate the influence of CFS sets, the ground truth measures were utilized to measure the impact of each CFS set of commenters on the entire co-commenter-channel network. For this purpose, the model suspended each CFS set from the network and then recalculated the GT measures to record the rate of the changes in the structure of the network. For example, when the model suspends CFS3 set shown in Figure 3 (top network), this set changed the structure of the network (**G**-CFS3) to a complete sparse co-commenter-channel network as shown in Figure 3 (bottom network). Furthermore, this set maximized the network's modularity values (GTMOD) from 0.7 to 0.957, and minimized the stability (GTNS) of the network (maximized number of communities) from 72 stable communities to 115 fragmented communities. Similarly, suspending CFS3 set from the network (G-CFS3) minimized the average clustering coefficient values (GTCC) from 0.029 to 0.0223.

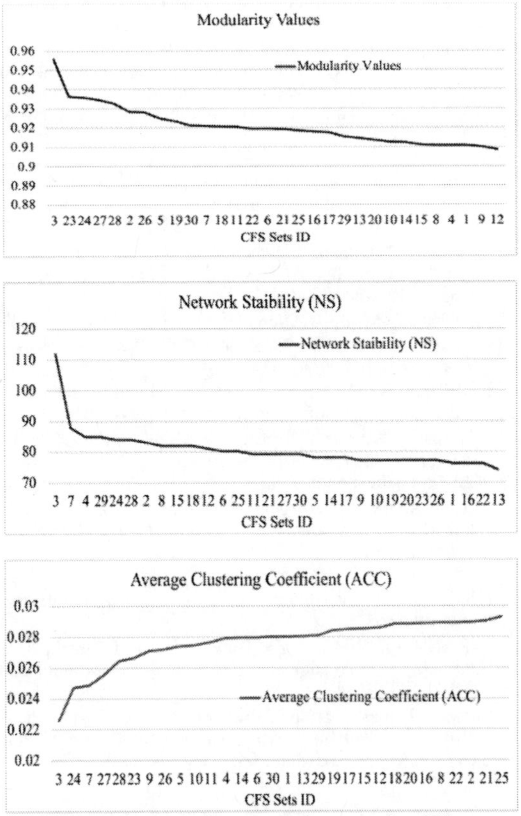

Figure 4. Changes in the network after suspending CFS sets.

Furthermore, to evaluate the quality of the other identified CFS sets, the employed method designed to suspend each CFS set, recalculates the changes in the modularity values, the changes in the number of communities, and the average clustering coefficient values. The model procedure have to recalculate these changes after suspending all CFS set from the co-commenter-channel network. Likewise, the changes in the co-commenter-channels YouTube networks where considered as Figure 4 shows the changes after suspending each CFS sets. Due to the space limit, we will skip presenting other changes in the co-commenter-channels values.

Additionally, from the GT analysis, we identified the top ten influential sets based on each GT values. The top ten sets had a greater impact on the co-commenter network compared to other sets, as shown in the following results.

- Top ten CFS set based on GTMOD: (CFS3, CFS23, CFS24, CFS27, CFS28, CFS2, CFS26, CFS5, CFS19, CFS30).
- Top ten CFS sets based on GTCC: (CFS3, CFS24, CFS7, CFS27, CFS28, CFS23, CFS9, CFS26, CFS5, CFS10).
- Top ten CFS sets based on GTNS: (CFS3, CFS7, CFS4, CFS29, CFS24, CFS28, CFS2, CFS8, CFS15, CFS18).

In summary, the model identified the top ten influential CFS sets based on three different criteria for further research and investigation. For example, CFS3, CFS24, and CFS28 were in the top ten CFS sets based on three sets of measures. In addition, CFS3 showed an interesting structure as this set impacted the co-commenter-channels network the most.

Moreover, this effort explored the utilization of multiplex networks and the focal structure analysis characteristics to detect the contextual focal structure sets on YouTube co-commenter networks. In a methodological practice, this study extended the structure of the information matrix to relax the complexity of the added information and help to interpret the contextual actions of the co-commenters on YouTube channels.

V. CONCLUSION AND FUTURE WORK

The CFSA model presented to reveal influential sets of YouTube commenters; where the co-commenter-channel multiplex network utilized to present their online contextual activities. Similarly, a participation layer representation is employed to capture the communication network among the commenters, posted videos, and the interconnection between the two layers (through co-commenter and YouTube channels). To measure the performance of the model, we utilized YouTube datasets related to the Indo-Pacific region, including Cheng Ho narrative videos. Additionally, we implemented a systematic procedure to measure each CFS set's impact on the co-commenter-channel network's stability. To accomplish this goal, the model temporarily removed each CFS set from the network and evaluated the alterations in modularity values, average clustering coefficient values, and network stability in the co-commenter-channels network. Finally, the model determined the top ten most influential CFS sets of co-commenters and their associated YouTube channels. Furthermore, the model revealed that the most influential set, CFS3, encompasses well-subscribed channels such as "Asumsi" [19], "Erwan Tuinesia"[23], "KOMPASTV" [20], and "metrotvnews" [21], primarily serving the Indonesian community in the Indo-Pacific region. Many of the channels are known to espouse misinformation.

Moreover, the characteristics of the CFSA model have practical implications and could be leveraged by social media platforms to develop and implement screening tools for users and communities' contextual activities on social networks. The CFSA model helps to distinguish contextual activities beyond the focal structures on social media. In addition, this study highlights the value of utilizing the multiplex network method and focal structure analysis models in revealing coordinating groups' contextual activities and information spread on social networks.

For future work, to improve the outcomes of the CFS model, we consider applying the model to small dynamic social networks. Next, implementing the CFSA model to analyze cross-platform scenarios, where this model could study contextual focal structure sets that simultaneously span across multiple social media platforms like Facebook, Twitter, Instagram, and YouTube.

Acknowledgment

This research is funded in part by the U.S. National Science Foundation (OIA-1946391, OIA-1920920, IIS-1636933, ACI- 1429160, and IIS-1110868), U.S. Office of the Under Secre- tary of Defense for Research and Engineering (FA9550-22- 1-0332), U.S. Office of Naval Research (N00014-10-1-0091, N00014-14-1-0489, N00014-15-P-1187, N00014-16-1-2016, N00014-16-1-2412, N00014-17-1-2675, N00014-17-1-2605, N68335-19-C-0359, N00014-19-1-2336, N68335-20-C-0540, N00014-21-1-2121, N00014-21-1-2765, N00014-22-1-2318), U.S. Air Force Research Laboratory, U.S. Army Research Office (W911NF-20-1-0262, W911NF-16-1-0189, W911NF- 23-1-0011), U.S. Defense Advanced Research Projects Agency (W31P4Q-17-C-0059), Arkansas Research Alliance, the Jerry L. Maulden/Entergy Endowment at the University of Arkansas at Little Rock, and the Australian Department of Defense Strategic Policy Grants Program (SPGP) (award number: 2020-106-094). Any opinions, findings, and conclusions or recommendations expressed in this material are those of the authors and do not necessarily reflect the views of the funding organizations. The researchers gratefully acknowledge the support.

References

[1] Global Affairs Canada, "Canada's Indo-Pacific Strategy," [retrieved: March, 2023]. [Online]. Available: https://www.international.gc.ca/transparency-transparence/indo-pacific-indo-pacifique/index.aspx?lang=eng.

[2] T. W. House, "Indo-Pacific Strategy of the United States," [retrieved: March, 2023], 2022. [Online]. Available: https://www.whitehouse.gov/wp-content/uploads/2022/02/U.S.-Indo-Pacific-Strategy.pdf.

[3] "Power shifts in the Indo-Pacific | Foreign Policy White Paper," [retrieved: March, 2023]. [Online]. Available: https://www.dfat.gov.au/sites/default/files/minisite/static/4ca0813c-585e-4fe1-86eb-de665e65001a/fpwhitepaper/foreign-policy-white-paper/chapter-two-contested-world/power-shifts-indo-pacific.html.

[4] "China's Rise and the Implications for the Indo-Pacific | ORF," [retrieved: March, 2023]. [Online]. Available: https://www.orfonline.org/expert-speak/chinas-rise-and-the-implications-for-the-indo-pacific/.

[5] "Social media in the Asia-Pacific region - statistics & facts | Statista," [retrieved: March, 2023]. [Online]. Available: https://www.statista.com/topics/6606/social-media-in-asia-pacific/#topicOverview.

[6] R. Chugh and U. Ruhi, "Social Media for Tertiary Education," Encycl. Educ. Inf. Technol., pp. 1–6, 2019.

[7] "YouTube – Myles Bassell, Official Website," [retrieved: March, 2023]. [Online]. Available: https://professorbassell.com/youtube-facts/.

[8] "Media | Statista," [retrieved: March, 2023]. [Online]. Available: https://www.statista.com/markets/417/media/.

[9] "Asia: category distribution of YouTube channels 2021 | Statista," [retrieved: March, 2023]. [Online]. Available: https://www.statista.com/statistics/1288302/asia-category-distribution-of-youtube-channels/.

[10] R. Zhou, S. Khemmarat, L. Gao, J. Wan, and J. Zhang, "How YouTube videos are discovered and its impact on video views," Multimed. Tools Appl., vol. 75, no. 10, pp. 6035–6058, 2016.

[11] "China's Columbus' Was an Imperialist Too: Contesting the Myth of Zheng He | Small Wars Journal," [retrieved: March, 2023]. [Online]. Available: https://smallwarsjournal.com/jrnl/art/chinas-columbus-was-imperialist-too-contesting-myth-zheng-he.

[12] M. Alassad and N. Agarwal, "Contextualizing focal structure analysis in social networks," Soc. Netw. Anal. Min., vol. 12, no. 1, pp. 1–26, Dec. 2022.

[13] F. Şen, R. Wigand, N. Agarwal, S. Tokdemir, and R. Kasprzyk, "Focal structures analysis: identifying influential sets of individuals in a social network," Soc. Netw. Anal. Min., vol. 6, no. 1, pp. 1–22, Dec. 2016.

[14] M. Alassad, N. Agarwal, and M. N. Hussain, "Examining Intensive Groups in YouTube Commenter Networks," in in proceedings of 12th International Conference, SBP-BRiMS 2019, no. 12, 2019, pp. 224–233.

[15] M. Alassad, B. Spann, and N. Agarwal, "Combining advanced computational social science and graph theoretic techniques to reveal adversarial information operations," Inf. Process. Manag., vol. 58, no. 1, p. 102385, Jan. 2021.

[16] M. E. J. Newman, "Detecting community structure in networks," Eur. Phys. J. B - Condens. Matter, vol. 38, no. 2, pp. 321–330, Mar. 2004.

[17] A. Clauset, M. E. J. Newman, and C. Moore, "Finding community structure in very large networks," Phys. Rev. E, vol. 70, no. 6, p. 066111, Dec. 2004.

[18] R. Zafarani, M. A. Abbasi, and H. Liu, Social Media Mining: An Introduction. Cambridge University Press, 2014.

[19] "Asumsi - YouTube," [retrieved: March, 2023]. [Online]. Available: https://www.youtube.com / @Asumsiasumsi/about.

[20] "KOMPASTV - YouTube," [retrieved: March, 2023]. [Online]. Available: https://www.youtube.com /c/kompastv/about.

[21] "METRO TV - YouTube," [retrieved: March, 2023]. [Online]. Available: https://www.youtube.com/ @metrotvnews.

[22] "TRANS7 OFFICIAL - YouTube," [retrieved: March, 2023]. [Online]. Available: https://www.youtube.com/ @TRANS7Official.

[23] "Erwan Tuinesia - YouTube," [retrieved: March, 2023]. [Online]. Available: https://www.youtube.com/channel/ UCuf-elLAvonX65UMupYfPbg?app=desktop.

VR-EDStream+EDA: Immersively Visualizing and Animating Event and Data Streams and Event-Driven Architectures in Virtual Reality

Roy Oberhauser[0000-0002-7606-8226]
Computer Science Dept.
Aalen University
Aalen, Germany
e-mail: roy.oberhauser@hs-aalen.de

***Abstract*—With increasing digitalization, the importance of data and events, which comprise its most fundamental level, cannot be overemphasized. All types of organizations, including enterprises, business, government, manufacturing, and the supporting IT, are dependent on these fundamental building blocks. Thus, evidence-based comprehension and analysis of the underlying data and events, their stream processing, and correlation with enterprise events and activities becomes vital for an increasing set of (grassroot or citizen) stakeholders. Thus, further investigation of accessible alternatives to visually support analysis of data and events is needed. This paper contributes VR-EDStream+EDA, a solution for immersively visualizing and interacting with data and event streams or pipelines and generically visualizing Event-Driven Architecture (EDA) in Virtual Reality (VR). Our realization shows its feasibility, and a case-based evaluation provides insights into its capabilities.**

Keywords - virtual reality; event-driven architecture; data pipelines; event stream processing; data stream processing; software architecture; visualization.

I. INTRODUCTION

It is said that "data is the new oil", with data playing a fundamental role in the digitalization and automation in various organizations, including enterprises, business, government, manufacturing, and IT. Events (a.k.a. record or message) are specific data consisting of a record of an occurrence. Modern software architectures, in the form of microservices or other decoupled reactive apps, are often event-driven, and microservice adoption in enterprises is growing, with IDC reporting 77% and GitLab reporting 71% of organizations (partially) using microservices [1][2].

The size of software applications has grown in size and complexity over the years and decades, as has the number of different apps or services and their interdependence or coupling in enterprises. Enterprise Service Buses (ESBs) are one example of how different apps and services can be coupled with each other without them even being aware of it. For example, it is said 57% of enterprises use between 1000-5000 business applications [3]. Consequently, more coupling and software reuse of (micro)services results in additional coupling and additional data and event traffic. At the business or enterprise level, each execution of an activity within a business process leaves a digital footprint of process-related events and the timepoint of execution, typically contained in various log files across the various IT systems or services. Analogous to the increase in and monitoring of network traffic, where network analysis supports analysis down to the packet level, an application- and tool-independent capability for equivalent data or event stream analysis is thus requisite.

Furthermore, as digitalization expands, various stakeholders (besides IT operators) may desire insight into the interactions between software and any related data and event processing. For example, developer responsibilities are expanding to include deployment, automation, performance management, user experience, and security, and increasingly responsible for the entire lifecycle of application development and operations [4].

Visualization and analysis of large dynamic data and event sets and their relations remains a challenge. While various specialized data tooling is available, alternative accessible generic (tool-independent) approaches for immersively visualizing and analyzing such (data or event) streams has not been sufficiently investigated. Furthermore, as data and processes become more relevant to the digital enterprise and stakeholders become more digitally savvy (grassroots or enterprise citizens), it is all the more relevant and challenging to include non-expert stakeholders in such data and event analysis. By leveraging Virtual Reality (VR), data and event analysis can be made more accessible to a wider set of stakeholders beyond the more specialized data scientists or software developers.

In prior VR-related work, in the area of processes we developed VR-BPMN [5] to visualize Business Process Modeling Notation (BPMN) models, while VR-ProcessMine [6] addressed process mining. In the area of Enterprise Architecture (EA), VR-EA [7] contributed a VR solution for ArchiMate EA models, VR-EAT [8] presented a VR-based solution for integrating dynamically-generated EA tool diagrams in VR, while VR-EA+TCK [9] integrated enterprise content and knowledge management systems in VR. In the software architecture and software engineering area, VR-UML [10] supports the Unified Modeling Language (UML) and VR-SysML [11] supports the Systems Modeling Language (SysML), while VR-Git [12] supports Git repositories. This paper contributes VR-EDStream+EDA, a solution for immersively visualizing and interacting with data, events, and generically visualize EDA in VR. Our prototype realization shows its feasibility, and a case-based evaluation provides insights into its capabilities for addressing the aforementioned challenges.

The remainder of this paper is structured as follows: Section 2 discusses related work. In Section 3, the solution is described. Section 4 provides details about the realization. The evaluation is described in Section 5 followed by a conclusion.

II. Related Work

Our search for related work includes the data visualization survey by Qin et al. [13] only mention events streams with regard to SQL-like query support. A survey on immersive analytics by Fonnet and Prié [14] includes no citations related to streams, and only two related to events: IDEA [15], which depicts user activity logs in a 3D cylindrical scatterplot while tracking a mobile chair, and DebugAR [16], which uses Augmented Reality (AR) for debugging.

As to immersive toolkits, the DXR toolkit [17] offers support for building immersive visualizations, and does not mention events nor streams. IATK [18] is another immersive analytics toolkit, whereby events, messages, and streams are not mentioned nor addressed. Stream [19] uses head-mounted AR devices to support visual data analysis. Spatially-aware tablets are used for interaction and input. In contrast, our solution does not necessitate additional AR hardware or a real tablet, since a virtual VR tablet is provided. Furthermore, our solution does not require or utilize individual linked 2D scatter plots. This would potentially impede scalability depending on the connectedness and grouping of the nodes involved.

Reactive Vega [20] is a streaming dataflow architecture that supports declarative interactive visualization. Its architecture and parser are implemented in JavaScript, and intended to run in a web browser or with Node.js. Popular tools for visualizing event systems, such as Kafka and RabbitMQ, include the web applications Grafana and Kibana, or some tool implementation in combination with D3.js.

In contrast to the above, VR-EDStream+EDA provides a generic (application and service independent, event platform independent, and programming language independent) approach for immersive event and data stream visualization and animation in VR.

III. Solution

VR is a mediated simulated visual environment in which the perceiver experiences telepresence. VR provides an unlimited space for visualizing a growing and complex set of enterprise models and processes and their interrelationships simultaneously in a spatial structure. As the importance, scale, inter-dependence, and coupling of data and events for IT infrastructure grows, an immersive environment can provide an additional visualization capability to comprehend and analyze both the structurally complex and interconnected static relations and the dynamic interactions between digital elements.

In support of the possible benefits of an immersive VR experience vs. 2D for performing an analysis task, Müller et al. [21] investigated a software analysis task that used a Famix metamodel of Apache Tomcat source code dependencies in a force-directed graph. They found that VR does not significantly decrease comprehension and analysis time nor significantly improve correctness (although fewer errors were made). While interaction time was less efficient, VR improved the UX (user experience), being more motivating, less demanding, more inventive/innovative, and more clearly structured.

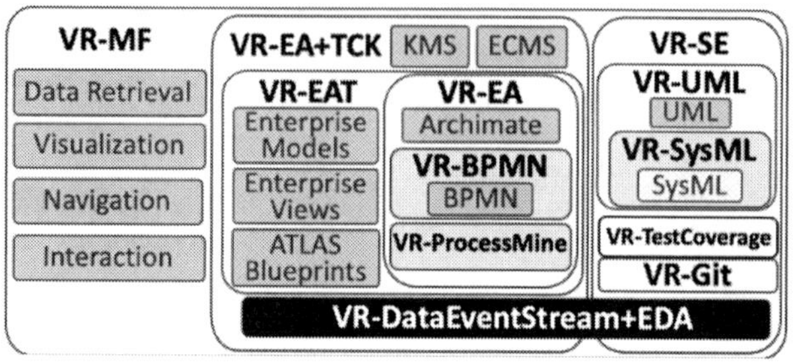

Figure 1. The VR-EDStream+EDA solution concept (black) in relation to our prior VR solution concepts.

To provide a context and background for our generalized solution concept for VR-EDStream+EDA we refer to Figure 1. VR-EDStream+EDA utilizes our generalized VR Modeling Framework (VR-MF) [6], which provides a VR-based domain-independent hypermodeling framework, which addresses four primary aspects that require special attention when modeling in VR: visualization, navigation, interaction, and data retrieval. VR-EA [6] provides specialized direct support and mapping for EA models in VR, including both ArchiMate as well as BPMN via VR-BPMN [5]. VR-ProcessMine [6] provides support for (business or software) process mining in VR. VR-EAT [8] extends this further with integration of EA tools for accessing dynamically generated diagrams and models from an EA tool in VR. VR-EA+TCK [9] extends these capabilities by integrating further enterprise knowledge, information, and content repositories such as a Knowledge Management Systems (KMS) and Enterprise Content Management Systems (ECMS). Since data streams, event streams, and EDA involve data and/or software and inter-software communication, VR-EDStream+EDA (shown in black) spans both the enterprise and software engineering areas, applicable to relevant stakeholders depending on their focus and intention.

A. Visualization in VR

A generic way of portraying an EDA or dynamic stream of data (records or packets) or events is as a set of nodes and a Directed Acyclic Graph (DAG) to indicate the producer (source) and consumer (sink), as exemplified in Figure 2. Events (messages) can be grouped and stored in topics, accessible to multiple producers or consumers. A 3D sphere is used to depict nodes, a 3D empty pipe (straw) is used for the graph, and the event is depicted as a 3D capsule that is dynamically animated within the pipe.

In the immersive space of VR, analysis is affected by the distance of objects, thus ideally an initial automatic placement should place them in relative proximity to avoid delays due to traveling to objects to interact with them. While a force-directed graph rebalances the distance of object automatically, it takes time to reach a steady state, while any manual element replacements by a user can cause side-effects. Inspired by 2D chord diagrams used in visual data analytics, we considered how to use the third dimension to reduce clutter, reduce connector collisions, and retain order and legibility. Thus, to support scalability while minimizing the collision of connectors, nodes are initially placed on the outer edge of an imaginary sphere, while node groups follow along a planar circle on the sphere's edge as shown in Figure 3. The largest sized group (based on number of nodes) is placed near the equator and serves as the basis for the sphere circumference, while smaller groups are placed accordingly closer to the poles. This grouping creates an implicit layering effect. Nodes in the same group have the same color, and the size of a node (sphere) is dependent on the number of connectors (streams), with the smallest having none.

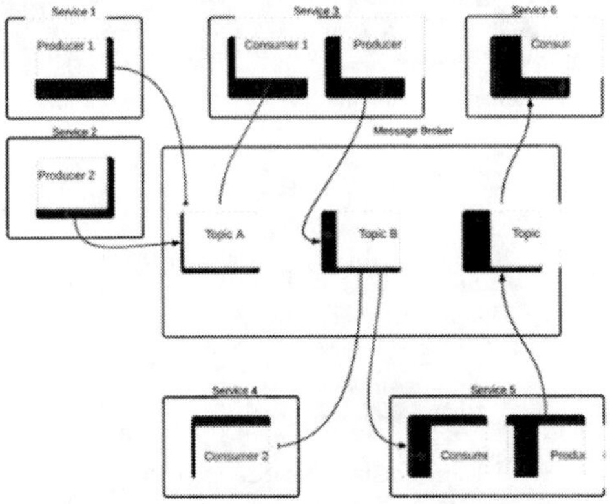

Figure 2. Example EDA couplings between services.

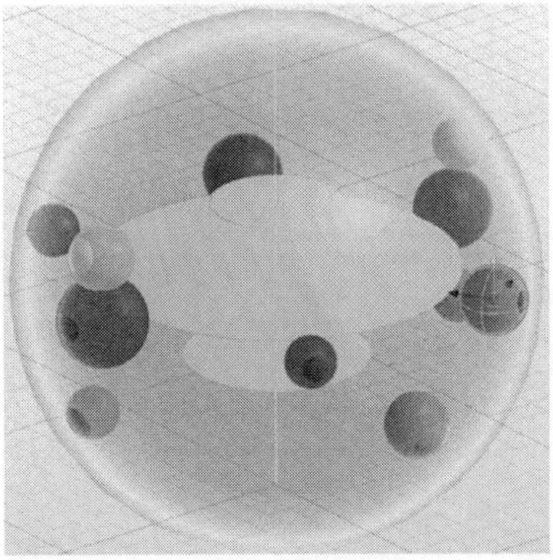

Figure 3. Node placement on spherical edge with groups on planar circles.

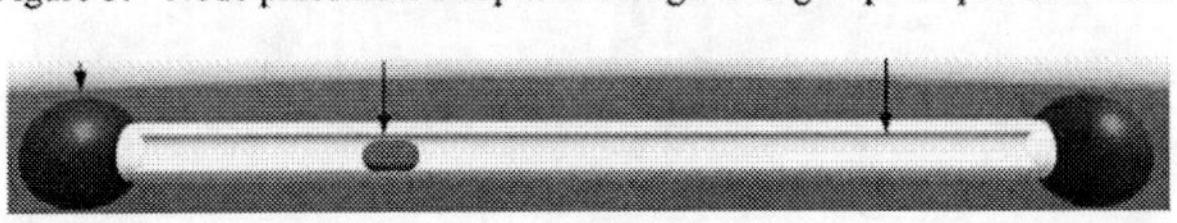

Figure 4. Event stream portrayal in VR: nodes as spheres (left arrow), semitransparent tube as stream (right arrow), and animated capsule as event (middle arrow).

To depict a stream, transmission, or processing of events or data in VR, a semi-transparent tube is used with nodes portrayed as spheres on both ends, and an animated capsule indicating the direction of source and sink, shown in Figure 4.

B. *Navigation in VR*

The immersion afforded by VR requires addressing how to navigate the space while reducing the likelihood of potential VR sickness symptoms. Thus, two navigation modes are included in the solution: the default uses gliding controls, enabling users to fly through the VR space and view objects from any angle they wish. Alternatively, teleporting permits a user to select a node or event and be instantly placed there (i.e., by instantly moving the camera to that position); while this can be disconcerting, it may reduce the susceptibility to VR sickness for those prone to it that can occur when moving through a virtual space.

C. *Interaction in VR*

Elements in the model can be freely moved. Since interaction with VR elements has not yet become standardized, in our VR concept, user-element interaction is handled primarily via the VR controllers and a virtual tablet. Our VR-Tablet provides detailed context-specific element information, and can provide a virtual keyboard for text entry fields (via laser pointer key selection) when needed.

D. *Capabilities*

Solution capabilities include:

- A network-based mechanism for monitoring and collecting data or events
- A common data and event storage mechanism
- EDA definition and configuration
- Node grouping, placement, naming, coloring
- Store and load VR model changes
- Define event flow time period
- Dynamic event flow step and speed control

IV. Realization

As a realization of our solution concept, our prototype is partitioned into a data hub, a backend for data processing, and a front end responsible for VR visualization.

The data hub was implemented as a microservice. For storage, the InfluxDB was used as a database due to: 1) its time series support and 2) since its storage requirements were deemed significantly smaller for large time series datasets than any alternatives, a benefit when scaling the solution. For receiving events generically, a microservice RESTful interface for receiving JSON event or data records was realized in Python using the FastAPI web framework. In addition to the REST interface, Telegraf - part of InfluxData platform, offers a open source server-based agent written in Go for collecting and sending metrics and events from databases, systems, and sensors to the InfluxDB. Either interface can be flexibly used to extract or collect events, applying an interceptor, proxy, or decorator pattern as appropriate.

VR was implemented with Unity and SteamVR. The main classes involved are shown in the class diagram in Figure 5. The NodeManager manages the overall configuration and portrayal of nodes and edges and passes events to the nodes. EventManager computes events based on the data records, and the NodeManager passes these to the appropriate Node, which generates and fires a visual capsule. Timeline manages the animation including timepoint and speed of events. DataHubManager is used for accessing the datasets.

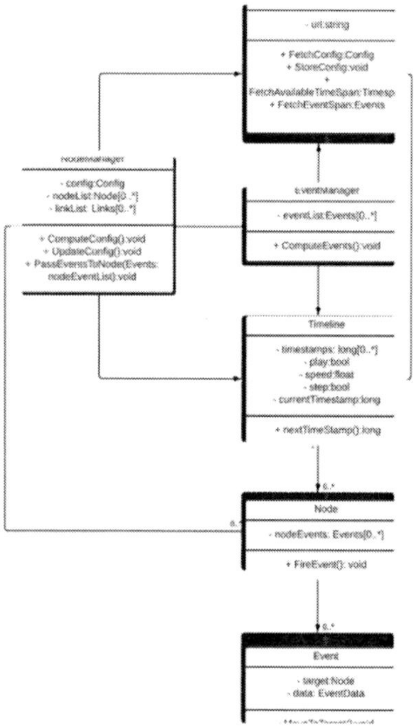

Figure 5. Class diagram for VR visualization support.

Integration with two different event systems was performed. Apache Kafka is an open-source distributed event streaming platform implementing the message broker pattern. Kafka Connect supports data integration between databases, key-value stores, search indexes, and file systems. The connectors receive and transmit data to and from topics as a source or sink, and various extensible implementations are available. Examples include a Source Connector that streams database updates to a topic, collect server metrics to a topic, forward topic records to Elasticsearch, etc. Confluent ksqlDB was used in the test applications as a database supporting queries in SQL syntax for stream processing applications based on Kafka Streams. To ensure a generic solution, a second popular publish/subscribe message broker event system, RabbitMQ, was also utilized in the evaluation. For more details and a comparison of these distributed event systems, we refer to Dobbelaere & Esmaili [22].

Metainformation collected via REST or Telegraf and retained in the database with each record are as follows: source, target, timestamp, payload. Thus, the payload can be data, an event, a message, etc. If no target exists, then any null or fake named node can be used (equivalent to a null device in Unix).

For interaction support with the data, a VR-Tablet menu offers these display modes:

- Animated Timeline for controlling dynamic stored or real-time playback (Figure 6 left),
- Querying the event or data store (Figure 6 right),
- Color customization (Figure 7),
- Object Details for a selected node (Figure 8) or capsule (i.e., event or data record, Figure 9), and
- Settings for storing and fetching configurations (not shown).

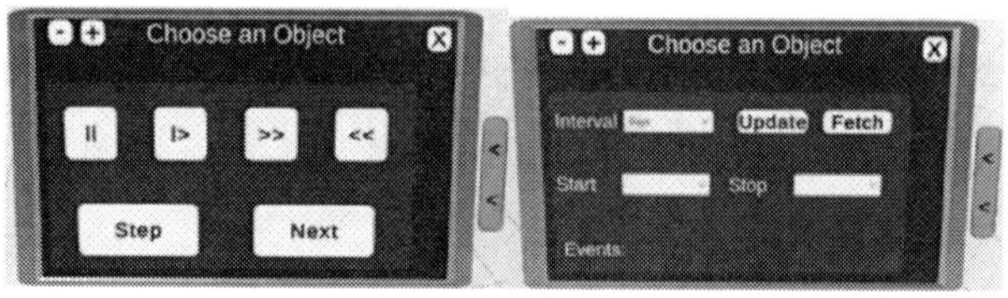

Figure 6. Dynamic animation interface (left) and Query interface (right).

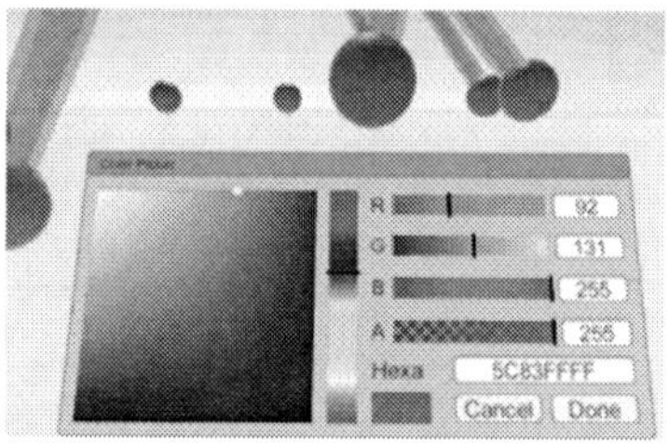

Figure 7. Object color customization.

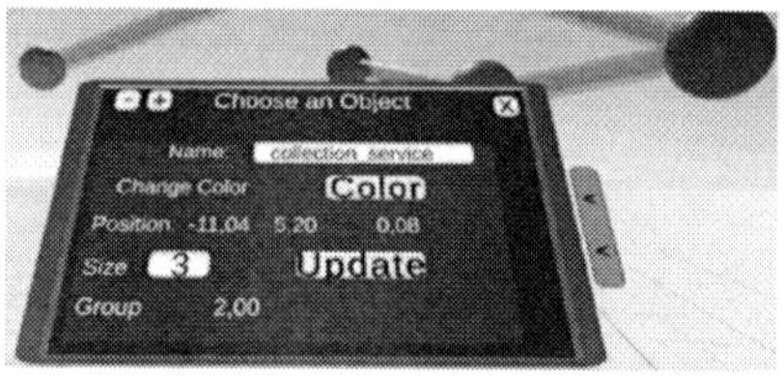

Figure 8. Node detail interface after node selection.

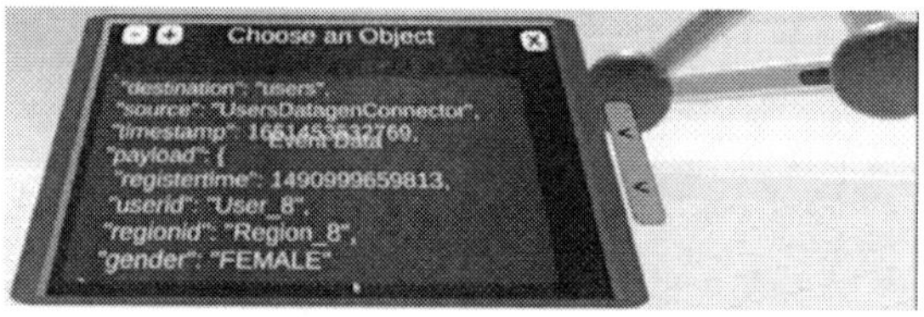

Figure 9. Example event details after selecting red capsule.

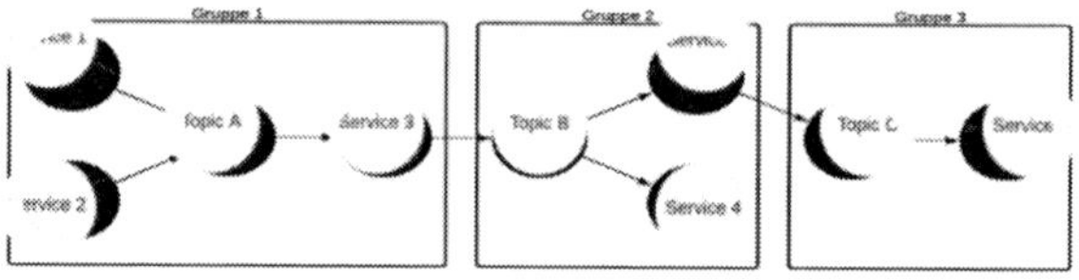

Figure 10. Abstracted node grouping EDA example.

Configurations stored in JSON format permit stakeholders to flexibly group nodes and streams, in essence defining the EDA (e.g., based on microservices) the way they wish based on their interst. An example cross-service EDA is shown in Figure 10. Nodes in a group are assigned the same color.

V. EVALUATION

The evaluation of the solution concept is based on design science method and principles [23], in particular, a viable artifact, problem relevance, and design evaluation (utility, quality, efficacy). For this, a case study based on scenarios is used, as our evaluation focuses on visual support for a variety of generic EDA configurations via node groupings and streams. These visual scenarios consisted of various node grouping and coupling configuration.

A. Event System Integration Tests

For generating event data for the evaluation, the Confluent Quickstart Demo using ksqlDB in combination with Kafka Connect was used with two connectors to the topics pageviews und users. A second configuration based on Confluent Kafka consisted of one producer and three consumers in Python. To ensure the solution was not Kafka dependent, a third configuration using only RabbitMQ with our microservice was also tested.

B. Single Large Group Connected to One Node

As a scalability scenario, a single group of 100 nodes all connected is shown in Figure 11. Note that in VR, due to its unlimited space, there are no actual limitations in navigating to nodes and comprehending large models.

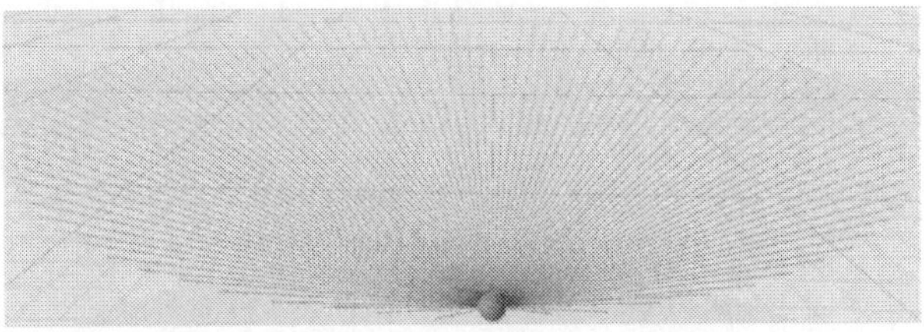

Figure 11. Scalability test: a group of 100 nodes connected to one node.

C. Unbalanced Groups Randomly Interconnected

This scenario consisted of three unbalanced groups: one group with 20 randomly intra-connected nodes, and two inter-connected groups consisting of a single node each, as portrayed in Figure 12. Note each group has a different node color, and more connected nodes are larger, and smaller groups are near the poles of the sphere, with the largest group at the equator.

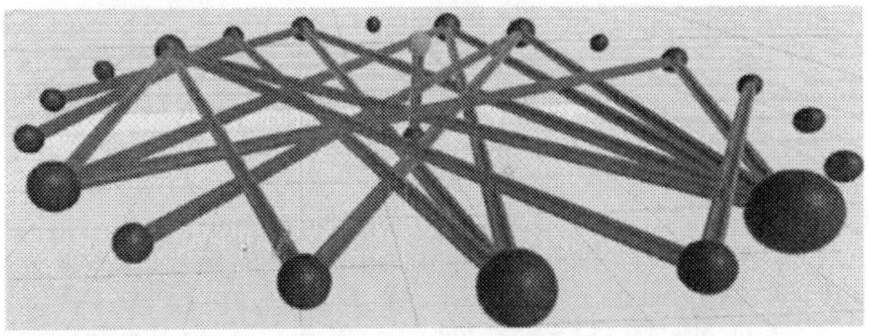

Figure 12. Three groups: one with 20 randomly intra-connected nodes and two inter-connected groups consisting of a single node each.

D. Multiple Balanced Highly Interconnected Groups

In this scenario, three balanced groups of 20 nodes each are randomly inter- and intra- connected with other nodes, as shown in Figure 13.

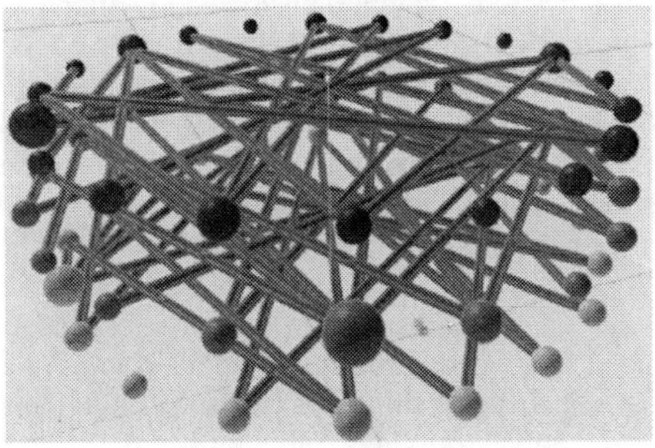

Figure 13. Three groups of 20 nodes each with random coupling.

E. Multiple Unbalanced Groups Irregularly Interconnected

To test many unbalanced groups with different degrees of connectedness, this scenario had five groups, one group with 20 nodes and the rest consisting of 5-10 nodes with random unbalanced coupling. The result is shown in Figure 14.

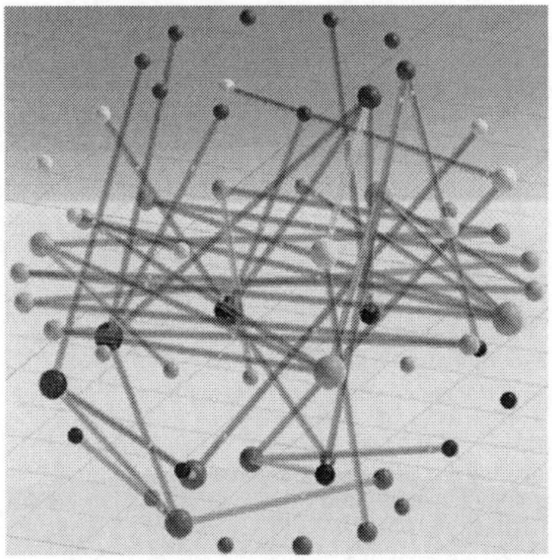

Figure 14. Five groups (with 20 and 5-10 nodes) and random coupling.

F. Discussion

The scenarios with their various node grouping configurations show various possibilities and capabilities of the generic solution concept. Our concept generically simplifies the understanding of complex software systems for those stakeholders only concerned with event and data flow. It does this by immersively depicting sources and sinks as nodes in a spatially compact (3D spherical) layout, and animating any interaction between them.

flows and communication streams for data and events by focusing only on the essential and removing all else, yet is scalable and immersive. By immersively visualizing these key aspects, various (grassroot) stakeholders can now access and comprehend the flow of event data in an animated fashion. The default placement of an EDA configuration provides a starting point for analysis, and users can move and recolor nodes as desired, and query applicable datasets.

VI. CONCLUSION

Access to and comprehension and analysis of the underlying events and data, their stream processing, and correlation with enterprise events and activities will become increasingly vital for a larger set of stakeholders. This paper contributed VR-EDStream+EDA, a VR solution for immersively visualizing and interacting with event and data streams or pipelines and EDA. Our realization showed its feasibility. A case-based evaluation provided insights into its capabilities, showing its ability to deal with balanced and unbalanced node group configurations and various coupling scenarios. Its customizable node placement in addition to the event animation provides an immersive visualization alternative for various stakeholders to comprehend the dynamic event and data flow data that form the basis of the IT system interactions in enterprises.

Future work includes adding additional data analyses, integration with our other enterprise hypermodeling VR solutions, an interview study with experts, and a comprehensive industry empirical study.

ACKNOWLEDGMENT

The authors thank Markus Harder for his assistance with the design, implementation, evaluation, and diagrams.

REFERENCES

[1] M. Loukides and S. Swoyer, "Microservices Adoption in 2020," O'Reilly Media, Inc., 2020. [Online]. Available from: https://www.oreilly.com/radar/microservices-adoption-in-2020/ 2023.03.25

[2] GitLab, "A Maturing DevSecOps Landscape," 2021. [Online]. Available from: https://about.gitlab.com/images/developer-survey/gitlab-devsecops-2021-survey-results.pdf 2023.03.25

[3] "New Ponemon Study Reveals Application Security Risk At All Time High: 1 in 2 Enterprises Need Better Protection," 2015. [Online]. Available from: https://www.businesswire.com/news/home/20151210006098/en/New-Ponemon-Study-Reveals-Application-Security-Risk-At-All-Time-High-1-in-2-Enterprises-Need-Better-Protection 2023.03.25

[4] M. Shirer, "IDC Survey Illustrates the Growing Importance of Developers to the Modern Enterprise," IDC, 2021. [Online]. Available from: https://www.idc.com/getdoc.jsp?containerId=prUS48058021 2023.03.25

[5] R. Oberhauser, C. Pogolski, and A. Matic, "VR-BPMN: Visualizing BPMN models in Virtual Reality," In: Shishkov, B. (ed.) Business Modeling and Software Design (BMSD 2018), LNBIP, vol. 319. Springer, Cham, 2018, pp. 83–97, doi.org/10.1007/978-3-319-94214-8_6.

[6] R. Oberhauser, "VR-ProcessMine: Immersive Process Mining Visualization and Analysis in Virtual Reality," the Fourteenth International Conf. on Information, Process, and Knowledge Management (eKNOW 2022), IARIA, 2022, pp. 29-36.

[7] R. Oberhauser and C. Pogolski, "VR-EA: Virtual Reality Visualization of Enterprise Architecture Models with ArchiMate and BPMN," In: Shishkov, B. (ed.) Business Modeling and Software Design (BMSD 2019), LNBIP, vol. 356, Springer, Cham, 2019, pp. 170–187, doi.org/10.1007/978-3-030-24854-3_11.

[8] R. Oberhauser, P. Sousa, and F. Michel, "VR-EAT: Visualization of Enterprise Architecture Tool Diagrams in Virtual Reality," In: Shishkov B. (eds) Business Modeling and Software Design (BMSD 2020), LNBIP, vol 391, Springer, Cham, 2020, pp. 221-239, doi.org/10.1007/978-3-030-52306-0_14.

[9] R. Oberhauser, M. Baehre, and P. Sousa: VR-EA+TCK: Visualizing Enterprise Architecture, Content, and Knowledge in Virtual Reality. In: Shishkov, B. (eds) Business Modeling and Software Design (BMSD 2022), LNBIP, vol 453, Springer, Cham, 2022, pp. 122-140, doi.org/10.1007/978-3-031-11510-3_8.

[10] R. Oberhauser, "VR-UML: The unified modeling language in virtual reality – an immersive modeling experience," International Symposium on Business Modeling and Software Design (BMSD 2021), Springer, Cham, 2021, pp. 40-58, doi.org/10.1007/978-3-030-79976-2_3

[11] R. Oberhauser, "VR-SysML: SysML Model Visualization and Immersion in Virtual Reality," International Conference of Modern Systems Engineering Solutions (MODERN SYSTEMS 2022), IARIA, 2022, pp. 59-64.

[12] R. Oberhauser, "VR-Git: Git Repository Visualization and Immersion in Virtual Reality," The Seventeenth International Conference on Software Engineering Advances (ICSEA 2022), IARIA, 2022, pp. 9-14.

[13] X. Qin, Y. Luo, N. Tang, and G. Li, "Making data visualization more efficient and effective: a survey," The VLDB Journal, 29, pp.93-117, 2020.

[14] A. Fonnet and Y. Prié, "Survey of Immersive Analytics," in IEEE Transactions on Visualization and Computer Graphics, vol. 27, no. 3, pp. 2101-2122, 2021.

[15] A. Fonnet, F. Melki, Y. Prié, F. Picarougne, and G. Cliquet, "Immersive Data Exploration and Analysis," Student Interaction Design Research Conference, Helsinki, Finland, hal-01798681, 2018, https://hal.science/hal-01798681.

[16] P. Reipschläger et al., "DebugAR: Mixed dimensional displays for immersive debugging of distributed systems," In: Extended Abstracts of the 2018 CHI Conference on Human Factors in Computing Systems, 2018, pp. 1-6.

[17] R. Sicat et al., "DXR: A toolkit for building immersive data visualizations," IEEE transactions on visualization and computer graphics, 25(1), 2018, pp.715-725.

[18] M. Cordeil et al., "IATK: An Immersive Analytics Toolkit," 2019 IEEE Conference on Virtual Reality and 3D User Interfaces (VR), Osaka, Japan, 2019, pp. 200-209, doi: 10.1109/VR.2019.8797978.

[19] S. Hubenschmid, J.Zagermann, S. Butscher, and H. Reiterer, "Stream: Exploring the combination of spatially-aware tablets with augmented reality head-mounted displays for immersive analytics," Proc. 2021 CHI Conference on Human Factors in Computing Systems, 2021, pp. 1-14.

[20] A. Satyanarayan, R. Russell, J. Hoffswell, and J. Heer, "Reactive Vega: A Streaming Dataflow Architecture for Declarative Interactive Visualization," In: IEEE Transactions on Visualization and Computer Graphics, vol. 22, no. 1, pp. 659-668, 2016, doi: 10.1109/TVCG.2015.2467091.

[21] R. Müller, P. Kovacs, J. Schilbach, and D. Zeckzer, "How to master challenges in experimental evaluation of 2D versus 3D software visualizations," In: 2014 IEEE VIS International Workshop on 3Dvis (3Dvis), IEEE, 2014, pp. 33-36.

[22] P. Dobbelaere and K.S. Esmaili, "Kafka versus RabbitMQ: A comparative study of two industry reference publish/subscribe implementations," In: Proc. 11th ACM int'l conference on distributed and event-based systems, 2017, pp. 227-238.

[23] A.R. Hevner, S.T. March, J. Park, and S. Ram, "Design science in information systems research," MIS Quarterly, 28(1), 2004, pp. 75-105.